Through the Russian Prism

Through the Russian Prism

ESSAYS ON LITERATURE AND CULTURE

Joseph Frank

PRINCETON UNIVERSITY PRESS
PRINCETON, NEW JERSEY

Library of Congress Cataloging-in-Publication Data

Frank, Joseph, 1918–
    Through the Russian prism : essays on literature and culture / Joseph Frank.
        p.   cm.
    Includes index.
    ISBN 0-691-06821-6 (alk. paper)
    ISBN 0-691-01456-6 (pbk.)
    1. Russian literature—19th century—History and criticism. 2. Russian literature—
20th century—History and criticism. 3. Soviet Union—Intellectual life—1801–1917.
4. Soviet Union—Intellectual life—1917–   I. Title.
PG3012.F7   1990   89-33185
891.709—dc20   CIP

Grateful acknowledgment is made to the following periodicals for granting permission to reprint articles that were first published in their pages:

"Dostoevsky's Realism" was first published in *Encounter*, March 1973, pp. 31–38.

"The Birth of Russian Socialism" first appeared in *Partisan Review* 29, no. 2 (1962).

"Deadly Idealist," first appeared in the *New Republic*, February 21, 1983. Reprinted with permission of The New Republic, © 1983, The New Republic, Inc.

"Fathers and Sons" and "From Gogol to the Gulag Archipelago" first appeared in the *Sewanee Review* 73 (fall 1965) and 84 (spring 1976). Copyright 1965 and 1976 by the University of the South. Reprinted by permission of the editor.

"Ralph Ellison and Dostoevsky" and "Alexander Herzen" first appeared in the *New Criterion*, September 1983 and September 1985. Reprinted by permission of the editor.

"N. G. Chernyshevsky: A Russian Utopia," first appeared in the *Southern Review*, January 1967.

"Roman Jakobson: The Master Linguist" and "Voices of Mikhail Bakhtin" are reprinted with permission of the *New York Review of Books*. Copyright © 1984–86 Nyrev, Inc.

"Freud's Case History of Dostoevsky," "Dostoevsky and the European Romantics," "The Search for a Positive Hero," and "The Road to Revolution" first appeared in the *Times Literary Supplement*, July 18, 1975; February 20, 1976; September 17, 1976; November 13, 1981, and are reprinted with permission of the editor.

"Russian Populism" first appeared in the *Slavic Review*, December 1961, and is reprinted with permission of the editor.

"A Word on Leskov" is reprinted from the *American Scholar* 48, no. 1 (Winter 1978–79), with permission of the editor.

THIS BOOK IS DEDICATED TO PAULETTE

For her ninetieth birthday.

Contents

Preface

THE ESSAYS and reviews collected here are all concerned with the problems of Russian culture, literature, and history, and are the offshoots of my work on Dostoevsky. A number of them deal directly with Dostoevsky's own writings, or with opinions about him; others discuss the manner in which his presence, and the issues raised by his work, continue to remain central to the Russian literature of the present and the recent past; still others are inspired by a general fascination with the Russian cultural history that has played so decisive a role in shaping our modern world. This is the double sense of my title, *Through the Russian Prism*, which is meant to stress not only the fateful influence of Western ideas in Russia—an influence with which Dostoevsky was so memorably concerned—but also the equally fateful, if less recognized, way in which such ideas, in their Russian metamorphosis, have returned to affect their original progenitors. The chapters are printed largely as originally written, though I have done some editing to bring them up to date and added new material here and there to turn a limited review into a more substantial consideration of the subject.

The present volume became more than an idea when Walter H. Lippincott told me that he would be happy to add such a collection to the Princeton list. This provided the stimulus for me to set to work in earnest, and I am very grateful for his energizing remark. My friends and colleagues in the Stanford Slavic Department—Edward J. Brown, Gregory Freidin, Lazar Fleishman, William Mills Todd III (now at Harvard), Richard J. Schupbach—have also provided important intellectual support and personal encouragement. It has been a privilege to be able to work in their midst. To these names I should add Victoria Bonnell (Mrs. Gregory Freidin), who in her capacity as a historian of Russia vigorously urged, during a memorable (for me) walk at Sea Ranch, that I collect my incidental pieces on Russian topics.

The funds for research of Stanford University helped to defray the expenses of preparing the manuscript, and Karen Rezendes typed a good part of it with efficient good humor. The reader of the manuscript, Hugh McLean, placed me in his debt both for his appreciation and by the many helpful suggestions he made for the improvement of the text. My copy editor, Lois Krieger, worked very hard to unscramble the tangle of spellings and transliterations caused by first publication in differing periodicals, and in general to rectify my unscholarly habits. My warmest thanks to them for their aid.

And most thanks of all, finally and once again, to my wife Marguerite, whose untiring insistence over the years that I take the trouble to bring together my scattered writings furnished the initial and sustaining impulse for thinking about what became this collection.

Joseph Frank
Stanford, California, July 1989

"Please note, gentlemen, that all those high European teachers, our light and our hope—all those Mills, Darwins and Strausses—sometimes consider the moral obligations of modern man in a most astonishing manner. . . . You will start laughing and you will ask: why did it occur to you to start talking precisely about those names?—For the reason that it is even difficult to conceive—speaking of our intelligent, enthusiastic and studious youth—that these names, for instance, would escape them during the initial stages of their lives. Is it possible to conceive that a Russian youth would remain indifferent to the influence of these and similar leaders of European progressive thought, especially to the Russian aspect of their doctrines?—this is a funny expression: 'Russian aspect of their doctrines'; let people excuse it; I am using it solely because this Russian aspect does actually exist in those doctrines. It consists of those inferences from these doctrines which, in the form of unshakable axioms, are drawn only in Russia, whereas in Europe, it is said, the possibility of such deductions is not even being suspected."

F. M. Dostoevsky, *Diary of a Writer* (1873)

PART ONE

Contemporaries

CHAPTER ONE

Roman Jakobson: The Master Linguist

No SCHOLAR of modern times has done more to revitalize the study of what has come to be called "the human sciences"—and particularly the science of language—than Roman Jakobson; and it is good to have this summary of his career (*Dialogues*, 1983) in the form of question-and-answer sessions with his former student and then wife, Krystyna Pomorska. The sessions took place in 1980, two years before Jakobson's death. First published in French, the dialogues are now made available in English—the language in which Jakobson wrote most of his works after coming to the United States in 1941.[1]

Jakobson of course was a formidable polyglot, who published first in his native Russian and could shift easily into French, German, and Czech, among other languages, as the occasion required. Tzvetan Todorov, who first heard him lecture in Bulgarian, and then came to know him well, has estimated that he could command about twenty languages—all of the Slavic group, all of the Romance group, and most of the Germanic family.[2] Indeed, his writings are so scattered, exist in so many languages, and cover so many disciplines that the condensed overview of his activity offered by *Dialogues* is more than welcome.

All the same, these dialogues are not as illuminating as they might have been—for a perfectly comprehensible and easily forgivable reason. Books composed of conversations with well-known representatives of thought are a form much cultivated by the French, who delight in the thrust and parry of verbal controversy; and these works are at their best when the questioner probes at the weak spots of whatever ideas and positions are being offered. Examples of such successful dialogues, where the subject was forced to stretch or defend his own views, are the conversations between Lévi-Strauss and Georges Charbonnier, or the dialogues between Raymond Aron and two young ex-Maoists who had taken part in the febrile spring uprising of 1968 in Paris.[3]

No such challenge, of course, is posed here to Jakobson by his wife; it

[1] Roman Jakobson and Krystyna Pomorska, *Dialogues* (Cambridge, Mass., 1983).

[2] Tzvetan Todorov, "L'Heritage formaliste," in Robert Georgin et al., *Jakobson*, Cahiers cistre no. 5 (Lausanne, 1978), 51.

[3] Georges Charbonnier, *Entretiens avec Claude Lévi-Strauss* (1961; reprinted, Paris, 1969); Raymond Aron, *Le Spectateur éngagé: Entretiens avec Jean-Louis Missika et Dominique Wolton* (Paris, 1981).

is, touchingly, rather the opposite that occurs. For when, occasionally, she feels that he has not given himself enough credit on one or another score, she supplements his account by her own. The result is rather a celebration than a conversation or true dialogue. But since the emphasis remains strictly on Jakobson's work, which there are certainly reasons enough to celebrate, the tone does not become too adulatory. And since he is allowed to speak at length, and uninterruptedly, on all the phases of his multifarious activities and interests, the book has the additional value of providing some final thoughts on the issues that preoccupied him all his life and have had such momentous consequences for contemporary culture.

Jakobson was, if one must place him in some conventional category, by profession a linguist. But he had a bold and wide-ranging speculative mind, which was constantly seeking to extend the limits of his linguistic inquiries and to examine their relations with other spheres of culture. He was anything but a narrow specialist, and he combined, to an unusual degree, a passion for scientific exactitude, for precision and clarity of thought, with an equal passion for Slavic literature, history and folklore, avant-garde painting and poetry, and the technique of the cinema. Readers of his work will be constantly surprised by the breadth of his range of reference, and by the startling ingeniousness of a mind capable of seeing relationships that nobody had previously suspected to exist. It is little wonder that, touching as he did on so many fields (and even creating the new discipline of neurolinguistics), the name of Jakobson should gradually have become known far beyond the area of his major professional preoccupation.

Some of Jakobson's fame, to be sure, may be attributed to historical chance. It was an accident, but a very happy one, that he was teaching in the same École Libre des Hautes Études, founded in New York during the Second World War by French and Belgian refugees, where Lévi-Strauss was also giving courses in anthropology. Each attended the other's lectures, and Lévi-Strauss, as a result, began to see how Jakobson's linguistic views could help him to solve some of the anthropological problems he was then wrestling with.[4] It was this encounter that gave birth to French structuralism.

Before very long structural linguistics was thus projected into the limelight as the key science for our time, whose postulates could furnish a new foundation for the study of culture much as Darwinian evolution had done for the latter half of the nineteenth century. Such an influence would scarcely have been possible, however, if Jakobson had not already worked out his linguistic theories at a philosophical level that made their general implications readily apparent. And Jakobson himself, in addition to his

[4] Jakobson's course has since been published in English: Roman Jakobson, *Six Lectures on Sound and Meaning*, trans. John Mepham (Cambridge, Mass., 1978).

researches on linguistics, carried on a steady activity all his life as a cultural essayist and literary critic, whose writings are accessible to an audience of nonspecialists and whose theories raise fundamental issues in aesthetics and literary criticism. Indeed, during his last years he devoted much of his attention to applying linguistics to the interpretation of poetry; and this effort gave rise to more public controversy than perhaps any other feature of his activity.

Certainly one of the major reasons for Jakobson's impressive scope, and his openness to the widest cultural perspectives, was his early contact with the explosion of Russian avant-garde art in the first quarter of the present century. Much to the astonishment—and perhaps amusement—of his staider scientific colleagues, the mature Jakobson always attributed the highest importance to his immersion in this bohemian climate when he was a young man; and he continues to do so in the dialogues. When not much older than an adolescent, he had been an intimate friend of the mysterious and vagabond Futurist poet Velimir Khlebnikov (whom he continued to call "the greatest Russian poet of our century"), a poet who had not only sought "the philosopher's stone" by creating neologisms that would transform all Slavic words into one another, but also dreamed of finding "the unity of world languages in general."[5] Much better known was another close friend, Vladimir Mayakovsky, who, for a short while before his suicide, came to be regarded almost as the Bard of the Bolshevik revolution. Jakobson was equally intimate with the Suprematist painter Kazimir Malevich and other young experimental painters then at the start of distinguished careers, such as Mikhail Larionov and Natalya Goncharova.

Moreover, Jakobson continued to remain faithful to these companions of his youth; in an informative afterword, Pomorska includes a touching portrait of his visits, when he returned to the Soviet Union after 1956 as an international celebrity, to the last survivor of the Futurist group, Alexis Kruchenykh, with whom the twenty-year-old Jakobson had once published a joint volume of poetry under a pseudonym and with a punning title. Then living in abject poverty in Moscow, Kruchenykh had remained an impenitent Futurist to the end, continuing to incarnate some of the jesting, irreverent, high-spirited but, all the same, intensely dedicated atmosphere of the bygone years before the First World War.

Those were the years, Jakobson recalls, when "Russian futurist poetry . . . was beginning to take hold"; and this "blossoming of modern Russian poetry followed the remarkable developments of modern painting, in particular French postimpressionism and its crowning achievement, Cubism." Russian culture at this time, as Jakobson rightly observes, had "acquired a

[5] Cited in Vahad D. Barooshian, *Russian Cubo-Futurism, 1910–1930* (The Hague, 1974), 11–12.

truly world-wide significance"; it was not only imitating Western developments but carrying them forward along original lines. For the Russians were beginning to think about these problems theoretically to a much greater extent than their European counterparts, and to place them in a broad scientific-philosophical framework. In an interview given in 1978 to a French questioner, Jakobson stressed precisely this point. The French avant-garde of the 1920s, he said, had been pursuing much the same artistic path as the Russians; but while the French "limited themselves to the arts and literature," the aspirations of the Russian avant-garde also "flowed into science."[6]

Jakobson may well have been thinking of himself here, and of the anomalies of his own career, but his remark is more than just another example of the retrospective illusion. For if we turn back to his article "Futurism" (1919), a defiantly youthful manifesto in the aggressive style of Futurist polemics, we find a defense of Cubism coupled with extensive quotations from two Russian expounders of Einstein's theory of relativity.[7] Since time and space no longer had fixed determinants, and the category of substance had lost all meaning, reality could only be represented, as the Cubists were showing it, from multiple points of view simultaneously. Remembering those exciting days, Jakobson here comments: "Such important experiments as non-objective abstract painting and 'supraconscious' (*zaumnyj*) verbal art, by respectively cancelling the represented or designated object, strikingly raised the problem of the nature and significance of the elements that exercise a semantic function in spatial figures on the one hand, and in language on the other" (7).

It was from this cultural climate that Jakobson took his point of departure, and his first important work—a study of Khlebnikov's linguistic innovations—contained one of the most intransigent declarations of early Russian Formalism. "Poetry," he declared, "is language in its aesthetic function," which means that it is "nothing other than an enunciation aiming at expression" and controlled solely by its own immanent laws. In poetry, the function of language as communication is reduced to a minimum,

[6] R. and R. Georgin, "Entretien avec Roman Jakobson," in Georgin, *Jakobson*, 11–12.

[7] Jakobson's *Selected Writings* have been published in six large volumes, and in the original language of composition, by Mouton in The Hague, but are so expensive that no ordinary book buyer can afford them. Smaller selections of his work in translation have appeared in numerous languages. I use the French *Questions de poétique* (Paris, 1973), translated by various hands and edited by Tzvetan Todorov, as well as the *Essais de linguistique générale*, trans. Nicholas Ruwet (Paris, 1963).

In its original form, this article contained a protest against the failure of American publishers, especially university presses, to make Jakobson's less technical writings available, as foreign publishers had done, in reasonably priced editions. Since then, I am happy to say, several such collections have appeared. See Roman Jakobson, *Verbal Art, Verbal Sign, Verbal Time* (Minneapolis, Minn., 1985); and *Language in Literature*, (Cambridge, Mass., 1987).

since poetry "is indifferent with regard to the object of the enunciation."
These words represent Jakobson's recasting, in terms of linguistics, of the
attitude toward language common to much modern experimental poetry
at least beginning with Mallarmé (whose work Jakobson knew and loved,
and who is cited twice in this essay). It would be only a slight exaggeration
to say that, in some sense, he spent much of his formidable intellectual
energy attempting to provide the Formalist aesthetics of modernism with
scientific respectability.

Jakobson traveled to Czechoslovakia in 1920 as part of an official Soviet
mission to the Red Cross, and, after becoming one of the main animators
of the famous Prague Linguistic Circle, finally decided not to return to his
homeland. His distinctive linguistic theories were developed during these
years, and the direction they took was clearly an outgrowth of his previous
poetic orientation. Traditional linguistics at that time, except for the work
of a few isolated precursors such as Ferdinand de Saussure and Baudouin
de Courtenay, the Polish linguist teaching in Russia, had been concerned
either with tracing historically the form of language changes, or with analyzing the physiological basis of sound production (phonetics). "They
studied language," Jakobson wrote in *Six Lectures*, "but never stopped to
ask how it satisfied cultural needs." As an erstwhile Russian Futurist, Jakobson was also fascinated with the sound level of language—but of course
from an entirely different point of view. For him, the sound level of language was important primarily as a shaper of poetic significance.

As a result, his next important work—a study of the differences between
the metric systems of Czech and Russian poetry—"brought out the role of
rhythmic variations that is played in Czech versification by such significa-
tive elements as the contraposition of long and short vowels. All of this
obliged me to work methodically at the systematization of the phonic elements of language" (23). Jakobson's attention thus became focused on
phonemes, the smallest sound segments of words, which, though they
mean nothing by themselves, allow the meaning of the word to be differ-
entiated from all other words in the same language. Phonemes, of course,
had been noted before in linguistics, but nobody had really centered on
them, or considered all their theoretical implications. It was Jakobson—
along with his boyhood friend Nicholas Trubetzkoy, then teaching at the
University of Vienna—who firmly established, in place of old-fashioned
phonetics (which Jakobson labels "prelinguistic"), the new discipline of
phonology, "the linguistic study of sounds, the study of sounds in the light
of the work they perform in language."

The analysis and systematization of phonic relations were carried on initially only for the sounds of vowels. Soon, however, Jakobson turned to
the consonants, which were of particular importance to him because Russian Futurism, reacting against the preference for vocalic euphony among

the Symbolists (Russian and otherwise), had particularly stressed that consonants were the backbone of poetic language. As Pomorska reminds Jakobson, "In your youth, you wrote verse based on the strangest combinations of consonants"(4).

Even though Trubetzkoy expressed some skepticism about the possibility of systematizing the consonants, since so diversified a mass of physiological data had been accumulated concerning them, Jakobson pressed ahead, aided by "X-ray pictures of spoken sounds and their measurements," which "made it possible to outline the major articulatory prerequisites of the most characteristic acoustic differences within the consonantal pattern"(31).

On this basis, and by a rigorous logical analysis of the differential properties of various classes of phonemes, Jakobson succeeded (at least to his own satisfaction, if not to that of linguists of other persuasions) in working out twelve binary oppositions that are sufficient to analyze all known languages and may be thought of as linguistic universals.[8] Examples of such oppositions are vocalic versus nonvocalic, tense versus lax, and grave versus acute, which are defined in terms of their acoustic correlates in speech production. In this way—though Jakobson never makes such a comparison himself—he realized the poetic dream that had haunted Khlebnikov of discovering the roots of a universal language.

Forced to flee Czechoslovakia in 1939, Jakobson first went to Denmark and Norway. He worked indefatigably with linguists in both countries, and plans were broached for a phonological atlas of the world that would have clarified many of the questions raised by his theories; but the occupation of Norway put an end to this project, and Jakobson moved on to find refuge in Sweden. Here, since Swedish linguists showed no interest in phonology, and since he could take advantage of the wealth of medical literature in Stockholm, he embarked on a pathbreaking linguistic study of aphasia, that is, the loss of the power to use words correctly, and the relation of this loss to the process of language acquisition by children.

Jakobson merely remarks that this was "a project I had cherished for many years"; but once again we can note the continuing influence of his early Futurist enthusiasms. For in their determination to free art and literature from conventional canons, the Futurists had organized exhibitions of children's art and had published poems and stories by children; even more, they had imitated the aphasic deformations of children's language in their own poetry.[9] Jakobson discovered, or confirmed his conjecture, that

[8] See Giulio C. Lepschy, *A Survey of Structural Linguistics* (London, 1970), 98–99.

[9] A. A. Hansen-Löve, *Der Russische Formalismus* (Vienna, 1978), 67. This monumental and extremely good book, unfortunately written in a very laborious German, is a mine of information about every aspect of Russian culture connected with the activity of the Formalist group and its relation to Futurism.

"a mirror-image relationship" existed "between phonological losses in aphasia and the order of acquisitions of distinctive oppositions by children." In his later years, working very closely with neurologists on the question of aphasia, Jakobson found some remarkable correlations between his own linguistic typology of aphasic impairments and neurological discoveries about the topography of brain lesions; his results were thus an important force in establishing the necessity of such collaborative neurolinguistic efforts.[10]

Upon arriving in the United States in 1941, Jakobson was introduced by Alexander Koyré to Lévi-Strauss, who had never heard of him but wanted to learn something about linguistics. (Koyré, also of Russian origin but a French national, was a great historian of philosophy who became an even greater historian of science.) In the preface he wrote for *Six Lectures*, thirty years later, Lévi-Strauss recalls the powerful impression that Jakobson made on him. His "innovatory ideas," he writes, "were all the more convincing in that Jakobson's exposition of them was performed with that incomparable art which made him the most dazzling teacher and lecturer that I had ever been lucky enough to hear" (xiv).

More important, Lévi-Strauss himself was then lecturing on kinship systems, and struggling to organize the "stunning multitude of variations" in the material that had been accumulated by ethnographers in the field. Jakobson's demonstration of how a limited number of phonemes, defined according to their mutually opposite—or "binary"—relations to one another, could be used to organize the multiplicity of phonic data into a coherent language system provided the anthropologist with the clue he was seeking:

> However much ideas such as those of the phoneme and of the prohibition of incest might seem incongruous, the conception which I was to form of the latter was inspired by the role assigned by linguists to the former. Just like the phoneme, which though it has no meaning of its own serves as a means by which meanings can be found, the incest prohibition seemed to me to be the link connecting the two domains hitherto held to be divorced from each other. To the articulation of sound with meaning there would thus correspond, on another level, that of nature with culture. And just as the form of the phoneme was the universal means, in all languages, whereby linguistic communication is established, so the incest prohibition, which, if we limit ourselves to its negative expression, is also found universally, also constitutes an empty form which is nevertheless indispensable if the articulation of biological groups into a network of exchanges whereby they can establish communication is to be both possible and necessary. (xviii)

[10] See the essays in Roman Jakobson, *Studies in Child Language and Aphasia* (The Hague, 1971); on the correlation with brain lesions, 93.

Lévi-Strauss later followed the same guideline in his studies of mythology, inventing the neologism "mytheme," on the analogy of phoneme, to designate the smallest unit of meaning in mythic discourse. "These are the elements from which mythic discourse is constructed, and they also are entities which are at one and the same time oppositive, relative, and negative; they are, to use the formula applied by Jakobson to phonemes, 'purely differential and contentless signs' " (xxii). Whether such mythemes can be distinguished with the same relative precision as phonemes—which are, after all, used to construct languages already known—is of course a much debated issue; but it was Jakobson, in any case, who paved the way for this daring attempt to unravel the mysterious origins of human culture.

Once he was established in the United States, Jakobson continued to pursue the main lines of research he had already initiated in technical linguistics, in the application of linguistic ideas to literature, and in other fields as well. Folklore had always interested him, he observes, ever since, as a schoolboy, he and his friends had gone out to collect songs and stories from the people in the immediate vicinity of Moscow. Folklore was also very popular with the Futurists, who saw in the glossolalia of some of the Russian religous sects a precursor of their own "supraconscious" use of language. Jakobson had studied examples of the Russian oral epic with the members of the Moscow Linguistic Circle as far back as 1915, and continued to do so in the intervening years. In 1929, he had written an article, "Folklore as a Specific Form of Creation," arguing against using categories taken from the written literary tradition to analyze oral literature. A whole volume of his *Selected Writings* is devoted to "Slavic Epic Studies"; and during his first years in this country he labored at a new edition of *The Lay of the Host of Igor*, the twelfth-century Russian epic whose authenticity had been questioned, but of which Jakobson produced a restored text with a historical commentary of enormous erudition.[11]

It is obviously impossible to follow Jakobson through all the many facets of his extraordinary career, each one of which would have been enough to occupy the entire life of any ordinary mortal. But the rise of French structuralism as primarily a *literary* movement, despite the initial impetus given

[11] Edward J. Brown of Stanford University, one of the most eminent American Slavists and a specialist in Soviet literature, was a student of Jakobson's at this time and has evoked him engagingly in an obituary: "When I first met him in 1946 he was in hot pursuit of true readings in many passages of the twelfth-century epic that had been misconstructed or misconstrued. Reconstruction of those passages required linguistic, literary, and folkloric erudition of extraordinary dimensions. In private conversations, in lectures and seminars, in the course of doctoral examinations, Jakobson would regularly announce sudden insights into the correct reading of a recalcitrant passage, with the result that his friends and students became his passive amazed companions in an enterprise that absorbed all his waking, no doubt also his sleeping hours." Edward J. Brown, "Roman Osipovich Jakobson: 1896–1982," *Russian Review* 41 (January 1983):91–99, citation on 98.

by the anthropologist Lévi-Strauss, focused increasing attention on Jakobson's more strictly literary ideas. Also, he too addressed himself more and more frequently to literary criticism and the interpretation of poetry. This was, in a sense, a return to his origins; but he was now far from being the brash young Formalist who had refused to regard poetry as anything but a set of linguistic devices, and who had insisted, surely hoping to irritate his elders, that "to incriminate the poet with ideas and feelings [expressed in his work] is just as absurd as the behavior of the medieval public which beat up the actor who played Judas" (*Questions*, 16).

By 1928, Jakobson had already broadened his perspective, as is plain from the famous theses that he wrote, in collaboration with Yury Tynyanov, while the latter was on a visit to Prague. Jakobson was then occupied with the problem of phonological change, and he addressed the same issue of change in relation to literature. The theses maintain, to be sure, that it is necessary to clarify the immanent laws of what is called "the literary series"; but these laws are now said to be "intimately linked to other historical series," such as politics, economics, philosophy, religion, and all the various dimensions of culture, so that there is no clear-cut opposition between the synchronic (static) study of language or literature and its diachronic (dynamic or historical) study. "Every synchronic system contains its past and its future, which are inherent structural elements." Even though the stress still remains on literature as a system, of crucial importance is the recognition that "while the discovery of the immanent laws of literary history (or languages) allows the characterization of each concrete literary change . . . it does not offer the possibility of clarifying the rhythm of evolution or the choice of the path taken by such evolution in the presence of several theoretically possible paths of evolution (*Questions*, 56–57). In other words, only the correlation of the literary series with other aspects of culture can explain historical movement.

In the brilliant literary criticism that Jakobson wrote during the 1930s, he was too powerful a creative thinker to allow himself to be hamstrung by theoretical preconceptions. Grief-stricken at the suicide of his old friend Mayakovsky, and enraged at the chorus of condemnatory stupidities uttered by official Party hacks, he quickly wrote "On the Generation That Squandered Its Poets," an intensely moving litany to the riches of the past that he had once known and that had been wasted by the prodigal hand of Russian history. Jakobson refers to this essay—one of the finest accounts of modern Russian poetry—in *Dialogues*, but cites only a part of the following revealing passage: "We threw ourselves toward the future with too much passion and avidity to be able to retain a past. The ligature of time was torn. We lived too much for the future, thought of it too much, believed in it, we no longer had the sensation of an actuality that was sufficient unto itself, we lost the feeling for the present" (138; *Questions*, 101).

Summarizing, fifty years later, what he had depicted as Mayakovsky's "personal mythology," he speaks of "the monolithic myth of the poet, a zealot in the name of the revolution of the spirit, a martyr condemned to cruel and hostile incomprehension and rejection." And he recalls that Mayakovsky himself wrote: "The massacre was over. . . . Alone above the Kremlin, the shreds of the poet waved in the wind like a red flag"(139). The article itself has a much larger, more magisterial canvas, documenting the constant recurrence of the theme of suicide in Mayakovsky's poetry, where the immensity of individual desire, extending even to the unquenchable craving for a literal personal immortality, is allied to a hatred of the quotidian that Jakobson sees as peculiarly Russian, and that Mayakovsky more and more came to identify with the world emerging from the Bolshevik revolution. Art and life in this instance cannot be disentangled, and the old Formalist Jakobson speaks, with perceptible pathos, of "the atrocious agony" of suddenly discovering "the transparency of the [poetic] pseudonym, when the phantoms of art, wiping out the frontiers, cross over into life, like the young girl in an old scenario of Mayakovsky, who is kidnapped from a film by a mad painter" (*Questions*, 94).

Jakobson wrote several other essays during these years (one devoted to the Czech romantic poet Mácha, another to the symbolism of the malevolent statue in Pushkin's poetry, a third on the prevalence of metonymy in Pasternak), all of them devoted to illustrating the intricacies of the relations between art and life. In each case, he attacks "the vulgar conception of poetic fiction as a mechanical superstructure on reality, as well as . . . the equally vulgar dogma that I call 'anti-biographism,' which rejects any relation between art and its personal and social background" (*Questions*, 154). For Jakobson, a poet's life was not an independent variable in relation to his art. The intermixture of the two was so manifold and subtle that the boundaries between them inevitably became blurred on closer inspection.

It was impossible to tell, Jakobson argued, whether Mácha's diaries and letters were "truer" than his verses, just as Pushkin's myth of the demonic statue not only appears in three poems but in his letters and the events of his own life as well. Similarly, the use of metonymy in Pasternak, where the personality of the poet seems to dissolve in the contiguous context of the world surrounding him, can, he argued, easily be linked to a certain passivity in his character and to the powerlessness of the social milieu from which he came. But Jakobson also insists on placing Pasternak in the literary tradition of his time, which imposed its imperatives on all poets independent of their volition. What Jakobson wished to safeguard is the complexity of the relation between art and life, the multiple ways in which they interact; no mechanical juxtaposition, no model of "base" and "superstructure" along positivist or Marxist lines, can portray this relation adequately. Jakobson's attempts to do so are immensely suggestive, and these remarkable contributions to the theory of literary biography have not received the attention they deserve.

Always alert to new advances in linguistics, Jakobson kept abreast of the theories of communication that emerged after the Second World War. During the 1950s he began to rework his ideas by showing their relation to codes and to the process of receiving and sending messages. In his classic article "Linguistics and Poetics" (1960), he reformulated some of his key principles from this new perspective. "A sender," he writes,

> sends a message to a receiver. In order to be received, the message requires, first, a context to which it refers (this is what one calls, in a somewhat ambiguous terminology, the "referent"), a context understood by the receiver, and which is either verbal or capable of being verbalized; then, the message requires a code, which is common, in whole or in part, to the sender and receiver (or, in other terms, to the coder and decoder of the message); finally, the message requires a contact, a physical channel and a psychological connection between the sender and receiver that permits them to establish and maintain communication. (*Essais*, 213–14)

Each of these six features gives birth to a different linguistic function; but while these functions can be theoretically distinguished, it would be difficult to find pure examples of any in an actual message. "The diversity of messages lies not in the monopoly of one or another function, but in the differences of hierarchy between them."

One of Jakobson's aims in this essay—given as a concluding speech at an interdisciplinary conference of linguists, anthropologists, psychologists, and literary critics—was to persuade his audience of the importance of studying the poetic function of language. This he defined, quite in line with his earlier notions, as "placing the accent on the message itself for its own sake," or, to use his old terminology, "language in its aesthetic function." But Jakobson no longer insists on any sharp separation between poetry and ordinary language; rather, he stresses quite the opposite—the subordinate use of the poetic function in all sorts of other messages. Taking one of the political slogans of the time ("I like Ike"), he gives a sparkling and amusing analysis of the sound pattern to show how it conveys the image of a loving subject ("I") enveloped by the loved object (the repetition of the vowel and consonant sequence, with "I" now included in "Ike"). It is in this way that the poetic function of language reinforces the effectiveness of the political slogan.

In its pure state, however, the poetic function brings such expressive aspects of language itself to the foreground, and Jakobson defines this process by means of his frequently used distinction between metaphor and metonymy: the first based on relations of similarity or equivalence, as in "All the world's a stage," the second on relations of contiguity, as when we say "White House" for the president. "The poetic function," he wrote, "projects the principle of equivalence from the axis of selection to the axis of combination." The axis of selection is the choice of a range of alternative words for any particular message; the axis of combination is the grammatical sequence required by whatever language is being used to convey the message in a coherent form. So that, in poetic language, the choice of words is governed by relations of symmetry and dissymmetry, or metaphorical linkages, which take precedence over the syntactical structure required to convey the meaning of the message with maximum clarity and efficiency. The use of parallelisms in folk poetry, where the same basic idea is repeated several times in the same rhythmic form, but with new examples, is an instance of relations of symmetry governing the axis of combination.

This "law of projection," as it has come to be called, provides a fundamental insight into poetry, particularly of modern poetry, and will certainly remain as one of the foundations of the poetics of the future. But while Jakobson's thesis was immediately accepted as throwing a flood of light on the linguistic underpinnings of poetic creation, his attempt to apply it to particular poems aroused a great deal of opposition. Some of this, as he claimed, simply sprang from the narrowness and prejudice of old-fashioned humanists, who resented a "scientific" intruder into their privileged domain; but since other skeptical critics were also distinctly sympathetic to his efforts, not all could be brushed off with the charge of bias. The only chapter of *Dialogues* in which he seems embattled is the one devoted to what he called "the poetry of grammar and the grammar of poetry" (also the title of one of the volumes in his *Selected Writings*). Jakobson usually treats opposition to his theories with the superior affability of a *grand seigneur*; but in this instance he becomes acrimonious. Perhaps the failure to carry his point, at such a late stage of his career, proved to be particularly galling.

What happened, as he tells us, was that after "Linguistics and Poetics," "I concentrated on the distribution and artistic function of the different grammatical categories within single poetic works and was surprised to observe from the outset the symmetry and regularity of grammatical oppositions among the most diverse poets, from every period and every language" (112). No explanation is offered here of the relation between this endeavor and his "law of projection"; but it is clearly stated in an article also dating from 1960: "one may propose that, in poetry, similarity is superimposed on contiguity, and therefore 'equivalence is promoted to the rank of a constitutive principle of the sequence.' In these conditions, every repetition of the same grammatical concept capable of attracting attention becomes an effective poetic device" (*Questions*, 225). Hence it is not only word choice but also grammatical structure itself, in all its multiform varieties, that is dominated by equivalence.[12]

Jakobson's method is difficult to illustrate briefly because it depends on a careful and exhaustive detailing of minutiae; but to give some idea, we may take the following passage from his analysis of Shakespeare's sonnet number 129, "Th'expence of Spirit in a waste of shame."

> As shown by many four-strophe poems in world literature, the outer strophes carry a higher syntactic rank than the inner ones. The inner strophes are devoid of finites, but comprise ten (6 + 4) participles. On the other hand, the outer strophes are deprived of participles, but each of these strophes contains one finite which occurs twice in the coordinate clauses linked by a conjunction: I_1 *Th'expense***$_2$Is lust***and***lust$_3$ Is perjurd;* IV_1 *the world well knowes yet none knowes well.* In each of these instances both clauses display a metathesis: I_1 *Is lust in action—till action lust$_3$ Is;* IV_1 *well knowes—knowes well.* In the first strophe *lust* occurs in two different syntactic functions.[13]

Jakobson applied his vast ingenuity and linguistic learning in this way in order to exhibit "the distribution and artistic function of the different grammatical categories within single poetic works," analyzing examples from, on his own count, sixteen languages.

No one had ever before paid such exacting attention to this aspect of poetic form, though Jakobson was fond of citing remarks from Baudelaire, Edgar Allan Poe, and Gerard Manley Hopkins as precursors of his own efforts. There is no question that Jakobson succeeded in establishing the existence of a dense network of such equivalences in the poetry he has treated; but the *importance* of these relationships for the interpretation of the poetic text is quite another matter. He was fond of arguing that such patterns work in a manner analogous to music, where the experience of the composition can be conveyed without any conscious or abstract knowledge of the underlying form; but such a comparison reveals one of the weaknesses of his own position. For music does not have, in addition to

[12] Here too Jakobson was returning, armed with his later linguistics, to the principles of early Futurist and Formalist poetics. Hansen-Löve points out the importance of the concept of repetition for the poetics of "Belyj as well as of O. Brik, Jakobson, Shklovskij and other Formalists," who saw in repetition "that 'power' which creates an intimate linkage between the optic-imaginative perceptibility of the metaphoric level and the 'primary acoustic phenomena' of assonance, etc. The repetition of sound leads to a repetition of word, and from here to all other forms and figures of repetition (*figura povtora*), which constructively organize the subject." *Der Russische Formalismus*, 128.

[13] Roman Jakobson and Lawrence G. Jones, *Shakespeare's Verbal Art in Th'Expence of Spirit* (The Hague, 1970), 23.

its formal structure, the complication of semantic meaning conveyed by words.

Up until the end, Jakobson was never able to convince his numerous critics that the grammatical relations on which he was concentrating are crucial for the comprehension of the poem and contain the secret of its interpretation. As the best American student of Russian Formalism, Victor Erlich, has recently written of Jakobson's readings, "Typically, a meticulous linguistic description of the poem would be followed by a sound and perceptive overall interpretation. But more often than not, only some elements of the latter could be shown to depend on, or derive from, the former."[14] Jonathan Culler, with whom Jakobson takes irritable issue by name in *Dialogues*, makes the essential point when he remarks that "poems contain, by virtue of the fact that they are read as poems, structures other than the grammatical, and the resulting interplay may give the grammatical structures a function which is not at all what the linguist expected."[15]

Jakobson's final remarks on this thorny problem seem, at first sight, to be simply a vigorous defense of his own claims; but a closer reading suggests that he may have begun to retreat. "If a critic reads into studies of the grammar of poetry a secret intention on the part of the analyst to reduce poetry to a grammar," he now says, "he is engaging in idle fantasy. In studying rhyme, no one went so far as to claim that poetry equals rhyme, just as one could never reduce poetry to a system of metaphors, or to a complex of stanzas, or to any other form and its various effects." A few sentences later, he defends the study of grammatical figures as "an interesting and useful undertaking, independent of the further question of the contributing role of these properties in the general 'effect' of the poetic work" (118). One can hardly quarrel with such a position.

Despite the sorrowful ruminations of "On the Generation That Squandered Its Poets," Jakobson never renounced his origins in Russian Futurism and never lost that hopeful élan which he noted as one of the characteristics of his own generation.[16] It is typical that, in discussing the ideas of Charles Sanders Peirce, whom he considered the greatest American philosopher, he placed particular emphasis on Peirce's concept of the linguistic symbol, the word, because this is related to an indefinite future. "The word and the future are indissolubly linked," he writes, and he sees this as "the essence of the science of creative language in general, and of poetic lan-

[14] This remark is contained in the new preface to the third edition of Victor Erlich, *Russian Formalism* (New Haven, Conn., 1981), 14.

[15] Jonathan Culler, *Structuralist Poetics* (Ithaca, N.Y., 1975), 73.

[16] In the interview already cited with R. and R. Georgin, Jakobson says: "Once again the young are beginning to play the role of innovators, although there is an essential difference. You wish to know what that difference is? We were much more optimistic and sure of ourselves. What predominates today is doubt and dismay." Georgin, *Jakobson*, 12.

guage in particular." Jakobson himself was always looking toward the future, and it is especially fitting that so much of his work, rather than being closed and definitive, opened up new paths for the future to explore. Pomorska in her afterword quotes a well-known poem of Mayakovsky, "To Comrade Nette—Steamship and Man," which depicts the poet and Nette, a Soviet diplomatic courier, traveling together in the special railroad car that Nette had at his disposal. To pass the time, they talk of a mutual friend:

> *One eye*
>> *crossing at the wax seal*
>> *you chatted all night of Romka*
>>> *Jakobson. . . .*

Many people will continue to carry on this conversation about the physically absent but indelibly present Roman Jakobson, whose vast life's work will provide inspiration to others for many years to come.

CHAPTER TWO

The Voices of Mikhail Bakhtin

1

TWENTY YEARS ago, the name of Mikhail Bakhtin would hardly have been known outside Russia except to Slavic scholars, and even then only to those with a special interest in Dostoevsky. At the present time, however, the works of Bakhtin are exercising a considerable influence among literary critics and cultural historians not only in his native land but in Europe and the United States as well. Bakhtin is the only Soviet Russian scholar one can think of whose writings have radiated so far and so extensively beyond their native borders; and the phenomenon is all the more surprising because Bakhtin, though hardly a conventional Marxist-Leninist, did all he could to avoid conflict with the Soviet state while maintaining his intellectual independence.

The prestige his work enjoys in the West thus does not derive from any overt political dissidence or opposition to Soviet authority. It is purely a product of the appeal of his ideas and the insights they offer into issues that occupy his Western admirers. The situation is somewhat different in the Soviet Union, where his belated fame does originate, at least in part, from his struggle to evade the straitjacket of Soviet official thinking, and to keep alive some of the élan of the apocalyptic and millenarian Russian culture of the early part of this century and the immediate post-Revolutionary years—the culture that was suppressed by Stalinism. But if Bakhtin can be considered to have been unhappy with the narrowness and dogmatism of the Soviet cultural establishment, there is not the slightest reason to believe that he ever doubted the wisdom and ultimate validity of the Bolshevik revolution.

Bakhtin, however, is not a product of the Revolution itself; he was formed in the ferment of the years immediately preceding this great upheaval. Very little about him personally was known until quite recently; but thanks to the researches of the husband-and-wife team of Katerina Clark and Michael Holquist, readers of their pioneering and enthusiastic critical biography now have more information at their disposal than the Russians themselves possess (at least in public print).[1] Indeed, the work of

---

[1] Katerina Clark and Michael Holquist, *Mikhail Bakhtin* (Cambridge, Mass., 1984); Tzvetan Todorov, *Mikhail Bakhtin: The Dialogical Principle*, trans. Wlad Godzich (Minneapolis, Minn., 1984).

Clark and Holquist, which is based on research in obscure Russian archives, and on personal interviews in the Soviet Union with people who knew Bakhtin personally or had the opportunity to obtain information about him, uncovers a hidden corner of Russian cultural life that continued to survive through the 1920s. In addition to Bakhtin himself, his milieu will prove of great fascination to all students of Russian culture; and the account given of it here enables us to catch a rare glimpse of oe among (the probably numerous) underground groups who, without being hostile to Bolshevik political power, refused to tailor their spiritual needs to its stifling moral and philosophical confines. By contrast, Tzvetan Todorov's book, *Mikhail Bakhtin: The Dialogical Principle*, is a slighter but valuable and scrupulous attempt to scrutinize Bakhtin's thought in a more systematic fashion; the two works thus complement each other very neatly.

Born in 1895, Bakhtin sprang from an old noble family that had deigned to soil its hands with commerce; his grandfather had founded a bank, and his father worked as manager in various branches. His parents were cultivated and liberal, and the Bakhtin children (he had three sisters and an older brother, Nikolay, who went into exile and ended his days in England as chairman of the linguistics department at the University of Birmingham)[2] were given a careful and superior education. Mikhail learned German at a very early age from a governess, who also instilled in the brothers a reverence for classical culture. Both eventually became classical scholars, and Bakhtin's extensive knowledge of Greek and Latin literature is everywhere evident in his work. Clark and Holquist also note the influence of Nietzsche and of Russian Symbolism (particularly of the poet and scholar Vyacheslav Ivanov, whose writings on Dostoevsky anticipate Bakhtin's own views). At age fifteen Mikhail also began to read Martin Buber and Kierkegaard, and was so impressed with the second that he tried to learn Danish.[3]

---

[2] It is fascinating to learn that Nikolay Bakhtin was a friend of the philosopher Ludwig Wittgenstein when they were together at Cambridge in the 1930s. Clark and Holquist report that Bakhtin's "conversations with Wittgenstein were one of the factors influencing the philosopher's shift from the logical positivism of the *Tractatus* to the more broadly speculative *Philosophical Investigations.*"

Brian McGuinness of Oxford University, an authority on Wittgenstein's life, was kind enough to inform me that there is a solid basis for believing the influence of Nikolay Bakhtin on Wittgenstein to have been considerable.

[3] An article that appeared in an émigré journal simultaneously with Clark and Holquist's book indicates that Bakhtin preserved his admiration for Martin Buber to the very end of his life. The author, who visited Bakhtin in a hospital sometime between 1979 and 1981 (the dates can be established because his wife was still present at his bedside), recalls another visitor asking the ailing scholar what he thought about Buber. The question was posed because a mutual friend, when queried about Bakhtin's opinion of this thinker, had remained strangely silent.

Bakhtin responded wearily that this mutual friend, being an anti-Semite, would not have wished to dwell on such a connection. But then he gave his own view: "Of Buber Mikhail Mikhailovich thinks that he—Buber—is the greatest philosopher of the twentieth century,

Bakhtin studied at the University of St. Petersburg between 1914 and 1918, and there came into contact with the person he called "the closest thing to a teacher I ever had." He was referring to F. F. Zelinsky, a Polish-Russian classicist of international reputation, whose ideas, in some sense, Bakhtin can be said to have drawn on all his life, though he extended them in ways going far beyond the study of the past. Zelinsky had conjectured that "all types of literature were already present in antiquity," and Bakhtin maintains that the modern novel (particularly beginning with Dostoevsky) is really a latter-day version of the Menippean satire, which goes back to the third century B.C. For Zelinsky, the dialogue form was "the literary expression of philosophical freedom," and Bakhtin elevated the notion of dialogue into the basis of a world view incorporating a metaphysics of freedom. Zelinsky also stressed the importance of the folk element in the culture of antiquity, particularly the subversive role of the satyr play in undermining the official culture—just as Bakhtin was to do with the folk elements in Rabelais that parodied and exploded the high culture of the Renaissance.

On graduating from the university in 1918, Bakhtin lived for two years in the provincial town of Nevel and then moved to neighboring Vitebsk, which had by then become a center of avant-garde art. Chagall, who was born there, had returned to found a museum and academy of art, which then was taken over by Kazimir Malevich and turned into a cradle of the Suprematist style. Sergey Eisenstein, who passed through Vitebsk in 1920, noted with astonishment that the walls of the houses had been whitewashed and were covered with "green circles, orange squares and blue rectangles." Bakhtin and his friends (the first of the circles that were to form around him) read Kant and Hegel, Saint Augustine and Vladimir Soloviev, and Vyacheslav Ivanov's books on the dionysiac elements of Greek religion that bore such strong and strange resemblances to the dying God of Christianity. To keep alive, Bakhtin taught in a high school, gave numerous lectures, and worked as a bookkeeper and economic consultant. Having suffered from a bone disease since childhood, he also received a small pension as an invalid, which was his only regular income for many years. Luckily, his devoted wife, Elena Aleksandrovna, whose image appears in a

---

and perhaps, in this philosophically puny century, perhaps the sole philosopher on the scene." Bakhtin then went on to explain that while Nicholas Berdyaev, Lev Shestov, and Jean-Paul Sartre are all excellent examples of thinkers, there is a difference between them and philosophers. "But Buber is a philosopher. And I am very much indebted to him. In particular, for the idea of dialogue. Of course, this is obvious to anyone who reads Buber."

See Mariya Kaganskaya, "Shutovskoi Khorovod," *Sintaksis* 121 (1984):141. I am greatly indebted to my colleague at Stanford University, Gregory Freidin, for his kindness in having called my attention to this article and providing me with a copy.

touching photograph snapped shortly after their marriage, took charge of their finances and miraculously managed to make ends meet.

Four years later Bakhtin moved to Leningrad, where most of his original circle were already living. Clark and Holquist's chapters on these Leningrad years provides a more detailed account of the Bakhtin circle, which now included musicians, writers, natural scientists, and scholars in diverse disciplines, some of extraordinary gifts and considerable attainments. One member later became artistic director of the Leningrad Philharmonic; another was a famous pianist (whose talent, if rumor is right, was appreciated by Stalin), and who played Shostakovich, Hindemith, and Bartók when it was hardly politic to do so; a third translated Spengler and Wölfflin into Russian; and there was, as well, a petroleum geologist, a biologist, and a specialist in Buddhism and ancient Indian and Bengali literature. What united all these people, aside from friendship, was an intense spiritual need and an intellectual curiosity that could not find nourishment in the prevailing cultural climate; and so they supplied what was lacking by their own efforts.

Here is one description of the activities of the group given by Clark and Holquist:

> The Bakhtin circle was not in any sense a fixed organization. They were simply a group of friends who loved to meet and debate ideas and who had philosophical interests in common. . . . Usually one of the group prepared a short synopsis or review of a philosophical work and read this to the circle as a basis for discussion. The range of topics covered was wide, including Proust, Bergson, Freud, and above all questions of theology. Occasionally one member gave a lecture series to the others. The most famous of these was a course of eight lectures on Kant's *Critique of Judgment* given by Bakhtin in early 1925. (103)

None of this was in accord with the Marxist ideas favored by the reigning authorities, and the pronounced interest in theology would of course have been particularly suspect. Indeed, it was Bakhtin's theological orientation that soon led to his fateful brush with the power of the state.

Despite all their laudable efforts, which produce a good deal of quite interesting information about minuscule religious groups of the 1920s, Clark and Holquist are unable to turn up much solid material concerning Bakhtin's religious convictions. Aside from the indisputable fact that he was known to be "a believer in the Orthodox tradition," very little can be said specifically about the doctrinal nature of this allegiance. He was, however, associated with the *Voskresenie* group (the word means "resurrection"), one of whose animators was Georgey P. Fedotov, later a professor at St. Vladimir's Orthodox Theological Seminary in the United States, who wrote what is unquestionably one of the great modern analyses of Russian culture, *The Russian Religious Mind* (unfortunately left incomplete at the time of his death in 1951). This is not primarily a study of theology, but a brilliant example of what now would be called *histoire des mentalités*.

Fedotov believed at that time that "revolutionary Marxism [was] a Judeo-Christian apocalyptic sect," and that it was inspired, particularly in Russia, by a "religious idea" that "hides a potential for Orthodoxy." Bakhtin presumably felt much the same, though such a conclusion can only be inferential; and like Fedotov he probably "saw in communism the seeds of a superior social order." Other members of the Bakhtin circle also attended meetings of the same *Voskresenie* group, whose social program "envisaged something like the communist ideal of the early church fathers" and was based on the Russian Orthodox conception of *sobornost*, or "togetherness"—a "true sense of community" whose initial Russian advocates, as Clark and Holquist regrettably fail to mention, had been the Slavophiles. Bakhtin's affiliation with such conventicles finally involved him in the Josephite schism of 1928, which refused to accept the decision of the Orthodox patriarch acknowledging the temporal power of the state over the Church. The October Revolution had freed the Church from the state control that had existed under tsarism, and the Josephites did not wish to see it reestablished.

Arrested and sentenced to a prison term in the arctic Solovetsky Islands, which would have meant a speedy death, Bakhtin was saved by a series of circumstances. Mutual friends enlisted the aid of Aleksey Tolstoy and Maxim Gorky; and a favorable review of Bakhtin's book on Dostoevsky happily appeared, written by no less a personage than the then commissar of enlightenment, Anatoly Lunacharsky. A man of letters himself, about whom Clark and Holquist might have furnished a little more information, Lunacharsky could appreciate literary quality when he came across it and knew immediately that Bakhtin was no run-of-the-mill scholar. Since Lunacharsky had once written a large treatise on *Religion and Socialism* (1908), in which he had identified Marxism with true Christianity, he would have been especially responsive both to the underlying moral-religious implications of Bakhtin's views and his attempt to disengage Dostoevsky's works from those particular ideological elements manifestly unacceptable to the Soviets.

Bakhtin was thus exiled to Kazakhstan for four years, where he again used his bookkeeping skills to stay alive and taught the subject to the cadres of collective farms engaged in implementing Stalin's disastrous agricultural policy. In 1936 he obtained a teaching post in a lowly pedagogical institute buried in the provinces of European Russia, which he left voluntarily a year later for fear of being purged. His past history of arrest always made him suspect, and although he wrote his book on Rabelais for a doctorate at the Gorky Institute of World Literature in Moscow, he was only allowed to teach foreign languages in high school during the Second World War. After the war, he returned to the pedagogical institute, which eventually became a university, and served very conscientiously as chairman of the department of Russian and foreign literature until his retirement in 1961.

Bakhtin lived in almost complete obscurity until the late 1950s, when references to his Dostoevsky book began to appear both abroad and in the Soviet Union. Some graduate students at the Gorky Institute, discovering that he was still alive, organized a campaign for the republication of the Dostoevsky text (which he substantially revised), and also worked successfully to publish the Rabelais manuscript, which had been reposing all this while in the files of their alma mater. Other essays also began to appear, written at various periods; one collection was published in 1975, the year of Bakhtin's death, and another collection, containing mostly early work, was issued in 1979. During these later years Bakhtin enjoyed extraordinary prestige among the younger Soviet intelligentsia, and "had . . . become a veritable guru" for them according to Clark and Holquist. Besides the intrinsic interest of his writings, he was also, in the eyes of the younger generation, the survivor of an almost legendary past; and they could still hear in his words the voice of that lost pre-Revolutionary world with whose values they wished to renew contact.

2

One problem that immediately arises in any approach to Bakhtin's work is that of authorship. Bakhtin published only three books under his own name during his lifetime—the one on Dostoevsky, the study of Rabelais, and the volume of essays that he saw through publication the year of his death. But in 1971, a well-known Soviet semiotician V. V. Ivanov, who was close to Bakhtin, stated unequivocally that he was also the author of three other books and several essays signed by two members of the Bakhtin circle, V. N. Voloshinov and Pavel Medvedev.[4] To what extent these works were written by Bakhtin himself, or were collaborative efforts, remains a matter of dispute. Clark and Holquist are inclined to accept them as entirely the work of Bakhtin; Todorov is more circumspect. But there is little doubt that the leading ideas can be attributed to Bakhtin if we assume, as is generally accepted, that he was "the philosopher" of the circle and supplied the dominating intellectual inspiration for views that might equally well be taken up and applied by others.

Much light has recently been cast on such views by the publication in

[4] All three books have been translated into English. See V. N. Voloshinov, *Freudianism: A Marxist Critique*, trans. I. R. Titunik (New York, 1973); P. N. Medvedev and M. M. Bakhtin (IP), *The Formal Method in Literary Scholarship: A Critical Introduction to Sociological Poetics*, trans. Albert C. Wehrle (Baltimore, Md., 1978); V. N. Voloshinov, *Marxism and the Philosophy of Language*, trans. Ladislav Matejka and I. R. Titunik (New York, 1973).

1979 of a volume of Bakhtin's essays, *Estetika Slovesnogo Tvorchestva*, which included an unfinished philosophical work on which he had labored in the early 1920s. Left untitled, and not yet published in English, it contains the ideas that Clark and Holquist, as well as Todorov, all agree remain central to Bakhtin's thought throughout his career. Bakhtin's fragmentary text is a work of both aesthetics and moral-religious philosophy—a combination that will continue to remain typical, since Bakhtin's linguistic and literary categories, however neutral they seem, will always have a moral meaning. His manuscript deals primarily with the relations between the individual self and the world formed by other human beings. Some of Bakhtin's analyses of these interpersonal relations anticipate those of Heidegger and Sartre, though he hardly works them out with the same degree of philosophical rigor; and Clark and Holquist seem to me to exaggerate the importance of Bakhtin's strictly philosophical ideas. Other remarks of theirs, however, agree with Todorov in the more persuasive view that Bakhtin's achievement lies in his ability to translate his philosophical intuitions into the terms of psychology, the philosophy of language, literary criticism, and cultural history.

At the center of Bakhtin's thought, which can be described as a variety of religious existentialism, is the paradigm of Christ. "Christ gave up the privileges of divinity, his uniqueness," explain Clark and Holquist, "to share the general condition of humanity, a model establishing the priority of shared as opposed to individual values." But, at the same time, Christ also infinitely deepened the sense of human self-consciousness. As Bakhtin himself wrote, "In Christ we find a synthesis—unique in its profundity . . . for the first time there appears an infinitely deepened I-for-myself [individual self-consciousness], yet not a cold I-for-myself, but one which is boundlessly good toward the other." Christ thus supplied the ideal model of all human relationships and, to cite Bakhtin again, "what I must be for the other [person], God is for me [for my I-for-myself]" (*Estetika*, 51–52).

Bakhtin thus conceives the self and the other as inseparably linked, the medium of this linkage being language. It is through language that self-consciousness achieves expression; it is language that defines the relations between the self and the other, which, ideally, should mirror the modality of the dialogue between man and God. Whatever hinders or blocks this dialogue is necessarily blameworthy; whatever favors or facilitates it is automatically to be preferred. These are the polarities of Bakhtin's thought, which work everywhere in and through his other seemingly descriptive and value-free categories.

The first three works published by the Bakhtin circle (whose titles are given in note 4), all sprang from the application of such ideas. In psychology, Freudianism was criticized for reducing consciousness to a complex of biological drives and neglecting its social dimension, which is present both in the language through which consciousness has been formed and in the verbal exchanges of the patient-analyst relationship. The same point is made in the work on Marxism and the philosophy of language, which quarrels with all contemporary schools of linguistics. It takes issue with those linguists like Ferdinand de Saussure who, studying language solely as a mechanism for the production of meaning, eliminate actual usage from consideration; but it also criticizes "Romantic subjectivists" like Karl Vossler and Leo Spitzer, who are quite arbitrarily charged with being concerned *only* with usage and individual linguistic creation.[5] Language for the Bakhtinians is "utterance," which involves the relation between the self and the other person; it is a living word exchanged between existing people, and can only be properly understood in the full range and richness of the moral and social meanings contained in discourse.

The members of the Bakhtin circle next moved from linguistics to literary criticism; and their book on Russian Formalism, which created a small stir on publication, is now recognized as among the most effective contemporary polemics (written from an extremely flexible and nondogmatic Marxist point of view) against the first phase of that movement. Bakhtin and Medvedev forcefully attack the Formalist separation of art from any specific content, the exclusive concentration on technical devices and on an "aesthetics of the material" (in the case of literature, the purely phonic and perceptual qualities of language). The work of art, they argue, is not simply an artifact but a medium of communication—like language itself, it is an "utterance" involving an exchange between the (artistic) self and the other, and must be understood within the ideological context of its time. But Bakhtin and Medvedev are equally criticial of vulgar Marxism, which interprets ideological content as a direct reflection of social reality and pays no attention to how such content is mediated through the work of art as a whole; it is the work of art as a unity that constitutes a response to its time,

---

[5] Such a charge hardly does justice to such major works of Vossler as his magisterial book on Dante, *Die Gottliche Komödie*, 2 vols. (Heidelberg, 1907–1910), which contains an entire history of Western culture up to Dante's time, or to his book on the evolution of the French language as part of the history of French culture, *Frankreich's Kultur in Spiegel seiner Sprachentwicklung* (Heidelberg, 1921). Vossler's Dante opus was translated into English as *Medieval Culture*, trans. Willian Cranston Lawton, 2 vols. (New York, 1929), a title that gives a better idea of its scope.

Spitzer is more concerned with the analysis of individual linguistic creation in poetry, but even he invariably places every text in a larger literary-cultural context provided by his prodigious erudition. A convenient collection of Spitzer's superb essays has recently become available again in *Representative Essays*, ed. Alban K. Forcione, Herbert Lindenberger, and Madeleine Sutherland (Stanford, Calif., 1988).

Readers of Bakhtin and the Bakhtinians should be very wary of accepting their evaluation of other critics and linguists at face value, and would do well to keep in mind that their remarks are polemical rather than descriptive.

not one or another of its aspects taken in abstraction. As Todorov remarks, one of Bakhtin's "major options" is a systematic refusal to separate form and content; and the attempt to apply this principle lies at the heart of his Dostoevsky book.

In the course of their polemic, Bakhtin and Medvedev compare the Russian Formalists with those whom they consider to be their European counterparts. And they point out that while the Russians, in their reaction against all types of academic and positivist scholarship and criticism, simply abandoned the issue of semantic or ideological content altogether, the European Formalists (they cite primarily specialists in art history like Konrad Fiedler, "Heinrich Wölfflin, and especially Wilhelm Worringer) interpret form itself as containing an ideological meaning. It is for this reason that the Europeans do not eliminate semantic significance in favor of formal interests. Inspired by this example, Bakhtin is one of the few literary critics who has nourished the ambition to demonstrate the ideological import of a purely formal *literary* style or technique; and this is exactly what he tried to do in the case of Dostoevsky. For Bakhtin claims that Dostoevsky created a new novelistic form (he calls it the "polyphonic novel"), which transposes in its technical features the moral-religious values also expressed in the content of the work. And these moral-religious values are precisely the ones that Bakhtin had previously spoken of as appearing in the world with the advent of Christ—a sense of the infinity of human personality, and thus the moral task of relating to this infinity not coldly and externally but with an attitude of boundless goodness.[6]

3

Bakhtin's study of Dostoevsky's poetics, now available in an excellent English version, is such a rich work, and raises so many issues—not only involving the interpretation of Dostoevsky but also fundamental questions of literary genre and narrative theory—that only scant justice can be done

[6] No one seems to be aware, to my knowledge, that Bakhtin was following Worringer in assigning an ideological (in this case a moral-religious) significance to a pure literary form (a particular modality of the relation between author and character). My own insistence on this point certainly stems from a personal reason that I cannot resist mentioning in this context.

Many years ago, also inspired by a reading of Wilhelm Worringer, I made a somewhat similar attempt myself—not for an individual writer but for an entire style, the style of modern experiments with language in both poetry and prose. This was the origin of my concept of "spatial form," the tendency of modernist writers to undo or circumvent the linear time-nature of language, which I interpreted as the expression of a negation of history and a return to the mythical imagination. See "Spatial Form in Modern Literature" in *The Widening Gyre* (New Brunswick, N.J., 1963). For further consideration of the problem by myself and others, see *Spatial Form in Narrative*, ed. Jeffrey R. Smitten and Ann Daghistany (Ithaca, N.Y., 1981).

to it in these brief remarks dealing mainly with his central thesis.[7] The first chapter, which contains a survey of the previous critics (mostly Russian) whom Bakhtin deems worthy of consideration, charges them all with the same error of which the vulgar Marxists had been accused earlier. Just as the Marxists had ripped certain elements of a work out of their artistic context and seen them as a direct reflection of social reality, so critics had taken one or another of Dostoevsky's characters as a direct reflection of the author's ideas. Bakhtin quite justifiably dismisses what he calls this "path of philosophical monologization" as an inadequate approach, even though, one should add, it has led to some sharp insights into Dostoevsky's thematics. Even Bakhtin, as a matter of fact, admits that he has found helpful suggestions toward his own formulations in the "gropings" of Vyacheslav Ivanov.

Citing and paraphrasing Ivanov, Bakhtin writes that

> to affirm someone else's "I" not as an object but as another subject—this is the principle governing Dostoevsky's worldview. To affirm someone else's "I"—"thou art"—is a task that, according to Ivanov, Dostoevsky's characters must successfully accomplish if they are to . . . transform the other person from a shadow into an authentic reality. (10)

Bakhtin's conception of "the ethico-religious postulate determining the *content*" of Dostoevsky's novels is exactly the same, though with more emphasis on the personality; but where Ivanov falls short, as Bakhtin sees it, is in his failure to connect this content properly with its formal expression. Ivanov called Dostoevsky's works "novel-tragedies" (it is he who invented this widely used term), and Bakhtin considers that this generic hybrid misses the true nature of Dostoevsky's creation of form. In my view, Ivanov's term is preferable to the one by which Bakhtin replaces it (the "polyphonic novel"), and Bakhtin's arguments against Ivanov on this point are very far from being completely persuasive. He speaks himself of Dostoevsky's content as involving the "tragic catastrophe" of a consciousness that, disconnected from others, remains immured in "solipsistic separation"; and he also points out accurately that Dostoevsky "saw and conceived his world primarily in terms of space, not time. Hence, his deep affinity for the dramatic form." Why, then, the rejection of a term that brings these artistic qualities to the foreground?

Clearly, Bakhtin rejects the designation because he does not wish to define Dostoevsky's form in relation to the central conflict of his plots (a tragic catastrophe), or the extreme compression of his time sequence. Rather, he concentrates on the author-character relationship, which, in his

---

[7] Mikhail Bakhtin, *Problems of Dostoevsky's Poetics*, ed. and trans. Caryl Emerson, intro. Wayne C. Booth (Minneapolis, Minn., 1984).

interpretation, parallels Dostoevsky's thematic essence as defined by Ivanov (the affirmation of "someone else's 'I' not as an object but as another subject"). According to Bakhtin, this is exactly how Dostoevsky as author is related to his own creation of character. "Thus the new artistic position of the author with regard to the hero in Dostoevsky's polyphonic novel is a *fully realized and thoroughly consistent dialogic position*, one that affirms the independence, internal freedom, unfinalizability, and indeterminacy of the hero" (63). A few pages earlier, Bakhtin had written that "the genuine life of the personality [a term he distinguishes from literary "character," which lacks the dimension of inner freedom] is made available only through a *dialogic* penetration of that personality, during which it freely and reciprocally reveals itself" (59). Dostoevsky as author is thus assigned the function previously assumed by Christ in Bakhtin's thought; as literary creator he is connected to the I-for-myself of others (his characters) by an attitude of such "dialogic penetration."[8]

As a result, Bakhtin views the structure of Dostoevsky's novels as a polyphony of independent voices (hence his term), each of which is grasped from within his or her own world view and not arbitrarily merged into any single dominating (monologic) position of the author's. "Dostoevsky," Bakhtin declares, "created a fundamentally new novelistic genre"; all previous novelists had been monologic or homophonic (though the only instance given of this type is Tolstoy), while in Dostoevsky "a hero appears whose voice . . . is just as fully weighted as the author's voice usually is." Indeed, "it sounds, as it were, *alongside* the author's word and *in a special way* [my italics] combines both with it and with the full and equally valid voices of the characters" (7).

Bakhtin's historical claim is a very strong one, and though he leaves it unchanged in the revised second edition of his book, it is, all the same, considerably weakened by a new fourth chapter, in which he attempts to trace the origin of the polyphonic novel back to the Socratic dialogue and the Menippean satire. For some of the problems created by such a genealogy, the reader can consult Todorov, who gives Bakhtin's theories closer

---

[8] In view of the close relation between Fedotov and Bakhtin in the 1920s, one cannot help remarking how easy it is to harmonize the conception of Christ implied in Bakhtin's writings with the interpretation of Russian Christianity later developed in Fedotov's classic work. According to Fedotov, kenoticism—a reverence for the example of the humiliated and suffering Christ—is a particularly important and native feature of Russian Christianity. For those who follow the kenotic ideal, humility, charity, and boundless love and pity are the predominant virtues.

Such an ideal, of course, precludes maintaining strict standards by which others are judged, but rather follows Christ in accepting even suffering for the sake of wrongdoers. There is no "finalizing" of the human personality in such an attitude, but rather an infinite tolerance that might well be equated with "dialogic penetration." George P. Fedotov, *The Russian Religious Mind*, 2 vols. (Cambridge, Mass., 1946–1966), vol. 1, chap. 4 and passim.

scrutiny than the more or less uncritical Clark and Holquist. Todorov notes that Bakhtin defines the essence of the novel form through works with which "the genre of the novel is [not] ordinarily associated." His definition of its attributes actually represents "a massive and uncritical" borrowing, "without notable alteration, from the great Romantic aesthetic, the reflections of Goethe, Friedrich Schlegel, and Hegel" (particularly the little-known but highly influential Schlegel). But an evaluation of Bakhtin's extremely suggestive and stimulating theory of the novel would lead too far afield; it is with the novels of Dostoevsky that we are primarily concerned here.

Ever since the publication of Bakhtin's first edition, one of the issues constantly raised in the by now widespread critical reaction is that of the place of the author in his scheme. What becomes of him or her if, as Bakhtin claims, the author does not assert any dominating control or authority over the characters? Bakhtin's view contains a superficial plausibility because, as is well known, some of Dostoevsky's most powerful characters (the Underground Man, Raskolnikov, Ivan Karamazov) represent points of view that he wished to combat and dethrone. In this sense, Bakhtin is right in asserting their relative independence, and stressing Dostoevsky's remarkably sympathetic projection of them from within their own world view. But since his critical terms (dialogue, monologue) are ultimately grounded in the Christ-man paradigm of his philosophy, he is constantly tempted to suggest an absolute independence that cannot in fact exist (except perhaps in aleatory writing, of which Dostoevsky's novels are certainly not an example).

Bakhtin of course knew this as well as anyone else, and tried to circumvent the problem by vague phrases of the kind already underlined (that is, Dostoevsky combines his own voice and that of his characters "in a special way"). In the notes for his revised second edition, in which he specifically addresses such criticism, he writes: "The author is profoundly *active*, but his activity is of a special *dialogic* sort." Bakhtin was never able to get beyond such loose declarations, which clearly do not explain anything. And Caryl Emerson rightly points out that, in the preface to his second edition, Bakhtin honestly admits that his book does not contain any treatment of "questions as complex as that of *the whole* in a polyphonic novel." This failure leaves a gaping breach in Bakhtin's theory and nullifies his ambition to show the unity of form and content in Dostoevsky.

In fact, then, if we take the term "polyphonic novel" in the strong sense asserted by Bakhtin, it does not define a new form at all because he is unable to explain how the absolute independence of fictional character can combine with the unity of a work of art. In a weak sense, however, it does highlight Dostoevsky's ability to dramatize his themes without intrusive authorial intervention (though more exists than Bakhtin is willing to concede), and especially through the power with which each character expresses his own world view. These features of Dostoevsky's technique, however, have long been recognized in Anglo-American criticism, where Dostoevsky has been viewed as a precursor of the later stream-of-consciousness novel from which old-fashioned narrators have entirely vanished.[9] Indeed, Bakhtin's concept has been so successful precisely because it appears to turn Dostoevsky into our literary contemporary. But to take Bakhtin only on this purely formal level is to falsify both his own ambitions and those of Dostoevsky. For Bakhtin dearly desired that Dostoevsky's technical innovations should be seen as arising out of, and as carrying, the full ethical and religious import of his themes. Regrettably, too, as Todorov has more recently argued, Bakhtin's ambiguities are such that he opens the way to an erroneous view of Dostoevsky as a moral relativist, and scants the tragic dimension of his struggle to uphold the moral values of Christian conscience in an increasingly secularized world.[10]

But if, at least in my view, Bakhtin's theses about the polyphonic novel ultimately fail to carry conviction, this does not mean that his book is negligible; quite the contrary, it is, and will continue to remain, a classic of Dostoevsky criticism. What makes it so, however, is not the theory of the polyphonic novel but rather his detailed discussion of the self-other relations between Dostoevsky's characters, which no one else has ever explored with such care and insight. From his very first novel, *Poor Folk*, as Bakhtin points out, Dostoevsky's characters are afflicted with an excruciating self-consciousness; they constantly view themselves as they are reflected in the eyes of others, but just as constantly refuse to remain frozen in the definition of themselves offered by such reflections. Invariably they rise in revolt against them, and Bakhtin perceptively traces the various modalities of this revolt, showing how it develops from the initial reaction against a literary stereotype provided by Gogol into a struggle against *all* attempts to enclose them within "any externalizing and finalizing definitions." (Such definitions were provided—as Bakhtin well knew but was unable, or unwilling, to state—by the ideology of the radical intelligentsia of Dostoevsky's time.)

Bakhtin illustrates this point with a series of examples in his fifth chapter, which also contains a valuable typology of various kinds of discourse. Particular attention is paid to what he calls "double-voiced discourse," that is, linguistic usage affected and deflected by awareness of the discourse of another (examples might be an exchange in conversation, or a work written

[9] See Melvin Friedman, *Stream of Consciousness: A Study in Literary Method* (New Haven, Conn., 1955), 64–69.

[10] See Tzvetan Todorov, *Critique de la critique* (Paris, 1984). The penetrating discussion of Bakhtin, "L'Humain et l'interhumain," is on 83–103. This work is now available in English as *Literature and Its Theorists*, trans. Catherine Porter (Ithaca, N.Y., 1987).

with a parodistic relation to its model). Of great systematic and theoretical interest, this chapter has always been exempted from the criticism leveled at the theory of the polyphonic novel; and since it deals with the relations of characters inside the text, not with the relation of the author to his characters, it does not depend on that theory for its validity. Bakhtin here is primarily interested in illustrating the various means by which Dostoevsky's central figures react against all attempts to restrict and confine the freedom of their personalities, and in analyzing the various types of double-voiced discourse through which they assimilate the voices of others and respond to them in ways strongly affected by such assimilation. The rhetoric of the Underground Man, for example, is framed to take into account and to overthrow the anticipated responses of a hostile reader, even though the Underground Man pretends to be writing for himself alone. In the course of these analyses, however, and without making the point directly himself, Bakhtin nonetheless manages to illuminate one of the most striking features of Dostoevsky's art as a novelist.

No reader of Dostoevsky can have failed to experience the impression that his characters are linked together in a fashion different from the ordinary; they seem to exist, not only on the level of those commonplace social interactions standard for the novel of Realism, but also as bound together in some subterranean manner that imparts a special, almost hypnotic intensity to Dostoevsky's narration. Effects of this kind are quite well known in Gothic and Romantic novels, where the supernatural can be drawn on to motivate such mysteriously "magnetic" relations between characters. But while Dostoevsky was familiar with, and greatly admired, such a writer as E.T.A. Hoffman, he nonetheless took great pains (with the single exception of *The Double*) to remain within the conventions of verisimilitude dear to the nineteenth-century novel. Yet he managed to obtain the same effect by other means; and it is here that Bakhtin, more than any other critic, aids us in grasping exactly how this was accomplished.

By focusing on the acute sensitivity that each Dostoevsky character exhibits toward the others, and exploring how each echoes and vibrates in the others' psyches, Bakhtin hits on the secret that distinguishes Dostoevsky so perceptibly from other novelists working in the same tradition. "Two characters are always introduced by Dostoevsky," Bakhtin acutely remarks,

> in such a way that each of them is intimately linked with the internal voice of the other. . . . In their dialogue, therefore, the rejoinders of the one touch and even partially coincide with the rejoinders of the other's interior·dialogue. A deep essential bond or partial coincidence between the borrowed words of one hero and the internal and secret discourse of another hero—this is the indispensable element in all of Dostoevsky's crucial dialogues. (254–55)

As Bakhtin further says of Raskolnikov: "It is enough for a person to appear in his field of vision to become for him instantly an embodied solution to his own personal question, a solution different from the one at which he himself had arrived; therefore every person touches a sore spot in him and assumes a firm role in his inner speech" (238). These words contain a fundamental insight into an all-important aspect of Dostoevsky's method of creation, and they brilliantly clarify the close-knit texture of Dostoevsky's novels—the manner in which characters continually reflect aspects of one another rather than existing as self-enclosed psyches. Even though this was not his purpose, it is only Bakhtin who allows us to understand how Dostoevsky creates this inimitable impression of subliminal psychic interweaving, which again anticipates one of the features of the stream-of-consciousness novel.

4

As should by now be amply clear, Bakhtin's writings go far beyond the limited domain of literary criticism. One can well understand why the graduate students at the Gorky Institute, just emerging from Stalinism in the mid-1950s, should have responded with such fervor to Bakhtin's insistence on the infinite freedom of the human personality, and to his Kantian demand that mankind be treated as an end rather than as a means to be "finalized" in any manner agreeable to the authorities.[11] And Bakhtin's Rabelais book, with its glorification of an irreverent and bawdily obscene folk culture in revolt against all the sacred taboos of its time, could also be—and certainly was—read as an appeal against the stifling restrictions of the Soviet cultural establishment.

It was in 1968 that the Rabelais book was translated into English—the year of the student uprisings in Paris and elsewhere, in the midst of a period when street theater, riotous rock concerts, and orgiastic "happenings" were flourishing. Bakhtin's celebration of what he called "the carnival sense of life," which turns the ordinary world upside down and is not only per-

[11] Kaganskaya, "Shutovskoi Khorovod," contains a revealing glimpse into how Bakhtin's works were received and read in the Soviet Union. "Yes," she writes, "our relation to Bakhtin was not disinterested; his texts, already so packed, were overloaded with a subtext, and the criticism of the monologic form of artistic expression we took as the negation of monolithic ideology in general, and of the one that occupied us in particular (or, more exactly, that occupied itself with us); we read *The Problem of Dostoevsky's Poetics* like a novel: in L. N. Tolstoy, for example, we divined an allegory of Soviet power (which, speaking honestly, is not such a strained interpretation, if one keeps in view a structure whose basic categories, not political but aesthetic, are 'the people,' 'simplicity,' and 'moral benefit'). Dostoevsky was our positive hero (a symbol of spiritual freedom), and a personage by the name of 'Polyphony' stepped forward as an allegory for 'pluralism' and 'democracy.' Ridiculous?—Well, ridiculous. Painful?—Yes, painful" (152).

formed but *lived* by those who take part in it, could not have been more up to date; and he was instantly hailed as a genial precursor of the revolutionary cultural events that were presumably transforming the modern sensibility. Similarly, his Dostoevsky book was translated into French at a time when the French *nouveau roman*, following Sartre, had pronounced a death sentence on all omniscient narrators and dominating points of view. Immersion in the subjectivity of characters was declared to be the only legitimate fount of novelistic creation, and Bakhtin once again immediately took his place at the center of contemporary concerns. Once the earlier works of the Bakhtin circle began to appear, they were also eagerly read by Western Marxists laboring to create a sociology of culture that would go beyond the limits laid down in the Party prescriptions of the past.

The ideas of Bakhtin have thus now become a ferment within Western culture itself, and Clark and Holquist have performed an extremely valuable service in tracing them back to their Russian roots. For whatever reservations one may have about this or that particular thesis of Bakhtin, it is impossible to contemplate his life without feeling admiration and immense respect for his achievement. That he should have written so much of value under conditions that were so discouraging, amid hardship and neglect, and afflicted by a crippling bone disease; that he should have preserved and kept alight the incandescent spirit of the intelligentsia of the Russian Silver Age despite the pressures of the Iron Age of Sovietism—this can only be considered a triumph of private courage and unassuming integrity.

One catches in him a glimpse of the same culture that Pasternak recreated in *Dr. Zhivago*, and, in his lesser way, Bakhtin has also handed on some of the heritage of that culture to posterity. There was, as a matter of fact, some occasional personal contact between the two men through mutual friends, and there are strong specific resemblances both in their acceptance of the Russian Revolution as a temporal apocalypse and in their devotion to a Christianity that inspires and supports a reverence for the infinite value of the human personality. Most important, though, is that, like Yury Zhivago, Bakhtin remained true to his highest values and never allowed his mind or sensibility to be objectified, reified, closed. Not to hear his voice, and to carry on with him in friendship "the great dialogue" of which he saw all human life composed, would be to strengthen all those forces making for the impoverishment and diminution of the human spirit, in Russia and elsewhere, against which he labored so untiringly.

CHAPTER THREE

Ralph Ellison and Dostoevsky

When I was invited some time ago to contribute to a volume of essays honoring the achievements of Ralph Ellison, I very much wanted to add my voice to the tributes being assembled for an old friend and a writer of major stature. But I hesitated at first because, in the years since *Invisible Man* had been published, I had lost touch with the new wave of Afro-American literature in which Ellison now takes so prominent a place. But then, remembering his love for, and familiarity with, the writings of Dostoevsky, it occurred to me that I could perhaps combine my knowledge of the Russian author with the desire publicly to express all my admiration of Ellison's achievement. With this idea in mind, I began to reread his books, and was delighted to discover (or rediscover what had probably been forgotten) that my choice of subject was not as arbitrary as I had feared it might be. For in focusing on the relation between the two writers, I was only following a lead given by Ellison himself.

In his essay "The World and the Jug," Ralph Ellison makes an important distinction between what he calls his "relatives" and his "ancestors." Irving Howe had criticized him for not being enough of a "protest writer" to satisfy Howe's conception of what a Negro writer should be, Howe's ideal at the time being the highly politicized Richard Wright. In explaining why Wright had not influenced him in any significant fashion, despite his great respect for Wright's achievement, Ellison discriminates between various types of influence. "Relatives" are those with whom, by accident of birth, one is naturally associated. Negro authors like Wright and Langston Hughes, not to mention many others, are Ellison's "relatives." But, he remarks, "while one can do nothing about choosing one's relatives, one can, as an artist, choose one's ancestors." And among such "ancestors," among those who had truly stimulated his own artistic impulses and ambitions, he lists T. S. Eliot, Malraux, Hemingway, Faulkner—and Dostoevsky.[1]

The most obvious connection between Ellison and Dostoevsky, which has often been pointed out, is that between *Invisible Man* and *Notes from Underground*. Indeed, the resemblances between the two works are self-evident, although they should not be pushed too far. Both are written in the first-person confessional form; in both the narrator is filled with rage

---

[1] This essay is reprinted in Ralph Ellison, *Shadow and Act* (New York, 1972), 107–43. All the other essays I refer to and the interview with Ellison also cited, are included in this volume.

and indignation because of the humiliation he is forced to endure; in both he explodes with fury against those responsible for subjecting him to such indignities; and both characters finally retreat to their "underground." The underground man retreats symbolically, back to the squalid hole-in-the-corner where he lives; the invisible man retreats literally, first to the coal cellar into which he falls accidentally during the Harlem race riot, and then to the abandoned basement of the prologue, where he hibernates and meditates. (It should be remarked that, in the "underground railway," the metaphor of the underground has an indigenous American meaning far richer than anything that can be found in nineteenth-century Russia, and Ralph Ellison did not have to read Dostoevsky to become aware of its symbolic resonances; but his reading of Dostoevsky no doubt gave him a heightened sense of its literary possibilities.)

What stands out for me, however, is not so much the "underground" imagery of the two books, or the many similarities between the underground man's rejection of the world in which he lives and the invisible man's rejection of his. Much more fundamental is Ellison's profound grasp of the ideological inspiration of Dostoevsky's work, and his perception of its relevance to his own creative purposes—his perception of how he could use Dostoevsky's relation to the Russian culture of his time to express his own position as an American Negro writer in relation to the dominating white culture. Despite the vast differences in their two situations, Ralph Ellison was able to penetrate to the underlying structural similarities beneath the obvious surface disparities.

What, after all, motivates the revolt of Dostoevsky's underground man against his world? It is the impossibility he feels of being able to live humanly within categories that, although he has learned to accept them about himself, have been imposed on him by others. As Dostoevsky saw them, these categories had been imported into Russia from European culture. (Dostoevsky was far from being the only prominent Russian to take such a view; the revolutionary Alexander Herzen, for one, shared exactly the same idea.) As a result, they are categories that the underground man finds to be profoundly in contradiction with his moral being. The revolt of the underground man is a refusal to accept a definition of himself, a definition of his own nature, in terms imposed by the alien world of European culture. At the same time, like all other educated Russians, he has assimilated and accepted the ideas and values of this alien world (accepted them, that is, with the rational and self-conscious part of his personality) because of their superior authority and prestige.

This is the very situation in which the invisible man finds himself all through Ellison's book. The invisible man stands in relation to white American culture and *its* ideas and values as Dostoevsky's underground man stands in relation to West European culture. For the invisible man discovers that all of its definitions of himself, all the structures within which it wishes to place him as a Negro, violate some aspect of his own integrity. No more than the underground man is he willing to accept such a situation passively; and he rejects each of these structures in turn the moment he realizes their true import.

The form of *Invisible Man*, as an ideological novel, is essentially the same as that of *Notes from Underground*, though Ellison's work is conceived on a much larger scale. Each major sequence dramatizes the confrontation between the invisible man and some type of social or cultural trap—a road opens up before him only to end in a blind alley, a possibility of freedom tempts him but then only imprisons him once again. Similarly, each of the two episodes in Dostoevsky's work unmasks the morally detrimental consequences of the two dominating ideologies that, because of the force of European ideas on the Russian psyche, had ensnared the Russian intelligentsia. (The materialism and ethical utilitarianism of the 1860s is parodied in Part I of *Notes from Underground*; the "humanitarian" and "philanthropic" Utopian Socialism of the 1840s is the butt of Part II.)

The invisible man too is a member of the American Negro intelligentsia, or has at least been chosen to be educated as one; and his adventures reveal the bankruptcy of all the doctrines that this intelligentsia has accepted up to the present from the hands of the whites. Such doctrines include the assimilationism of the carefully tailored and prettified Negro college that the invisible man attends; the Africanism of Ras the Exhorter, which is finally only a mirror image of white racism despite the dignity and purity of the passion at its source; and the radical politics embodied in the Brotherhood. When the Brotherhood provokes a race riot, it is employing the very tactics of the-worse-the-better that Dostoevsky understood very well and had dramatized in *The Devils*, a novel that, among many other things, is a handbook of extremist politics.

Notes from Underground and *Invisible Man* thus undertake essentially the same task, and both perform it superbly. But one should not press the comparison too hard. Ellison took from Dostoevsky what he needed, but used it in his own way. Actually, *Invisible Man* is more an extrapolation than an imitation of *Notes from Underground*. Ellison portrays the *process* through which the invisible man becomes disillusioned with his previous conceptions, while this process is more or less taken for granted by Dostoevsky. We do not really follow the underground man stage by stage in his development; we never see him in that state of innocent acceptance typical of the invisible man. *Invisible Man* ends where *Notes from Underground* begins; the two works overlap only in the framing sections of *Invisible Man*, the prologue and epilogue. Here Ellison's narrator directly expresses the conflict in himself between his refusal *entirely* to abandon the ideals he has accepted up to this point (in the hope of fashioning some modus vivendi with the white world), and his rejection of all the forms in which this modus has presented itself to him. Dostoevsky's character is caught in exactly the same sort of conflict: his acceptance of European ideas is at war with his moral instincts. "Who knows but that, on the lower frequencies, I speak for you?" the invisible man suggests to his (white) reader, who is incapable of seeing him for what he truly is but nonetheless shares with him the same tragic dilemma. The underground man addressed himself to *his* scornful and mocking readers in exactly the same way at the conclusion of *Notes from Underground*. "We are even so tired of being men, men of real, *our own* flesh and blood, that we have reached the point of being ashamed of it," he says; "we consider it a disgrace, and aspire to dissolve into some sort of abstract man who has never existed." He does not exclude himself from this accusation, and speaks, at the same time, for all those who will sneer at his words.

Dostoevsky's novella is primarily a lengthy interior monologue of inner conflict, expressed in both ideological and psychological terms. *Invisible Man* is a negative Bildungsroman, in which the narrator-hero learns that everything he has been taught to believe by his various mentors is actually false and treacherous. His experiences can thus be considered to be those of a black Candide. There is, to be sure, very little of Candide in the underground man, but even when Ellison swerves from Dostoevsky, he instinctively moves in a direction Dostoevsky wished to take himself. For one of Dostoevsky's cherished literary projects—one that he never got around to realizing—was to write what he called in his notes "a Russian *Candide*."

A work of Dostoevsky's that bears a much less explicit connection with Ellison's *Invisible Man* is *House of the Dead*, Dostoevsky's sketches of life in the Siberian prison camp where he served a term of four years. There is certainly no obvious literary similarity between the two books; but Ellison himself points toward a connection by remarking, in *Shadow and Act*, on "Dostoevsky's profound study of the humanity of Russian criminals." For my part, I am convinced that the effect of *House of the Dead* on Ellison's sensibility was more profound than has ever been suspected. It affected him strongly and personally, and provided him with a powerful precedent for entering into a positive relation with the Negro folk culture he had imbibed from the cradle.

One of the outstanding characteristics of *Invisible Man* is its use of Negro folk culture, not as a source of quaint exoticism and "lowdown" local color, but as a symbol of a realm of values set off against the various ideologies with which the narrator becomes engaged. What these values are is expressed in Ellison's famous definition of "the blues": "an impulse to keep the painful details and episodes of a brutal experience alive in one's aching consciousness, to finger its jagged grain, and to transcend it, not by the consolation of philosophy but by squeezing from it a near-tragic, near-comic lyricism." (*Shadow and Act*, 78) It is this quality of American Negro folk sensibility that Ellison embodies in such a character as Peter Wheatstraw, who arouses the admiration of the still naive invisible man even though the latter has been taught, in accordance with the standards of educated white society, to look down on Wheatstraw's punning speech style and versifying idioms as primitive and demeaning. "God damn, I thought, they're a hell of a people!" writes the invisible man after this encounter. "And I didn't know whether it was pride or disgust that suddenly flashed over me."

This uncertainty represents the clash within the narrator of his instinctive response to the indigenous forms of cultural expression of his people, with all the toughness and resilience of spirit that they embody, and the response instilled by his education: "I'd known the stuff from childhood, but had forgotten it; had learned it *back of school*." Part of what he discovers in the course of the book is the value of what he had been taught to discard.

This is where *House of the Dead* enters the picture. For while it would be nonsensical to imagine that Ralph Ellison needed Dostoevsky to make him aware of the richness and depth of Negro folk culture, Dostoevsky could (and did) serve as an invaluable and prestigious literary "ancestor" who had had to fight the same battle on behalf of the Russian peasant culture of his own time.

American readers will find it difficult to imagine that Russians could once have looked down on their own peasant culture as whites (and Negroes wishing to conform to white cultural standards) looked down upon the Negro folk culture developed in the slave society of the American South. But such was the rage for Europeanization in Russia, such the rejection of all vestiges of the Russian past as "barbarous" and "regressive," that exactly the same prejudice prevailed. Anything not conforming to the standards of Europeanization was scorned and ridiculed. This situation reached such a degree of self-negation that the Russian upper class hardly spoke its own language any longer. (It will be recalled that, at the beginning of *War and Peace*, a discussion of the threat of Napoleon at an aristocratic gathering is conducted not in Russian but in French.) One of the most important works that broke the grip of this prejudice was *House of the Dead*, in which Dostoevsky not only depicts for the first time the "humanity" of "criminals" (the men he wrote about were criminals technically, but a good many had landed in Siberia only because they had reacted violently to the prevailing injustice and ill treatment of their class) but also uncovers the hidden treasures of Russian peasant culture.

Dostoevsky managed to keep a notebook while in prison camp in which he wrote down peasant expressions, proverbs, songs, and anecdotes. These revealed to him an independent, strong-willed, tough-minded outlook on life that he came to admire and even to think superior, in some of its moral aspects, to the advanced, "progressive" views he had once accepted. *House of the Dead* is really a story of his reeducation along such lines, which finally allowed him to recognize the riches of the way of life of his own people. Could not this be said as well to be one of the major thematic aims of *Invisible Man*? One can only speculate on the effect that reading such a work had on the young Ralph Ellison, wrestling with the problem of reconciling what he had learned in school (his first ambition, after all, had been to become a *classical* composer) with what he had picked up "back of school." We do know that he later became a writer who, while measuring himself by the highest standards of the great modern masters, refused to see any contradiction between his exalted literary ambitions and his admiration for the far from classical world of American Negro folk music and folk life.

Dostoevsky's book would thus unquestionably have helped Ellison to find his own way. And if we read *House of the Dead* from this angle, it is not too difficult to spot passages that might have had particular importance for him. Would he not have been struck, for example, by Dostoevsky's suggestion that, so far as the Russian educated class is concerned, the Russian peasant is really *invisible*? "You may have to do with peasants all your life," he tells his educated readers,

> you may associate with them every day for forty years, officially for instance, in the regulation and administrative forms, or even simply in a friendly way, as a benefactor or, in a certain sense, a father—you will never know them really. It will all be *an optical illusion*, and nothing more. I know that all who read will think I am exaggerating. But I am convinced of its truth. I have reached this conviction, not from books, not from abstract theory, but from reality, and I have had plenty of time to verify it.[2]

One can go through the whole book in this way and pick out episode after episode that could have impressed the young Ellison as being directly relevant to his own creative problems. There is the incident where Dostoevsky, who had formerly believed that the backward muzhik was a bungling and incompetent worker, suddenly discovers, because he is now a member of the work convoy himself, that the supposed "incompetence" is really a form of sabotage. When the peasant-convicts get the conditions they want, "there was no trace of laziness, no trace of incompetence. . . . The work went like wildfire. Everyone seemed wonderfully intelligent all of a sudden" (85). And there was the revelation of the peasant-convict orchestra "playing the simple peasant instruments," some of them homemade. "The blending and harmony of sounds, above all, the spirit, the character of the conception and rendering of the tune in its very essence were simply amazing. For the first time I realized all the reckless dash and

[2] Fyodor Dostoevsky, *The House of the Dead*, trans. Constance Garnett (New York, 1954), 236.

gaiety of the gay dashing Russian dance song" (143). The spirit of the people emerged and could be felt in their own music, which for the first time Dostoevsky—who had previously been an inveterate concertgoer—was able to estimate at its true worth. Such a passage would surely have strengthened Ralph Ellison's determination to win for the folk music of his own people (jazz, the blues, spirituals) the recognition it deserved as a valid artistic expression of their own complex sense of life.

Many other instances of the same kind could be adduced as Dostoevsky undergoes that transvaluation of values—the same transvaluation undergone by the invisible man—in favor of the peasant-convicts and against the "enlightened" and "civilized" standards of educated Russian society. The representatives of that society constantly speak of "justice," but assume that they have the right to a leading place in the world. How different from the peasant-convicts at the prison theatricals, who gave Dostoevsky a front-row seat because they feel it "just" to do so. Dostoevsky is a connoisseur of the theater, who could appreciate all the nuances of the performance; therefore he "deserves" a better place. "The highest and most striking characteristic of our people," Dostoevsky writes of this incident, "is just their sense of justice and their eagerness for it. There is no trace in the common people of the desire to be cock of the walk on all occasions and at all costs, whether they deserve to be or not. . . . There is not much our wise men could teach them. On the contrary, I think it is the wise men who ought to learn from the people" (141).

What is most important, however, is Dostoevsky's clear-eyed and unblinking ability to look the facts about the Russian peasant in the face; not to sentimentalize or gild or touch up their benightedness, backwardness, and sometimes terrible cruelty. And his ability to understand, at the same time, that these repulsive aspects of their lives were the result of the age-old oppression in which they had been forced to survive. He was capable of discerning whatever spark of humanity continued to exist under such conditions, and he believed that such a spark *must* exist somewhere no matter how much appearances might suggest its extinction. This same capacity is condensed in the observation of Ralph Ellison's that "the extent of beatings and psychological maiming meted out by southern Negro parents rivals those described by nineteenth-century Russian writers as characteristic of peasant life under the Czars. The horrible thing is that the cruelty is also an expression of concern, of love" (*Shadow and Act*, 91). Such a remark could only have come from Ellison's intimate identification with the spirit in which Dostoevsky had portrayed Russian peasant life, and Ellison's awareness of the extent to which it had helped him enter into a genuinely creative relation with his own world.

House of the Dead stands out from Dostoevsky's other books by its descriptive and plotless character. It is a series of sketches focusing on a milieu and a collectivity, and resembles a piece of reportage more than a novel. One would hardly think it written by the same author who gave us such febrile and tightly wound dramatizations of the philosophical and ideological dilemmas of the Russian intelligentsia. Its effect on Ralph Ellison is much more in the realm of attitudes and idea-feelings than in that of artistic technique. Yet there is one point at which *Invisible Man* and *House of the Dead* come together thematically in a remarkable fashion, and where a direct, artistic influence may be inferred. Or if not, the parallel is all the more worth mentioning because it reveals how close the two are in their grasp of human existence.

One of the high points of Ellison's narrative is Jim Trueblood's story about the violation of his daughter, with whom, while half asleep and dreaming, he unwittingly commits incest. Its parallel in *House of the Dead* is a narrative titled "Akulka's Husband." Both are written in the form of what is called a *skaz* in Russian criticism, that is, a first-person oral tale strongly colored by the speech style of the teller. In Ellison's story, the speaker is a southern Negro tenant farmer; in Dostoevsky's, it is a Russian peasant. Both recount what is, in fact, a criminal transgression of the laws of God and man—in the first case incest, in the second, the deliberate murder of an innocent wife by a craven, resentful, sadistic husband who had already beaten his victim half to death.

What unites the stories—and Dostoevsky's is by far the more frightful—is the unsparing way they depict the unforgivable and unredeemable, and yet manage to do so in a manner that affirms the humanity of the people involved rather than negating it. Jim Trueblood's deed is not an act of lust or animal passion, but an accident caused by being forced through poverty to sleep with his wife and grown-up daughter in the same bed. He tells what occurred as a deeply moral man, bewildered and disturbed by his own transgression, even ready to let his outraged wife chop off his head with an ax (though she is finally unable to bring herself to the act). He goes through a period of mortification ("I don't eat nothin' and caint sleep at night"). One night, looking up at the stars, he starts to sing, and "*ends up singin' the blues.*" He then returns to his family to begin life anew and shoulder the burden of what he had done—and yet not *really* done.

In Dostoevsky's tale, it is not the narrator whose ineradicable human quality emerges in this way, although we are made to realize that he kills because of intolerable personal humiliation—which at least saves him from being taken only as a bloodthirsty sadist. It is rather the murdered wife and the man she loves, Filka Morozov, who suddenly reveal a depth of sentiment that one would not have suspected. Until this happens, the wife has been only a piteous victim, Filka only a headstrong and reckless scoundrel who had slandered the girl unmercifully in order to take revenge on her domineering father, with whom he had quarreled. It is Filka who is responsible for all the torments she has had to endure, including a forced marriage to her weak-willed husband. But then, just before he is taken away for military service (which meant that he would probably never return), Filka proclaims her innocence to the entire village, bowing down at her feet; and she forgives him, declaring her love in the same ritual manner and in heightened poetic speech. The tale is suddenly lit up by a flash of the purest feeling and the tenderest human emotion, only to sink back into darkness again with the murder. But we do not forget, after this flash, that the participants are *people*, not inhuman monsters; and we derive this same knowledge from the narrative of Jim Trueblood. Ellison drives home to us as Americans the same point Dostoevsky had driven home to his Russian readers a hundred years earlier.

There is still another important relation between Ralph Ellison and Dostoevsky that should be discussed: the convergence of the two writers when they defend the integrity of art and the independence of the artist from the ideological dictates and constraints imposed by the guardians (unofficial in both cases, but not to remain so in Dostoevsky's homeland) of the collective conscience.

Most of the incidental journalism in which Dostoevsky defended his position has not been translated at all, or has been put into English rather recently. But Ralph Ellison did not have to read Dostoevsky's journalism to find himself confronted with the same problems. The attitude about art against which Dostoevsky had fought in the early 1860s has become, through the triumph and worldwide influence of Russian Communism, the dogma automatically imposed on artists anywhere who become involved with radical politics. Ralph Ellison, like so many others (and like Dostoevsky himself in the 1840s), went through such a phase. Finding himself subject to the authority and censure of the cultural commissars, he reacted against them exactly as Dostoevsky had done.

Very early in Dostoevsky's career, he ran into efforts to influence and control the nature of his literary production. The host of the radical circle whose meetings he attended, Mikhail Petrashevsky, criticized him for not writing overt social propaganda that would further the cause of progress. The best critic of the time, V. G. Belinsky, who had hailed Dostoevsky's first novel, *Poor Folk*, as a masterpiece, also thought that Dostoevsky's later work in the 1840s was deficient in social content. But Dostoevsky resisted the criticism of both men. He even told Belinsky that the influential critic "was giving literature a partial significance unworthy of it, degrading it to the description, if one may so express it, *solely of journalistic facts*, or scandalous occurrences."[3]

[3] For more information on these matters, see my *Dostoevsky: The Seeds of Liberation, 1821–1849* (Princeton, N.J., 1976), chaps. 13 and 17. Later, in the 1860s, the idea that literature

What is important about Dostoevsky's opposition to such views is that he did *not* defend the autonomy of art in the terms that have come to be known as "art for art's sake." He did not argue that, since art was its own supreme value, a writer could legitimately neglect the social arena in pursuit of its perfection. Dostoevsky accepted the premise of the radical critics that art had an important moral and social function to fulfill. But it was exactly for this reason that the artist was obliged never to sacrifice the standards of art in the interest of social utility. For even in the terms of social utility, Dostoevsky insisted, "a production without artistic value can never and in no way attain its goal; indeed, it does more harm than good to the cause. Consequently, in neglecting artistic value the Utilitarians take the lead in harming their own cause."

There is then, in Dostoevsky's view, no conflict between the belief that art has a supremely important moral and social mission and a determination not to turn art into a medium of propaganda. This is exactly the position that an embattled Ralph Ellison has defended so eloquently and staunchly in his criticism. No contemporary American writer has made out a stronger case for the moral function of art than Ralph Ellison in such essays as "Twentieth-Century Fiction and the Black Mask of Humanity" and "Stephen Crane and American Fiction." These critical pieces locate the greatness of such writers as Twain and Melville in their incessant moral preoccupation with the basic injustices of American life (preeminently slavery and, more generally, the race problem). Ellison admires their attempts to cope with such injustices, not politically but morally. Among his own contemporaries, only Faulkner, in Ellison's view, has taken up this task, accepting and transcending the southern stereotypes of his Negro characters and exploring the deep wounds inflicted on the southern white psyche by the tangled history of its relations with the Negro.

While himself engaged in wrestling artistically with these very themes, Ralph Ellison has energetically rejected all efforts to confuse the function of art with that of social agitation. In an important exchange with Irving Howe, Ellison draws a clear line between the obligations of art and those of social action.[4] "In his effort to resuscitate Wright," Ellison points out, "Irving Howe would designate the role which Negro writers are to play more rigidly than any southern politician—and for the best of reasons. We must express 'black' anger and 'clenched militancy'; most of all we should

---

should serve only as an auxiliary in the battle for a better social world was codified into an aesthetic theory by Nikolay Chernyshevsky. See the discussion of his views, especially my essay on Rufus Mathewson's book (Chapter 6, below), and also in my criticism of Walicki (Chapter 5, below).

[4] This exchange was initiated by an article of Irving Howe's "Black Boys and Native Sons," reprinted in his *Decline of the New* (New York, 1970), 167–89. Ellison's reply is included in *Shadow and Act*, 107–43.

not become too interested in the problems of the art of literature, even though it is through these that we seek our individual identities. And between writing well and being ideologically militant, we must choose militancy" (120). To which Ellison retorts: "I think that the writer's obligation in a struggle as broad and abiding as the one we are engaged in, which involves not merely Negroes but all Americans, is best carried out through his role as a writer. And if he chooses to stop writing and take to the platform, then it should be out of personal choice and not under pressure from would-be managers of society" (132).

I had read this exchange when it first appeared—in *Dissent* and *The New Leader* in 1963—and had written about it, upholding Ellison's position, in a review of *Shadow and Act* commissioned and accepted by *Partisan Review*. The piece, for some reason, was never published. I suspect that its disappearance may have had something to do with an idea expressed in the epigraph from Malraux that Ellison had appended to his reply to Howe: "What runs counter to the revolutionary convention is, in revolutionary histories, suppressed more imperiously than embarrassing episodes in private memoirs" (107).[5] In any case, it is impossible for me to read Ellison's words now without thinking of Dostoevsky's remarks on the advice given by the radical critic N. A. Dobrolyubov to the Russian poet I. S. Nikitin.

The descendant of a lowly merchant family, Nikitin was an admirer of Pushkin and an imitator of his lyrical style. Dobrolyubov found this taste deplorable, especially in view of Nikitin's class background; and the gist of his comments is summarized by Dostoevsky in the following fashion:

> "Write about your needs" Nikitin is told, "describe the needs and necessities of your condition, down with Pushkin, don't go into raptures over him, but go into raptures over this and over that and describe this and nothing else"—"But Pushkin has been my banner, my beacon, my master" cries Mr. Nikitin (or me for Mr. Nikitin). "I am a commoner, he has stretched out his hands to me from where there is light, where spiritual enlightenment exists, where one is not stifled by outrageous prejudices, at least not like those in my milieu; he has been my

[5] William Phillips, one of the editors of *Partisan Review*, has written a few sentences in his memoirs that may—or may not—have been provoked by my remarks here. I note them for the record, and because they are relevant to the question. Part of *Invisible Man* first appeared in *Partisan Review*, "but in 1964." Phillips writes, "we were unable to print a part of his book of essays, *Shadow and Act*, because we could not time it before the book came out, and when later we asked Joseph Frank, who reviewed the book, to make some changes to include a critical discussion of the questions raised by Ellison, our request was misunderstood and the review never appeared." William Phillips, *A Partisan View* (New York, 1983), 117.

My own recollection is that I was merely asked to shorten the piece, which I did, and then told later that it was no longer topical and would not be used. I do not recall any request for a more critical discussion of Ellison, though after twenty years I make no claim to certainty. Phillips's words, however, confirm my impression that the editors did not agree with my staunch support for Ellison's point of view.

spiritual food"—"You've gone wrong, and that's too bad! Write about the needs of your class."

This is the same sort of advice that Irving Howe was implicitly giving Ralph Ellison: forget about T. S. Eliot, Malraux, Hemingway, Faulkner, Dostoevsky; write about the struggle of the Negro for civil rights, and look at Negro life *only* in relation to that all-important struggle.[6]

What is involved here is much more than a quarrel over the role and function of art; it is really a disagreement about the range and dimension of human experience. No one knew this better than Dostoevsky, who refused to accept the reduction of possibility, the shrinking of the horizon of human concern, that lay at the root of the Russian radical doctrine of art. "The imagination builds castles in the air," Nikolay Chernyshevsky had written with heavy sarcasm in a treatise devoted to aesthetics, "when the dreamer lacks not only a good house, but even a tolerable hut." Hence a preoccupation with whatever transcends immediate physical and material need, or at best the concrete social issues of the moment, must be rejected as illusory and reprehensible. Dostoevsky replied to this position with a satirical skit in which he portrays a new contributor to a radical journal receiving instructions from the editors on how to toe the party line. "If a person," he is told, "says to you: I want to think, I torment myself with age-old problems that have remained unsolved; or, I want to live, I aspire to find a faith, I search for a moral ideal, I love art, or anything of this kind, always reply immediately, clearly, and without a moment's hesitation, that all this is stupidity, metaphysics, that all this is a luxury, childish dreams, senselessness."

Ralph Ellison again joins Dostoevsky at this point, but of course in the terms of his own special situation as a Negro-American writer. The white cultural world—especially those "friends" of the Negroes strongly influenced by Marxism-Leninism—has a tendency to insist that Negro experi-

[6] With his usual intellectual and moral scrupulosity, Irving Howe returns in his autobiography to make an observation very much worth citing about this old argument. In a chapter dealing with the rediscovery of their "Jewishness" by many on the radical Left, including himself, Howe recalls a response to Sartre's *Reflxions sur la question juive* made by Harold Rosenberg. Sartre had defined the Jews as a group whose identity was constituted by their "situation" in the eyes of others, and as having no true historical identity of their own. Howe found himself agreeing with Harold Rosenberg that such a position was sadly deficient in understanding the inner realities of Jewish self-consciousness; and many years later, he realized that, in his controversy with Ellison, he had been "cast, to my surprise, in a Sartre-like position." Howe continues: "Ellison claimed for the blacks, as Rosenberg had for the Jews, an autonomous culture that could not be fully apprehended through the lens of 'protest.' Surely there was some validity to Ellison's argument, yet I could not help thinking that the 'situation' of the blacks had generated more traumas, more scars than he was ready to admit. Perhaps, however, it was easier for me to see this with regard to blacks than Jews." See Irving Howe, *A Margin of Hope* (New York, 1982), 257.

ence in particular remain fixed within the confines laid down for human nature as a whole by Russian radical thought. But the Ralph Ellison who has written so touchingly about the ideal of "Renaissance man," cherished by himself and a few friends while they were growing up in Oklahoma, refused very early to accept any such limitations; and he has protested again and again when attempts have been made to impose it, or, even worse, when it has been accepted voluntarily. Indeed, Ellison's criticism of his close friend and erstwhile literary comrade-in-arms Richard Wright is precisely that after a certain point in his career Wright had tailored his creative imagination to such a pattern. Wright, Ellison remarked in an interview, "was committed to ideology—even though I, too, wanted many of the same things for our people." Fundamentally, he goes on, he and Wright had differed in their concept of the individual. "I, for instance, found it disturbing that Bigger Thomas (in Wright's *Native Son*) had none of the finer qualities of Richard Wright, none of the imagination, none of the sense of poetry, none of the gaiety. And I preferred Richard Wright to Bigger Thomas" (16).

Ellison makes the same sort of argument in an article on Wright's *Black Boy*, where he directs his polemical fire against those critics who had wondered in print how a mind and sensibility such as Wright's could have developed amid the appalling conditions of life, and out of the searing personal history, that he describes. These critics felt it to be a weakness in the book that no explanation was offered for this anomaly. Ellison retorts:

> The prevailing mood of American criticism has so thoroughly excluded the Negro that it fails to recognize some of the most basic tenets of Western democratic thought when encountering them in a black skin. They forget that human life possesses an innate dignity and mankind an innate sense of nobility; that all men possess the tendency to dream and the compulsion to make their dreams reality; that the need to be ever dissatisfied and the urge ever to seek satisfaction is implicit in the human organism, and that all men are the victims and beneficiaries of the goading, tormenting, commanding and informing activity of that imperious process known as the Mind—the Mind, as Valéry describes it, "armed with its inexhaustible questions" (80–81).

The final connection between Ralph Ellison and Dostoevsky that I wish to make concerns a certain similarity in the public status of their work and its relation to its audience. Dostoevsky has for so long been accepted as one of the dominating figures of world literature that it comes as something of a shock to realize how much hostility he encountered during his lifetime. His major novels were published in Russia at a time when liberal and radical opinion dominated among the intelligentsia; and each of his great works was ferociously attacked. (The inferior *A Raw Youth*, published in a left-wing journal, escaped such censure, while *Notes from Under-*

ground was simply ignored.) For conservatives, who wished only to let sleeping dogs lie and to defend the existing régime at all costs, Dostoevsky's books were hardly consoling either; they were too probing and raised far too many fundamental questions. His novels really satisfied nobody's politics; but they imposed themselves by the sheer power and force of their art and the profundity of their vision.

Today, the spiritual descendants of the Russian radicals of the 1860s form the ruling class of Dostoevsky's homeland. The very ideas against which he fought lie at the heart of the social and cultural ideology they have imposed. The guardians of official Soviet culture are perfectly aware that the later Dostoevsky undermines all their most cherished dogmas. They would dearly like to get him out of the way, and even tried to do so during the heyday of Stalin. But Dostoevsky adds too much glory to Russian literature to be lightly discarded. The Soviets have now almost completed the publication of a splendid collected edition of his works in thirty volumes, whose termination will constitute a remarkable achievement of Soviet scholarship. But most of the copies are sent abroad immediately, and those remaining in the Soviet Union are extremely difficult for the average citizen to procure. Until recently the later novels were rarely republished, although the earlier (socialist-influenced) work came out in editions of several hundred thousand. On my last visit to a Russian bookstore, however, I became aware that the later novels are now also being republished in cheap editions and in hundreds of thousands of copies. Dostoevsky is still a thorn in the flesh of the Soviet establishment, but he cannot simply be plucked out and thrown aside; his work refuses to be ignored or suppressed.

The position of Ralph Ellison in the United States is, happily, very different, and yet certain parallels exist all the same. *Invisible Man* was hailed as a masterpiece immediately on its publication, and Ralph Ellison's reputation has maintained its high stature through the intervening years. Yet, as the controversy with Irving Howe indicates, Ellison has come under fire for some of the same reasons that Dostoevsky was also assailed. During the turbulent 1960s, these attacks, launched by left-wing spokesmen for the new upsurge of black nationalism, mounted in frequency and ferocity. Ralph Ellison became the hated enemy against whom the new black nationalist literati felt it necessary to discharge their long pent-up resentment and rage. While he maintained a quiet dignity in the face of the storm, even managing to jest about it in conversation, he was deeply wounded by the unfair and intemperate charges leveled against him in print and in person when he appeared on the lecture platform.

The storm seems to have abated, though, and the wind to have shifted, if I am to judge by a thoughtful and informative article of John Wright in an issue of the *Carleton Miscellany* (Winter 1980) largely devoted to Ellison's work. Exactly as in the case of Dostoevsky, the power and profundity of his art have imposed themselves despite the onslaught of his ideological foes. It would even appear that some of those who had assailed Ellison most ferociously—not all, to be sure—have now begun to realize that the foundation of the new black American culture they are seeking has been laid down in his pages. In an excellent formulation, John Wright speaks of Ellison as "approaching Afro-American life through a psychology of survival and transcendence rather than through a psychology of oppression." Even Ellison's former opponents, he points out, now recognize him as providing "the new black literary radicals with a positive vision of black lifestyles as profoundly human and spiritually sustaining" (148).

It is good to know that at least some of "Uncle Tom's children" (to borrow a phrase from Richard Wright), much more refractory and rebellious than Richard Wright could possibly have believed, have begun to see what they can learn about themselves from Ellison's clear-eyed and vibrantly appreciative vision of Negro-American life and culture. As happened with Dostoevsky, this vision proved too impressive to be discarded or neglected; it simply had to be assimilated, and the process of reevaluation seems to be proceeding apace. As a result, a possibility once broached by Ellison is now well on its way to becoming a reality. "Perhaps," he remarked in his controversy with Howe, "if I write well enough the children of today's Negroes will be proud that I did, and so, perhaps, will Irving Howe's" (139). The classic status now unanimously accorded to *Invisible Man* would indicate that this generous hope has come true.

CHAPTER FOUR

The Lectures of Professor Pnin

IT MUST have been fun to have taken Vladimir Nabokov's classes in Russian literature at Wellesley and Cornell, but woe to the poor student who had to pass a major examination in the field under more conventional auspices! For Nabokov was of course not a professional pedagogue, concerned with imparting information and giving his listeners some acquaintance with a "field"—in this case, the Russian literature of which he was one of the most eminent living representatives. And so some of those whom Nabokov affectionately called "the backbone of the nation, the industrious army of grade C's," may have been a little put off by Professor Nabokov's freewheeling ways. But the majority probably found him as endearingly nutty as his own Professor Pnin. And what a feast he was for those with some literary sensibility, who were capable of appreciating his flashing wit, his pungently expressive language, and his keen insight into literature as a craft!

Lectures on Russian Literature is a carefully edited reconstruction, from notes and drafts left among Nabokov's papers, of the course he gave on Russian literature.[1] Putting them together was a daunting job, and the editor, Fredson Bowers, is to be congratulated that they read as well as they do. The prospective reader, however, should know that much of the book is quotation, since a good deal of classroom time was taken up with reading extracts aloud (of course in English) accompanied with a running fire of scornful remarks about the translation and appropriate corrections. Ample room is given to a fine display of Nabokov's usual crotchets and whimsies. He laboriously figures out the exact date on which the action of *Anna Karenin* (no "a," please) begins, even though Tolstoy did not think it important enough to mention. And Nabokov in one of his favorite roles—the mad pedant with a fanatical gleam in his eye—is fully evident in the thirty pages of commentary that he intended for a (never-published) edition of *Anna Karenin(a)*. For example, under the entry for "cabbage soup and groats," we learn that "in my time, forty years later [than the novel] to slurp *shchi* was as chic as to toy with any French fare."

The book, however, contains much more than such eccentricities. It begins with a superb and lively lecture, delivered in 1958, which views Rus-

[1] Vladimir Nabokov, *Lectures on Russian Literature*, ed. and intro. Fredson Bowers (New York, 1980).

sian literature as having been continuously subject to two censorships in the nineteenth century—that of the tsarist state on the one hand, and of the radical critics on the other. The first insisted that writers be loyal to the state, the second to the welfare of the masses. "The two lines of thought were bound to meet and join forces when at last, in our times, a new kind of régime, the synthesis of a Hegelian triad, combined the idea of the masses with the idea of the state" (5). No better description has ever been given of the situation that produced so much dreadfully didactic Soviet literature, whose absurdities Nabokov punctures with a few selected quotations. Nor, it should be noted, does he accept the fashionable cant that the indirect pressures of the marketplace on writers in free countries amounts to the same thing as the direct pressures of the police state.

Individual chapters are then devoted to Gogol, Turgenev, Dostoevsky, Tolstoy, Chekhov, and Gorky. Usually one or two works are discussed, though overall impressions are also briefly conveyed, and after a few background facts Nabokov gets down to textual details. For as he writes, "Let us not look for the soul of Russia in the Russian novel: let us look for the individual genius. Look at the masterpiece, and not the frame—and not at the faces of the people looking at the frame" (11). This is Nabokov's response to the overwhelming demand on Russian writers, both by the radical critics of the past and the state-supported critics of the present, to concern themselves with a "message" of some kind and write "special delivery" works (as he calls them). As a reaction, both Nabokov and the Russian Formalist critics who were his contemporaries desired to free art from such ideological constraints and to view it in terms of a series of technical "devices." One can understand this response and sympathize with it, without believing it necessary to import so stringent a conception into our own more liberal cultural climate of ideas, or finding that the taste in literature it engenders is necessarily compelling or definitive.

Gogol of course is one of Nabokov's favorite writers, whose stylistic antics in *Dead Souls* and *The Overcoat* he explores lovingly while carrying on a polemic both with translators and the standard view of Gogol as a "realist."[2] He focuses mainly on what he calls Gogol's "life-generating syntax," the manner in which "the peripheral characters of his novel [*Dead Souls*] are engendered by the subordinate clauses of his various metaphors, comparisons and lyrical outbursts." But he also considers the main character Chichikov, as Russian Symbolist critics had done earlier, to be "an ill-paid representative of the Devil, a traveling salesman from Hades," who works to extend the influence of Satan & Co. through "the essential stupidity of universal *poshlost* [mediocrity, philistinism]." Nabokov also remarks, at the

[2] These pages are excerpted from Nabokov's sprightly critical masterpiece, *Nikolai Gogol* (Norfolk, Conn., 1944), which he wrote in English.

end of his consideration of *The Overcoat*, that the work "approaches to that secret depth of the human soul where the shadows of other worlds pass like the shadows of nameless and soundless ships." The Devil and "the shadows of other worlds" may not be "the Russian soul," but we seem to be getting dangerously close to its vicinity all the same.

Nabokov then moves on to Turgenev, whom he labels "not a great writer but a pleasant one," and who is admired rather patronizingly for the delicacy of his landscapes and his feel for textures and colors. But he finds his style patchy—some passages are too highly worked over—and, since Turgenev lacked "'literary imagination," he could never discover "ways of telling the story which would equal the originality of his descriptions." These are shrewd and telling observations, but despite such weaknesses Nabokov still considers *Fathers and Sons* "one of the most brilliant novels of the nineteenth century," and he works through it perceptively. Turgenev also inspires him to one of his most delightful and sustained outbursts of criticism by unerringly aimed parodistic summary:

> Russia in those days was one huge dream: the masses slept—figuratively; the intellectuals spent sleepless nights—literally—sitting up and talking about things, or just meditating until five in the morning and then going out for a walk. There was a lot of flinging-oneself-down-on-one's-bed without undressing and sinking-into-a-heavy-slumber stuff, or jumping into one's clothes. Turgenev's maidens are generally good get-uppers, jumping into their crinolines, sprinkling their faces with cold water, and running out, as fresh as roses, into the garden, where the inevitable meeting takes place in a bower. (65–66)

After reading such a passage, few will ever be able to take certain scenes in Turgenev with the same solemnity as in the past.

Nabokov's invariably hostile pronouncements on Dostoevsky have always aroused much curiosity and opposition, and of course he did not miss the chance to take some healthy sideswipes in his classes at his perennial punching bag. His dislike of Dostoevsky goes back a long way, and may plausibly be traced to two causes. One is that Dostoevsky's works were used in turn-of-the-century Russian culture as reinforcement for the most reactionary elements of Russian society, and good Russian liberals like the Nabokov family would have naturally detested the harnessing of such a great writer to so sleazy a cause. One way of meeting the problem was thus to tear down his literary status. But, at the same time, Nabokov as a writer could not escape his enormous influence, and certain elements in his own work are unquestionably indebted to Dostoevsky. This only further increased his irritability and resentment, and it became all the more imperative to ridicule and denigrate those aspects of Dostoevsky that he deplored and could not use.

He does so, however, in terms that are hardly new in Russian criticism, though they have long since been out of date. Dostoevsky was heartily disliked, during his own lifetime, by a sizable section of critical opinion because of the crude sensationalism of his murder plots, his use of character types like the virtuous prostitute and the saintly idiot reminiscent of sentimental melodrama, and his general depiction of the more sordid sides of human existence. Such traits were unfavorably contrasted with the more elegant, aristocratic, country-house traditions of the Russian novel descending from Pushkin and carried on by Turgenev, Tolstoy, Goncharov, and many others. Nabokov simply revives this sort of critical nitpicking, based on a refined dislike of Dostoevsky's presumed artistic vulgarity, and refuses to see anything in his work except the plebeian origins of his raw materials and his unseemly display of a somewhat hysterical religiosity. Dostoevsky's genius, of course, consisted precisely in being able to take such crude materials and raise them to the level of high tragedy. But if you think that Raskolnikov's motivation in *Crime and Punishment* is "terribly muddled," and that *The Brothers Karamazov* "is a typical detective story, a riotous whodunit—in slow motion," then what is there to say in reply? Nothing at all, except to remark that, just as Nabokov admits that he lacks "an ear for music," so too he lacks whatever organ is necessary to appreciate Dostoevsky.

Or at least the art of the major Dostoevsky. He rates *The Double*, an early and relatively uncomplicated story, as Dostoevsky's finest achievement, no doubt because so many of his own characters are haunted by doubles both real and imaginary. And he praises the strain of furious grotesquerie in Dostoevsky, his "wonderful flair" for a "humor always on the verge of hysterics and people hurting each other in a wild exchange of insults." Grotesque comedy is also Nabokov's forte, though usually in a more restrained key. His dislike of Dostoevsky is so intense, though, that he even loses his abundant sense of humor while discussing him—or so it seems, unless he is once again pulling our leg. For he solemnly argues that Dostoevsky's major characters are all such "poor, deformed and warped souls" that their reactions can scarcely be accepted as human. And he goes on to list the various types of mental illness under which they can be classified, using categories culled from an article in—of all places, and despite his antipathy to Freud— the *Psychoanalytic Review*! Will wonders never cease, or are we hearing the voice of Dr. John Ray, Jr., Ph.D., the learned psychiatrist who prefaced *Lolita*? After all, what sort of characters does Nabokov himself portray? Pillars of mental health?

Nabokov is, of course, much more sympathetic to Tolstoy, whom he calls "the greatest Russian writer of prose fiction." In view of his dislike of writers with "messages," he has a little trouble here in adjusting his prejudices to his preferences; but he decides that Tolstoy's art "was so powerful, so tiger bright, so original and universal that it easily transcends the sermon." In any case, he only discusses *Anna Karenin(a)* and *The Death of Ivan Ilyich*; *War and Peace* would have been a tougher nut to crack. He has an interesting but rather obscure theory about Tolstoy's use of "time," penetratingly analyzes the many details foreshadowing Anna's suicide under a train, and rather unctuously states the theme of the book to be the contrast between metaphysical and carnal love. The first, "based on willingness for self-sacrifice, or mutual respect," is embodied in the Kitty-Levin relationship; "the Anna-Vronski alliance was founded only on carnal love and therein lay its doom."

Two short stories of Chekhov, and a long note on *The Seagull*, bring out some of Nabokov's most tender and evocative prose. He savors the casual delicacy of Chekhov's art, his use of throwaway detail to create mood, and most of all his unwillingness to take sides in the raging political warfare of his day, his preference for the sheerly human to the ideological. Chekhov also possesses that mixture of whimsicality and sadness that appeals so much to Nabokov's sensibility, and Chekhov was himself an archetypal Russian liberal (though personally a very successful one) who chronicled the strivings, illusions, and defeats of those close to Nabokov's heart. Nabokov's paean of praise for this type ("the intellectual, the Russian idealist . . . a good man who cannot make good") is too long to quote entire; but it reveals much about his own values. So does his celebration of "all this pathetic dimness, all this lovely weakness, all this Chekhovian dove-gray world," which "is worth treasuring in the glare of those strong, self-sufficient worlds that are promised us by the worshipers of totalitarian states."

The book concludes with a brief dismissal of Gorky as a writer, though the sketch of his life is respectful, a few amusing pages on *poshlost* again, and some familiar considerations on the art of translation. On the whole, it is more an anthology of great passages of Russian literature than a series of lectures; but the commentary is by Nabokov, and there is never a dull or conventional moment. One may agree or disagree, but the pleasure of being in such engaging and civilized company never flags. For all lovers of Russian literature, and for all those who aspire to be lovers of Russian literature, Nabokov's volume is a garden of delights.

PART TWO

Overviews

CHAPTER FIVE

Russian Thought: The Road to Revolution

1

ANYONE INTERESTED in the history of Russian culture has become aware that some of the best work in the field has been done, in the past fifteen years or so, by a Polish scholar named Andrzej Walicki. His first book, *Osobowóść a historia* (1969), a series of studies dealing with the Slavophiles, Belinsky, Turgenev, and Dostoevsky, has not been translated; but two later works, *The Slavophile Controversy* (1975) and *The Controversy over Capitalism* (1969), have made him better known to a larger international audience. Walicki's *A History of Russian Thought* (1973) should receive, and certainly deserves, a wide public among students of Russian culture, and all those readers of Russian nineteenth-century literature who wish to obtain some enlightenment on the sociocultural background from which it emerged.[1]

A knowledge of cultural history is of course indispensable for the study of any literature; but it may be argued that this is more true of Russian than of any other major European literature of the same period. Owing to the difficulty of expressing controversial ideas directly in public print (though it is amazing how many such ideas did manage to find their way into the journals because of the obtuseness—but sometimes also the tolerance—of the tsarist censorship), literature served more or less as a safety valve through which forbidden subjects could be presented or at least suggested. Hence the notorious ideological *density* of the best Russian literature—a trait that still continues to distinguish its writers, whether novelists or poets, from their freer confrères in the West, who sometimes envy the intensity of the Russian response to literature without fully understanding the reason for such fervor. It is, quite simply, that literature is not an adornment or accessory of everyday existence; it is the only form in which Russians can see discussed the true problems by which they are preoccupied, and of which their rulers have always thought it preferable to keep them ignorant.

If Russian literature was thus created in such close connection with Russian thought, it was also because this thought itself was so largely focused on the political and sociocultural concerns that occupied every thinking Russian; there was no incongruity involved in creating characters who

[1] Andrzej Walicki, *A History of Russian Thought*, trans. Hilda Andrews-Rusiecka (Stanford, Calif., 1979).

were consciously engrossed with such seemingly abstract, "philosophical" matters. It is primarily "thought" of this kind that Walicki places at the center of his considerations (as his original Polish title indicated more clearly, that is, *Russian Philosophy and Social Thought from the Enlightenment to Marxism*). And he argues, with a good deal of justice, that to write the history of Russian philosophy in any other way is "a particularly thankless task."

Professional philosophers in Russia, until the last quarter of the nineteenth century, were apt to be second- or third-rate Germans who conscientiously propounded one or another "system" acquired in their youth, or Orthodox theologians teaching in seminaries and turning their backs on the controversies racking the current scene. There were, of course, some exceptions, and Walicki makes brief mention of Pamphilus Yurkevich, whose polemic against Chernyshevsky's materialism deserves a little more extended treatment if only because it is so rarely taken seriously.[2] But he is right in maintaining that a parade of such figures, and a review of their works, would only reveal the appalling poverty of official Russian intellectual life. It is only when one turns from the schools and seminaries to the independent journals, and to the writings of those who would in the West be loosely called sociocultural essayists and publicists, that the genuine interest of Russian thought begins to appear. This is why, as Walicki contends, it is preferable to study it primarily as the history of *social* thought, and to set it, as he does, firmly in the context of sociopolitical history.

Seen from this point of view, in terms of "the issues that were closest to the hearts of the educated Russians of their time," the history of Russian thought takes on quite a new richness and importance, despite the lack of any truly outstanding philosopher of major stature. (The one possible ex-

[2] Yurkevich was a professor at the Kiev Theological Academy, who was then appointed to the chair of philosophy at the University of Moscow in 1861. Walicki recognizes him as "the most serious critic of Chernyshevsky, the leading radical thinker of the 1860s, but remarks that his "Platonic idealism was . . . too reminiscent of traditional Christian apologetics to have any wider influence in secular circles" (215).

This is unquestionably true, but says nothing about the value of Yurkevich's criticisms in themselves. They seem to have hit home pretty effectively, and to have left some scars, if we are to judge by the fact that G. V. Plekhanov still felt it necessary to answer them at the beginning of this century and devotes a whole chapter in his study of Chernyshevsky (1909) mainly to the polemics between the two. In a now almost forgotten but still very valuable book on the history of Russian criticism in the nineteenth century, one of the few not written from a radical materialist or (later) Marxist-Leninist point of view, the neo-Idealist critic A. Flekser (writing under the pseudonym of A. Volynsky), makes a very good case for taking Yurkevich seriously, and goes into depressing detail about the scurrilous campaign against him launched by the radical press. To reevaluate such neglected people, who were unable to obtain a hearing on their merits, would seem to be a task that Western Slavists might well undertake. See G. V. Plekhanov, *Izbrannye Filosofskie Proizvedeniya*, 5 vols. (Moscow, 1956–1958), 4:246–55; A. Volynsky, *Russkie Kritiki* (St. Petersburg, 1896), 261–368.

ception being Vladimir Soloviev at the end of the nineteenth century, though Alexander Herzen is also entitled to press a claim.) For we find in Russian thought, as Walicki sees it, "a most unusual cross-fertilization of ideas and influences; the rapid modernization of a great nation compressed into a short space of time; the curious co-existence of archaic and modern elements in the social structure and in ways of thinking; the rapid influx of outside influences and resistance to them; the impact on the intellectual élite of the social realities and ideas of Western Europe on the one hand, and their constant re-discovery of their own native tradition and social realities on the other" (XIV). This passage, from the preface to the Polish edition of the book, defines the larger horizon within which Russian thinkers debated the issues of their time. And one can agree with Walicki that "all these factors help to make the history of Russian ideas . . . more interesting and more dramatic than the intellectual history of many more advanced countries with richer philosophical traditions." It may be added that these factors also give Russian thought a special international relevance at the present time, when so many Third World peasant countries, entering the phase of modernization, are faced with exactly the same problems of assimilating alien ideas and asserting their own cultural identity.

Walicki is of course a Marxist, and an eminent member of the Polish Academy of Sciences; but the Marxism of Eastern Europe, or at least of Poland, is by no means that of the Soviet Union.[3] It is significant that, in his introduction to *The Slavophile Controversy*, he acknowledges his debts to such thinkers as Ferdinand Tönnies, Max Weber, and Karl Mannheim (or to such a freebooting Marxist as Lucien Goldmann) rather than making the usual obeisances to more orthodox authorities. To be sure, Marx, Engels, and Lenin are amply cited in his pages; but he always uses them appositely and for their genuine insights, never as sacred writ to close a question. Moreover, Walicki is careful to exclude any kind of "reductionism" in his approach, and even has the audacity (in *A History of Russian Thought*) to criticize Lenin for such a failing because of one of his remarks about the Populist theoretician N. K. Mikhailovsky.

Such a criticism stems from Walicki's acute awareness, expressed in *The Slavophile Controversy*, of the dangers of assuming "that an individual's ideas are directly dependent on the sum total of his social involvements (which are often quite fortuitous)"; and he explains that he prefers rather to seek "a correlation between structures of thought and imagination on the one hand and the social structures—and the types of human relationships determined by them—on the other." His own position is said to re-

---

[3] Walicki has spent a good deal of time outside of Poland in recent years, and has taught both in Australia and the United States, most recently at the University of Notre Dame. It is not clear, at least as far as my own knowledge goes, whether or not he has gone into exile.

sult "indirectly" from "the basic thesis of historical materialism," but Walicki chooses to name it "anthropocentric"—by which he means that "at the core of every view of the world lives a specific philosophy of man and society." Again, however, he hastens to add that "this does not mean that man's imaginative curiosity is confined to historical and social issues; it is only one of the consequences of the elementary truth that men belong to the world of human kind and in their reasoning reflect one or another of the laws governing this world." With such an "elementary truth" even non-Marxists can readily agree; and it is this freedom from dogmatic blinkers, combined with an ingenious ability to find fresh and illuminating "correlations," that gives special value to Walicki's contributions to the history of Russian culture.

2

A History of Russian Thought is written as a survey, and its task is primarily to convey information rather than to argue any particular thesis. The book is thus difficult to review in the sense that, covering as it does so wide a range of issues—and issues that in most cases have been hotly disputed now for more than a century—to deal adequately with all the questions it raises would require an extended commentary on every chapter. Walicki's point of view, however, has already been indicated in the quotation from his preface; it is clear that he sees the interest, and indeed what might be called the pathos, of Russian thought, in the effort to cope with "the social realities and ideas of Western Europe on the one hand, and [its] own native tradition and social realities on the other." Even though Walicki subordinates the task of interpretation to that of exposition, and his history includes much that cannot be directly included within the terms of his antithesis, a rapid scrutiny of the book from this point of view will not distort his basic approach and, at the same time, allow for more than a series of random notes on individual topics.

There is not much evidence of any reaction against European influence in the first two chapters, which deal primarily with the reign of Catherine the Great. Catherine herself was enamored of Enlightenment thought, and made efforts to encourage it until it became a threat to political stability. The two main figures of this period, N. I. Novikov and Alexander Radishchev, both ran afoul of her and landed either in prison or Siberia. Novikov was a satirical journalist and, later, an important force as a publisher; Radishchev's *A Journey from St. Petersburg to Moscow* contained an impassioned attack on serfdom. Walicki also believes that Radishchev's treatise on the immortality of the soul (written in Siberia) is "the highest achievement of Russian Enlightenment thought in the sphere of pure philosophical speculation." In addition, he discusses a few minor figures (recently disinterred by Soviet scholarship) who earnestly carried on in the Enlightenment tradition.

Some reaction against Enlightenment values can be observed in the second part of Catherine's reign, after the peasant revolt of Pugachev had temporarily shaken the foundations of the empire. Mostly, though, this took the form of Freemasonry, to which Walicki devotes a useful section. The influence of this movement, familiar to all readers of *War and Peace*, is explained as a reaction against the fright engendered by Pugachev among the enlightened aristocracy. This produced "an inducement to abandon liberal ideas," but it was impossible for such persons simply to return "to the previous matter-of-fact acceptance of the exploitation of the peasantry. . . . What remained was the flight into the realm of individual self-perfection, the 'inner life of the soul,' or, in other words, the Masonic lodge" (20). Even Catherine's aristocratic opposition, who saw themselves as representing the old Boyar tradition, did not appeal to Russian antiquity and simply desired a Western constitutional monarchy. The single exception is Prince Mikhail Shcherbatov, whose *A Discourse on the Corruption of Morals in Russia* (unpublished during his lifetime) deplored the moral disintegration that had resulted from Peter's reforms. Herzen published the text many years later as anticipating the Slavophiles; but Walicki finds too many Enlightenment ideas in Shcherbatov to accept this analogy without serious objections, and calls it "largely superficial and even unreliable."

With the reign of Alexander I, Walicki moves into the nineteenth century and will stay there for the remainder of his book. Gentry conservatives and gentry revolutionaries are here pitted against each other, the first represented by Nikolay Karamzin and the second by the Decembrists, who tried to prevent Nicholas I from acceding to the throne in their ill-fated one-day uprising. Karamzin, the first great Russian historian, was also an important man of letters; a Masonic liberal in his youth, he was frightened by the French Revolution, which he witnessed firsthand and described— among many other things, to be sure—in his still very readable *Letters of a Russian Traveller*. It is not true to say, as Walicki claims, that "he was completely uninterested in social problems"; and perhaps more emphasis could have been given to the tension between Karamzin's commitment to Westernization and his warning to his countrymen not to follow the disastrous European political path. Despite his defense of autocracy in his *Memoir on Ancient and Modern Russia*, he retained enough of his old liberalism to argue that the sphere of private life was outside the power even of the tsar. One should also note his sentimental fondness for the ancient Russian "merchant republics" of Novgorod and Pskov, whose absorption by the state he depicted "in a spirit of elegiac melancholy."

The Decembrists organized the first revolt of the Russian upper class against the throne that was more than a court conspiracy. Walicki discusses the various programs of the different sections of the movement, and concludes that, despite some statements appealing to a largely imaginary past (the inevitable "merchant republics," and the twelfth-century Boyar Duma), "Decembrist ideology was essentially an example of modern liberalism." Still, the most original mind among them—Colonel Pavel Pestel, the leader of the Southern Society—was the first to pay attention to the Russian peasant commune (*obshchina*); his plans called for the commune to be preserved, and to be used to guarantee everyone a minimum of subsistence. Another Decembrist "described the peasant commune with a self-governing *mir* [assembly] as 'tiny republics,' a living survival of ancient Russian liberty" (67). This discovery of the commune may be considered the effective beginning of the Russian effort to reexamine their own social realities; and as Walicki remarks, "the idea that the village commune contained the seeds of Russia's future social system was to have an astonishing career in the history of Russian ideas" (63).

The Decembrists, however, attached no real importance to the *obshchina* and had their eyes firmly fixed, as a model, on European social and political developments. Indeed, they are depicted by Walicki as the only—and very short-lived—group manifestation of classical liberalism on the Russian social scene, even though they have been claimed as predecessors by generations of Russian revolutionaries inspired by Socialist and Communist ideas (Lenin called them "the best sons of the gentry"). "The Decembrist ideology," Walicki comments, "found no continuators in later Russian revolutionary thought. No radical movement in Russia was to put forward a liberal or even a liberal-cum-aristocratic conception of freedom or to support economic liberalism" (69). The absence of such movements, indeed, constitutes one of the sharpest differences between Russian and Western European sociopolitical development.

3

After the dismal failure of the Decembrist revolt, the gentry intelligentsia sought consolation from the military-bureaucratic rigors of the regime of Nicholas I in German Idealism and Romantic literature. Anti-Enlightenment ideas were now the order of the day, and the secret "Society of Wisdom-Lovers" (they chose the Masonic term *lyubomudrie* in preference to the French "philosophy") initiated the vogue of Russian Schellingianism. The president of the society, V. F. Odoevsky, was a wide-ranging, philosophical dilettante who dabbled in theosophy and mysticism, and also a writer of merit admired by the young Dostoevsky. In his *Russian Nights*, he collected a series of stories, dialogues, and parables depicting the decline of European civilization as a result of the combined effects of rationalism, industrialism, and Utilitarianism. As a Romantic nationalist, Odoevsky believed that Russia's mission was to use its still-untapped resources of spirituality to renew a European civilization at the end of its tether.

It was, however, Peter Chaadaev, the most important thinker of this period, who first gave classic formulation to what Walicki calls "the privilege of backwardness," the thesis that Russia's lack of development along Western lines was really a tremendous advantage. An elegant dandy and idol of the Moscow intellectual salons, and a close friend of Pushkin, Chaadaev had been considered a liberal as a young man. But his philosophical writings show the influence of French Catholic traditionalists (de Bonald, de Maistre, the early Lamennais); and at first he took a totally despairing view of Russia as, so to speak, the stepchild of historical Providence. It was, he argued in the first of his *Philosophical Letters* (the only one published in his lifetime), a country without a "moral personality" because it has been cut off from the roots of Western civilization embodied and preserved in Roman Catholicism. An infuriated Nicholas I promptly had Chaadaev declared insane, and he was confined to house arrest (an administrative procedure that has since been democratized and put on a less impromptu medical footing).

Several years later, Chaadaev published his ironically titled *Apology of a Madman*, the result of further reflections and some discussion with his Slavophile friends. Maintaining most of his old ideas intact, he simply drew different conclusions from them in a dialectical somersault that was soon to find innumerable imitators. If Russia was a country without a true history, he now maintained, and had failed to take part in European civilization, this was really a great historical opportunity. For it meant that, in Walicki's summary, "in constructing their future, the Russian people can make use of the experience of European nations while avoiding their mistakes: they can be guided solely by 'the voice of enlightened reason and common will.' " As a result, Chaadaev concluded, Russia was destined "to resolve the greater part of the social problems, to perfect the greater part of the ideas which have arisen in older societies" (89). Such notions had of course been uttered before in Russia, but it was Chaadaev who gave them their most impressive formulation and provided Russian Messianism with an up-to-date philosophical foundation (its earlier religious sources have been brilliantly analyzed in Michael Cherniavsky's *Tsar and People*).[4]

[4] The subtitle of Cherniavsky's book is *Studies in Russian Myths*, and it is one of the most penetrating analyses of Russian culture I have ever come across. The myths he is concerned with derive from the sacred quality attributed to Russian sovereigns, who differed from Western rulers in a fundamental way. "In the West, the tension was between two unequal entities [embodied in the person of the ruler], one higher and one lower, a divine nature and a human one. In Russia, the tension was between the divine nature of princely power and the saintly nature of the prince as a man" (29). This made the Russian sovereign power completely identical with Christianity. "There was no concept of a secular state in Russia, no concept outside

The book now reaches the crucial period of the 1840s, and the next four chapters deal respectively with the Slavophiles, the Westernizers, and the Petrashevtsy. Here Walicki is on familiar territory, simply condensing much of the material expounded in *The Slavophile Controversy*. He places the Slavophiles both in the narrow context of "a reply to Chaadaev" and in the much wider one of a response to the evils of capitalist modernization that had already become evident in the more highly developed Western countries. If the Slavophiles drew so heavily on the ideas of the German conservative Romantics, it was because both Russia and Germany were relatively backward in industrial development, and "the new social and political system had already begun to reveal its negative features and had already come under attack by critics on the right as well as the left." This made it easier, in both cases, for conservative thinkers "to idealize the patriarchal traditions and archaic social structures that in their countries had shown an obstinate vitality."

The Slavophiles answered Chaadaev's initial glorification of European civilization by tracing its present difficulties to a classical past from which Russia—happily—had been excluded. The Roman state, Ivan Kireevsky argued, had been based on a "juridical rationalism" that presupposed the conflict of competing individuals; and only despotism, as in Roman Catholicism, could impose any sort of unity. The final result of European spiritual evolution, according to Aleksey Khomiakov, had been "the philosophy of the enlightenment, which paved the way for the French Revolution, German Idealism, and which ultimately led to Feuerbach's deification of man and Stirner's apotheois of egoism" (95). The Slavophiles, especially Kireevsky, also pointed out that the excessive rationalism of Western culture had destroyed the "integrity" of the self, and led to a profound inner split in the personality that could only be healed by faith. (The dramatization of this split, and the struggle to regain "integrality," is of course one of the great themes of Russian nineteenth-century literature.)

Opposed to all this was Holy Russia—at least the Russia of "the people"—whose adhesion to the Orthodox faith had saved them from the nox-

---

of Christianity and its purposes" (33), since the ruler never acted in any nonreligious capacity simply as a man.

This seamless equation between the Russian sovereign and divine purpose became the source of Russian Messianism as the Russian "lands" were amalgamated into a great state; and though its rulers were no longer prince-saints but imperial tsars, they were unfailingly characterized with the saintly appellation "most gentle" (44). When Peter the Great became a secular emperor instead of tsar, he caused a terrible crisis in Russian self-consciousness. The Messianic religiosity previously attached to the person of the ruler was now transferred to the notion of "Holy Russia" and finally to "the people" as the embodiment of "holy Russia." Cherniavsky's fascinating examination of this process throws a strong historical light on some of the obscurer corners of what used to be called "the Russian soul." Michael Cherniavsky, *Tsar and People* (New York, 1961).

ious effects of such ideas, and who lived a life based on mutual trust between ruler and ruled in which "the disintegrating egoism of private
ownership" divorced from social obligations was unknown. The basic social unit of Russian life was the *obshchina*, founded on the common use of
land and governed according to time-honored traditions and the principle
of unanimity; the same ethos was also embodied in the Orthodox doctrine
of *sobornost* ("conciliarity") which excluded "both self-willed individualism
and its restraint by coercion." This way of life had presumably existed in
pre-Petrine Russia and was preserved among the peasantry, even though,
since Peter the Great, upper-class society had been corrupted by Western
notions and values and had lost the sense of its Russian roots.

4

The Slavophiles have usually aroused passionately partisan interpretations
among the historians of Russian culture, but Walicki takes no part in such
quarrels. He is interested in analyzing the origins of their thought, and in
explaining its appeal in sociological terms, rather than in exposing its obvious fallacies and shortcomings. He views Slavophilism as being an image,
or myth, of a "conservative Utopia" (the notion is included in the Polish
title of his book about them), which furnished "a comprehensive and detailed vision of a social ideal sharply contrasted to existing realities"; and
while it can be seen merely as the nostalgia for an idealized past that never
existed, it also contains some elements of more lasting value. Walicki points
out the similarity of Slavophile ideas to those of Tönnies about "community and society"; and he notes that Max Weber had also seen the influence
of Roman law as responsible for the "progressive rationalization" of Western social institutions and the Western state. Moreover, even though Slavophile ideas were never widely accepted in their original form, they in-
jected an extraordinary ferment into Russian thought as the first large-scale
attempt to provide an alternative image to Western European sociocultural
models. And their influence has continued right up to the present, if we
are to judge from current reports of a renaissance of Slavophile ideas
among the restless Soviet intelligentsia. Nor is this really surprising, even
after half a century of Marxist indoctrination: it is only to the Slavophiles
that Russians can turn to define their own cultural identity.

The Westernizers, of course, took exactly the opposite tack, and the polemics between the two camps filled the journals of the period. The Westernizers are much better known (Bakunin, Belinsky, and Herzen are the
most important), and they all went through a roughly similar evolution.
They began with some form of social or philosophical Romanticism, absorbed themselves in Hegel, followed his injunction to pay attention to
"reality," and finally, inspired by the Left Hegelians and particularly Feu-

erbach, turned to a philosophy of political action so as to transform the world in the light of conscious reason. The ideal, as with the young Marx, was to fuse the results of German philosophy with French political activism. Bakunin remained fixed in the negative phase of this dialectic, and coined the famous slogan that adorned the walls of the Sorbonne in 1968: *Die Lust der Zerstörung is auch eine schaffende Lust* (The passion for destruction is also a creative passion). Belinsky, not really a philosopher but a brilliant literary critic, wrote his famous letter to V. P. Botkin denouncing the Hegelian universal in the name of the suffering individual (very probably one of the sources for Ivan Karamazov's revolt against God's world). Herzen made the most important contributions to what we call philosophy in his *Dilettantism in Science* and *Letters on the Study of Nature*, which look forward to the synthesis of empiricism (materialism) and idealism, that is, the Hegelian dialectic that Herzen called "the algebra of revolution."

Walicki sees the main issue at stake between the Westernizers and Slavophiles as being "the idea of personality," since the first took as crucial the emancipation of the individual from antiquated social bonds and the second insisted on the importance of maintaining intact the inherited traditions that had preserved Russian society from the upheavals of the West. But while the Westernizers wished to emancipate the individual, and idolized Peter the Great as the initiator of such emancipation for Russia, the form that individualism had taken in the West—the development of capitalism—was not at all to their taste. All were affected by Utopian Socialism to some degree, and perhaps Walicki does not stress this phase sufficiently (particularly in the case of Belinsky); but in any event they were faced with the problem of reconciling their theoretical "Westernism" with the actual shape of Western society. A conflict over capitalism thus raged among them in the late 1840s, with Herzen and Bakunin arguing that Russia should rely only on the peasants and the intelligentsia to shape the future, while others insisted, like some of the later Marxists, that a bourgeois capitalist phase of economic development was indispensable. Belinsky, after some wavering, finally rallied to this latter position, and could thus later be praised by Plekhanov for his sociological "intuition" and by Walicki for his "dialectical historicism."

Actually, the main course of Russian thought was to follow quite a different direction for a good many years. The path it took is already prefigured by the Petrashevsky Circle, whose ranks included Dostoevsky and who are best known as followers of Fourier. But one finds among them the idea that the *obshchina* and the Fourierist "phalanstery" were very much alike, and that the first could plausibly evolve into the second under the proper guidance. The linkage between Socialism and the *obshchina*, however, which had only been broached among the Petrashevsky, flowered into a full-scale doctrine in the writings of Alexander Herzen during the 1850s. Herzen had always been more sympathetic to the Slavophiles than the other Westernizers and, when he went to live in Europe, reacted to the vulgarity of bourgeois life there with a moral and aesthetic revulsion "not without a tinge of aristocratic superiority." The failure of the revolutions of 1848 convinced him that the bourgeoisie was invincible for the foreseeable future, and that Western Socialism had itself become bourgeois in character.

The only hope was in a "Russian Socialism" that would redeem the world, and that, as the *obshchina* seemed to indicate, would not have to be created artificially because it already existed as a way of life among the Russian people. They "had not been corrupted by the Roman juridical heritage and the individualistic view of property relations associated with it"; and their very absence from modern history, as Chaadaev had argued, had been a concealed blessing. Uniting the Messianism of Chaadaev with the Slavophile view of Western history and the *obshchina*, Herzen combined this with his previous Westernism by the role he assigned to the Russian intelligentsia. It was they, the product of the reforms of Peter the Great, who would bring the "personality principle" to the people and fuse it with "the communism of the common man." This was Herzen's vision of the future, which he expounded in such works as *From the Other Shore*, his open letters to Herwegh, Mazzini, and Michelet, and in *The Development of Revolutionary Ideas in Russia*.

Herzen was an extremely rich and complex personality, perhaps the most attractive figure humanly among a great generation of Russians (his friend Turgenev would be a close second), and the interest of his ideas is not exhausted by their immediate political significance. Walicki comments on his important rejection of the idea of historical inevitability in *From the Other Shore*; his criticism of mass, middle-class culture in *Ends and Beginnings*; and his *Letter on Free Will* in which, while maintaining his respect for the natural sciences, he argues that "the sense of freedom is a necessary attribute of the consciousness of men." Walicki interprets this as "the rejection of all theories that advised radicals in the name of 'objective laws' of physiology, history or economics to become reconciled to inevitable facts and abandon the struggle to realize their 'utopian' aims" (174). Later, however, in his *Letters to an Old Comrade* (Bakunin), Herzen limited such "freedom" by rejecting the attempt of a small group to take power and impose its revolutionary will on the masses; this could only lead, he said, to "communist serfdom." In practice, while still demanding a revolutionary transformation of society, he came to favor gradual reform because "it is not possible to liberate people further in their external circumstances than their *inner* freedom permits" (179).

5

Herzen dominated Russian culture in the mid-1850s and early 1860s; but he was soon replaced by the representatives of a new generation, the radical "enlighteners" of the 1860s, whose spokesmen were Nikolay Chernyshevsky and Nikolay Dobrolyubov. They are the successors of the former Westernizers and they idolized Belinsky; but they were much narrower in their views, much harsher in their personal outlook, and more determinedly revolutionary. Both were hardworking journalists who turned out an enormous amount of copy and hardly had the time to think very deeply about the matters on which they touched. Chernyshevsky, while in prison, turned to literature and produced an immensely successful didactic novel *What Is to Be Done?* Dobrolyubov was a mordant and slashing pamphleteer, who, unfortunately for the future of Russian literary criticism, was forced to use literature as the material for his diatribes against the system. Both were ex-seminarians, both came from priestly families, and both were atheists and materialists of the most simpleminded stripe. Chernyshevsky came closest to having a "philosophy," which combined Helvétius and Holbach with a dash of Feuerbach and, for good measure, the influence of Bentham's Utilitarianism in its crudest form. Walicki is of course obligated to expound their views, and he does so with a good deal of conscientiousness; perhaps too much, in my opinion, since he seriously exaggerates their intellectual stature.

This is particularly so in his discussion of Chernyshevsky's treatise *The Aesthetic Relations between Art and Reality*, which Walicki considers "close to the great humanist tradition in Germany represented by Goethe, Schiller and Hegel." To place in such company the man who declared that art was useful only as a "surrogate" for reality is almost grotesque; and Chernyshevsky meant exactly what he said. Just as Marx had learnt from Feuerbach that religion was the opium of the people, Chernyshevsky had arrived at the same conclusion about art: it could only be tolerated as a substitute, until what is depicted could be obtained in reality. Although a man of admirable courage and political dedication, Chernyshevsky's sensibility was drearily philistine; and the best writers of the period (Turgenev, Tolstoy, Dostoevsky) knew what they were about in considering his views to be outrageous and an implicit attack on the very right of art even to exist. His *Anthropological Principle in Philosophy* (the derivation from Feuerbach is obvious) is touchingly naive in its faith in the latest discoveries of science (particularly physiology) to solve all human problems; but it can hardly be taken seriously as "thought."

Despite his Westernism, however, Chernyshevsky defended the *obshchina* against attempts to dissolve it when the serfs were liberated in 1861; and he wrote an article to prove that Russia could "skip" the stage of capitalist development since "communal ownership of the land could serve as the basis for the Socialist development of agriculture." Dmitry Pisarev, the third of the "enlighteners" of the 1860s, was much more consistent in calling both for the "destruction of aesthetics" in favor of feeding the hungry masses, and also for the expansion of capitalism in Russia (of course under the leadership of "enlightened capitalists" with progressive opinions).

But Pisarev remained totally isolated in this respect, and the Populists of the 1870s continued in the channels already dug by the Slavophiles, Herzen, and Chernyshevsky. By this time capitalism had begun to make serious inroads in Russia, and the Populists devoted themselves to combating the idea that its further expansion was either inevitable or desirable. Lavrov's *Historical Letters* castigated "the cost of progress" and persuaded the conscience-stricken intelligentsia that, since their own advantages had been purchased at the price of terrible suffering by millions in the past, such a debt could only be repaid by dedicating themselves to alleviating any further suffering. (This was one of the sources inspiring the astonishing "going-to-the-people" movement of 1873–74, the "Populist crusade" in which thousands of young people flocked to the villages both to learn from Socialism in action and to help protect it from erosion.) Mikhailovsky wrote his influential "What Is Progress?" which insisted that Russia, while at a lower "level" of economic development than Europe, was actually a "higher" type of society because the Russian peasant had not been splintered as a personality by the division of labor and exercised all his faculties and capacities in his daily work. True "progress' consisted in preserving the *obshchina*; and this was "a conservative question because the solution depends on keeping the means of production in the hands of the producers, i.e., protecting the peasant proprietors against expropriation" (260). The Populists were familiar with Marx (Lavrov was even a personal friend), but the reading of *Capital* only convinced them that the horrors of "primitive accumulation" had to be avoided at all costs.

The Populists, with no clear political program, deprecated the struggle for political rights as linked with bourgeois capitalism and of benefit only to the educated class. But Peter Tkachev, the spokesman for a "Blanquist" or "Jacobin" Populism, argued that only by the seizure of power could the further depredations of capitalism be checked; and he declared that a revolutionary dictatorship would be necessary in order to transform all aspects of society in accordance with Populist ideals. One of these ideals was to institute the reign of "equality"; and, with admirable rigor, he affirmed that this could only be done if an "organic, physiological equality" were to be created "stemming from the same education and identical conditions of life." (Dostoevsky bitingly satirized this ambition to create a "biological" equality in the summary given of the ideas of Shigalev, the lame schoolteacher in *The Devils*, who is unfortunately never able to deliver his series of lectures on the perfect society.) Tkachev's relentless logic, however, does reveal one of the dilemmas that Populist thought was never able to resolve. What would be the place of "critical thinking individuals" in the ideal society it envisages? For it is only such individuals whose ideals and moral conscience impelled them to defend the village; and yet such ideals, obviously, were the product of that very Westernization that the Populists were pledged to fight against tooth and nail.

No such problem can be discerned in the "ideologies of reaction" that flourished during the last quarter of the nineteenth century; but it is striking to observe, on both sides of the Russian political spectrum, the same search for some definition of Russia's sociocultural "uniqueness" vis-à-vis Europe. Nikolay Danilevsky, once a fanatical Fourierist, worked out a doctrine of Pan-Slavism based on a theory of culture types anticipating Spengler and Toynbee. There was no universal law of historical evolution, and Russia would create an independent Slavic civilization that "was likely to be closest to the ideal of "all-humanity.'" Konstantin Pobedonostev, the sinister procurator of the Holy Synod in later life, also believed that each nation had its own organic laws of development that should not be infringed; autocracy was native to Russia, and he defended it with all the weapons at his command.

The most original and interesting of such thinkers was Konstantin Leontiev, the "Russian Nietzsche," whose loathing of bourgeois civilization was so great that he preferred the Ottoman Empire or China to Russia itself, which he thought already hopelessly infected with the dread "liberal-egalitarian" virus. Nonetheless, he imagined at first that Russia might still, after conquering Constantinople, create a neo-Byzantine civilization based on Orthodoxy and autocracy; but he later became convinced that the future belonged to Socialism. He speculated that perhaps "a Russian Tsar would stand at the head of the Socialist movement and would organize and discipline it"; and he was convinced that, in any case, the liberals whom he hated would be the first to suffer. For those Socialists who came to power, he said, "will require discipline; traditions of humility, the habit of obedience will be of use to them" (304–5). The isolated and intransigent Leontiev, who ended his days as a monk in the Optina cloister, certainly did not lack his moments of prophetic insight.

Nor, of course, did Dostoevsky and Tolstoy, who are linked together in a separate chapter titled "Two Prophetic Writers." The comparison between them has long been a set piece of criticism, and Walicki's sober discussion compares well with more flamboyant treatments. It is, indeed, valuable because of its very sobriety, and because it is useful to have both writers set so clearly in the context of the Russian ideas and problems that nourished their work. Walicki stresses Dostoevsky's affinities with the Slav-

ophiles in setting "against the rational egoism of European capitalism . . .
the ideal of the authentic fraternal community preserved in Orthodoxy and
Russian folk-traditions"; and he interprets the later novels as responses to
the dethronement of the God-man in Feuerbach and Stirner (312). All this
is relevant and accurate, but should be slightly qualified. For Walicki fails
to bring out sufficiently that, for Dostoevsky, "the rational egoism of European capitalism" was represented in Russia by the "enlighteners" of the
1860s. And while he was thoroughly familiar with Feuerbach and Stirner,
whose ideas he had encountered among the Petrashevtsy, he was primarily
concerned with exposing the effects of such ideas as he saw them appearing
in the various ideologies of the radical intelligentsia.

The treatment of Tolstoy is more concerned with his late publicistic
writings than with his novels, and is thus of less general interest. Walicki is
clearly more attracted to Dostoevsky, whose ideas for him still "have a remarkable freshness," while he senses in Tolstoy "a genuinely and not just
superficially archaic mode of thought" whose moral zeal is impressive but
irrelevant to modern concerns. It is interesting, though Walicki fails to
mention it, that Dostoevsky defined his own relation to Tolstoy in very
similar terms in the concluding pages of *A Raw Youth*.

6

The end of the century saw a revival of metaphysical idealism in the work
of Vladimir Soloviev, and was marked by the conflict between Populism
and Marxism that immediately preceded the Russian Revolution. Walicki
displays an unusual empathy for so theosophical a thinker as Soloviev, and
sketches an engaging portrait of this complex personality, inspired by mystical visions of *Sophia* (Divine Wisdom), and whose ideas exercised so remarkable an influence; they not only gave birth to a whole generation of
Idealist theologians and philosophers but also played an important role in
the poetic flights of Russian Symbolism. Metaphysical idealism, however,
"developed apart from the leading trends of social thought" (though it
exercised an indirect influence by turning intellectual energies away from
an exclusive interest in social problems), and it is with these latter that we
are primarily concerned here. The future of Russia was being decided at
this time in the battle between the Populists and the Marxists, who had
just arrived on the scene as a fully fledged sociopolitical tendency. Oddly
enough, while the Marxists emerged triumphant in the ideological struggle, it was the Populist conviction that Russia need not follow the tutelage
of the West that ultimately prevailed in practice.

By the 1880s, it was clear that large-scale industrialization could not be
avoided, and a group of economists known as "Legal Populists" were willing to concede the inevitable; but they insisted, all the same, that Russian

capitalism, not being able to compete successfully with more advanced economies, would unavoidably fail. The alternative was a noncapitalist industrialization that would take advantage of, and encourage, all the "socialized" forms of labor still existing in Russia, and aid their transition to more highly developed forms of production. In this way, Russia would still be able to lead the world to a Socialist industrialism while avoiding the evils of capitalism; and the old Messianic note is struck once again in the assertion that "it will be Russia's role to serve them [Western workers] as an example in their attempts to reorganize the social system." Lenin countered this position in *The Development of Capitalism in Russia*, which attempted to demonstrate that capitalism was already well established there and could hardly be avoided any longer.

A key figure in the debate was Georgy Plekhanov, an ex–Populist turned Marxist, who founded the first Marxist party in Russia and whose considerable merits as a historian of Russian and Western social thought, as well as a critic and writer on art and literature, we shall unfortunately have to neglect. Plekhanov firmly believed in the "iron necessity" of the Marxist laws of social-economic evolution, and he fought with great skill and erudition against any idea that they could be "skipped" or abrogated. (Actually, Marx himself did not personally believe in any such "iron necessity," as Walicki demonstrates briefly here and at greater length in his *Controversy over Capitalism*; but Marx's views became known too late to influence the position taken by the Russian Marxists.) Plekhanov was an impenitent Westernizer, who believed that the working class should take up the task of modernization first begun by Peter the Great; only when this was completed by a capitalist economic phase and the attainment of political democracy would a true Socialist régime be possible. Otherwise, he affirmed, those who tried to organize a Socialist system from above would be forced "to resort to the ideals of a patriarchal and authoritarian Communism; the only change would be that the Peruvian 'sons of the Sun' and their officials would be replaced by a Socialist cast." Plekhanov therefore found himself in "the tragic dilemma" of a Socialist "arguing for the capitalist development of his country"; and Walicki highlights all those aspects of his thought (such as his devotion to Spinoza and Hegel) that turn the conception of necessity into an ontological principle inherent in the nature of the universe.

The young Lenin was a disciple and ally of Plekhanov, but already differed from him in certain fundamental respects. He was always temperamentally closer to the Populists even while rejecting their "economic romanticism," and he regarded the peasantry as a revolutionary force, rather than, like Plekhanov, as the main prop of "Asiatic despotism." Marxism for him was not primarily a theory of economic development but of class struggle; and Walicki cites a post-Revolutionary article in which he ridiculed the idea that a Marxian textbook could foresee "all the forms of development of subsequent world history." In the same article Lenin quotes with approval Napoleon's maxim: "On s'engage et puis . . . on voit." Plekhanov was in favor of an alliance with the liberal bourgeoisie so as to further the Westernization of Russia, but Lenin wanted the Marxists to align themselves with "the democratic sections of the petty bourgeoisie and the peasantry." He was well aware of his debt to Populism, and remarked in 1912 that the Bolsheviks had extracted from Populist Utopianism its "valuable democratic kernel." The rest, of course, is history—a history that Walicki describes as Lenin's realization of "the Populist dream of a direct transition from the overthrow of the Tsarist autocracy to the building of Socialism" (448).

Plekhanov opposed the revolution when it arrived, and accused the Bolsheviks "of ignoring the concrete 'conditions of time and place' in seizing political power as the "Jacobin" wing of the Populists had always wished to do. "It is ironical (and part of his tragedy)," Walicki comments, "that the recognition of historical necessity, which he thought would save him from 'utopianism,' turned out to be the very essence of his own utopianism" (423). Such a judgment, to say the least, is rather disingenuous. In what sense was Plekhanov "utopian" in predicting that the revolution would necessarily become an "authoritarian Communism"? He did not, after all, maintain that the seizure of power was impossible; only that a revolution made under such conditions could not live up to its avowed democratic aims and ambitions. Who, in this sense, was more "Utopian," Plekhanov or Lenin? Can one "skip" the phase of bourgeois liberal democracy and yet establish a genuine (and not sham) Socialist democratic system? The experience of the past half century would not encourage one to believe so, and Plekhanov's predictions have invariably proved accurate.[5]

[5] Just as this book was going to press, I came across an article that furnished additional confirmation of Plekhanov's prescience. It is an interview with a prominent Chinese writer, Liu Binyan, who spent twenty years at exile and hard labor beginning in 1957, and then, after his return, fell afoul of the authorities again in the early 1980s and was expelled from the Chinese Communist Party. "No writer in the Western countries seems comparable to Liu," writes Merle Goldman. "His position in China resembles that of Eastern European intellectuals such as Vaclav Havel in Czechoslovakia. . . . The great respect now accorded him throughout China derives from his courage in saying what many believe and talk about privately but are afraid to say openly. Despite his persecution, however, Liu still considers himself to be a Marxist."

What Liu Binyan, on a visit to Harvard as a Nieman fellow, said in an interview was the following: "Stalin was the first to ruin Socialism. The second was Mao. Cambodia's Pol Pot was the third. . . . These men were not really Marxists at all. The ignored Marx's basic tenet that Socialism presupposed a high level of material development. The conditions in each of the countries where these men came to power were not economically mature enough to build a Socialist society." Liu also remarks that "the need to maintain state power persuaded Lenin to push aside the materialist science of Marxism and attempt to establish Socialism in one

Whether a Communist régime would behave any differently, if it came to power legitimately in a highly developed Western country with democratic traditions, still remains to be seen. But that such a question arises at all testifies to the effect of the Russian example, and the immense historical consequences of the paradoxical victory, under the guise of Marxism, of the Slavophile-Populist current of Russian thought.

---

backward country. The result was not true Socialism." One wonders if Liu Binyan has been reading Plekhanov. "The Price China Has Paid: An Interview with Liu Binyan," *New York Review of Books* 35, nos. 21–22 (January 19, 1989): 31.

CHAPTER SIX

The Search for a Positive Hero

IN ONE of the articles that he contributed in 1873 to *The Citizen*, the weekly journal he then edited, Dostoevsky threw out a remark on what he called "the Russian aspect" given to the doctrines of great European thinkers such as John Stuart Mill, Darwin, and D. F. Strauss whenever their influence spread eastward. When they came to Russia, the ideas of such men and others were never simply taken over and discussed as they were in the country of their origin, or in other European lands. Invariably, "the Russian aspect" of their transplantation would sooner or later emerge— and this consisted, to cite Dostoevsky, "of those consequences of their teachings, in the form of indestructible axioms, which are drawn only in Russia; in Europe the possibility of such consequences, it is said, could not even be suspected."

Dostoevsky was thus acutely aware of the manner in which European ideas suffered a sea-change when they passed through Russian minds and were applied to Russian problems. Their most extreme consequences would inevitably be drawn; they would be believed in and accepted with religious fervor; and they immediately would be given a practical application. As Dostoevsky remarks, Mill, Darwin, and Strauss were all men who unquestionably loved humanity; but in Russia their ideas had led straight to the Nechaev affair, in which a young student who had wished to resign from a secret revolutionary organization had been coldbloodedly murdered to bind the others through terror. Ideas that in Europe only aroused scholarly controversy, or at most some serious heart-searching in the depth of troubled consciences, in Russia might and probably would result in mayhem.

No one paid much attention to Dostoevsky's article at the time, and one might be inclined to dismiss it even today merely as part of his reactionary campaign to blame the struggle against the tsarist régime on the nefarious influence of foreign ideas. But Dostoevsky had a deep insight into the psychology of his countrymen and their culture; and even though we may suspect this particular application of his thesis, the fact remains that he hit upon something that is more and more thrusting itself upon the consciousness of the Western world.

Ever since the Bolsheviks took power in Russia and became the leaders of world revolution, European Communists have had to struggle with the problem of adapting themselves to Russian conceptions of what Marxism means in practice. And not so long ago, in the heyday of Eurocommunism, the Communist parties of the West (particularly the Italian) began to reject the Russian model of a Communist society because this model was too *Russian* to suit other countries with different national histories. It should thus now hardly be necessary to argue in favor of Dostoevsky's view that "the Russian aspect" of European ideas is something not to be overlooked. Indeed, this "Russian aspect" has proven to be so powerful that, when Europeans receive their own theory of Marxism back in the Russian form of Marxism-Leninism, they are increasingly reluctant to recognize their own values in what is presented to them as a universal image of the radiant Communist future.

Nothing can therefore be of greater interest right now, when under Mikhail Gorbachev's leadership the Russians themselves appear to be engaged in a process of profound self-questioning, than to study the origins of this divergence or, to use another image, this refraction—to see just what happens to Western ideas when they pass through the Russian prism. A good ideal of information on this subject is already contained in the countless works that trace the transmutation of the sociopolitical ideas of German Marxism into Russian Communism. The great value of Rufus Mathewson's *The Positive Hero in Russian Literature*—a revised, second edition of a work first published in 1958—is that it performs the far more delicate task of tracing the same transmutation as it occurs in relation to literature.[1] To be sure, it has always been difficult for Western artists and writers, even those with overt and proclaimed Communist sympathies, to accept the doctrines of Marxist-Leninist orthodoxy in their domain (one thinks, among others, of the French Surrealists, Picasso, and more recently, Sartre). But it has not been generally understood to what extent this reluctance has been caused by specific Russian attitudes that, as a result of the triumph of the Bolshevik revolution in Russia, have then been accepted as Marxist dogma by the (until very recently) compliant Communist parties and their fellow-traveling intellectuals in the West.

On its original publication, Mathewson's book was recognized as the most serious, best-informed, and most penetrating study yet to have appeared in English (or, so far as my knowledge goes, in any other language) of the origins and consequences of the Marxist-Leninist doctrine of art within its Russian context. At that time, after detailing the baneful effects of its dogmas in reducing Soviet literature to mediocrity, he held out little hope for the future. But, he added, it could be that "a series of brilliant literary works, provided they were allowed to see the daylight, might suddenly render the entire structure of Socialist Realism obsolete, another monument to Russia's agony and servitude" (X). The works of Pasternak,

---

[1] Rufus W. Mathewson, Jr., *The Positive Hero in Russian Literature* (Stanford, Calif., 1975).

Solzhenitsyn, and Sinyavsky have since arrived to fulfill the prediction. And the ease with which Mathewson could integrate a new section on these writers into his earlier text illustrates how well he had grasped the inner strains and stresses of Soviet Russian culture to which they at last gave utterance.[2]

What has become known as the Marxist-Leninist view of art, as Mathewson amply demonstrates, really has very little to do with Marx or classical Marxism at all, and much more with a set of attitudes hammered out in Russia between the 1840s and 1860s. Trotsky once remarked that, in his native land, "literary criticism took the place of politics and was a preparation for it"; and this had already begun to be true in the writings of V. G. Belinsky, even though Belinsky was a genuine literary critic of international stature whose work still commands respect for its insight. But, after his conversion to Utopian Socialism in the early 1840s, he more and more began to judge literature in terms of its value in furthering the cause of moral-social progress as he understood it. This feature of his work was then strongly accentuated in the 1860s by his self-proclaimed disciples, the radical publicists Nikolay Dobrolyubov and Nikolay Chernyshevsky, who saw no other role for literature (and art in general) except that of social propaganda to enlighten the masses. Influenced—oddly enough for Russian radicals—by Bentham's Utilitarianism, they applied a strict Utilitarian doctrine to art, just as Bentham had done himself. But where the quirky Englishman simply decided that poetry and the game of pushpin were

---

[2] Rufus Mathewson, who died in 1978, was an outstanding member of the generation of American Slavists that emerged after the Second World War, and who gave a vital impetus to Slavic studies in this country at a moment when the knowledge of Russian culture took on a new international importance. A vibrant and ebullient personality, a brilliant and amusing talker, his wide-ranging mind made his conversation as informative and provocative as it was lively, and his mordant wit was the merciless enemy of any sort of cant and pretense. Wherever he went, he never failed to gather round him a circle brought into existence and animated by his magnetic presence.

His sensibility had been schooled in the contemporary writing that expressed the social and cultural turmoil of the 1920s and 1930s, such as the novels of Ernest Hemingway and André Malraux, but he also approached Russian literature with a freshness of response and a critical acuity springing from his intense love for, and intimate familiarity with, the great writers of the Modernist canon such as Yeats, Eliot, Joyce, and Wallace Stevens. Without neglecting history, he made Russian literature come alive for his students at Columbia (to whom he gave much more of himself than was perhaps beneficial for his own work) as part of their present rather than as the product of a remote past or of an alien world; and he was rightly revered and cherished by all those devoted younger scholars whom he helped to form. As one of them, Robin Feuer Miller, wrote three years after his death, "He left behind him, like ripples emanating from a stone dropped in water, several generations of students whose paths, however varied, had always continued, in one way or another, to orbit around him." His friends, among whom I was privileged to be included, have never ceased to mourn his untimely passing. See Robin Feuer Miller, "Recollections of Rufus Mathewson, 1918–1978," *Ulbandus Review* 2, no. 1 (1979):5.

much the same, the Russians, deprived of any other means of getting revolutionary ideas into public print, seized on literature and literary criticism
as an invaluable instrument in the struggle.

This peculiarity of Russian cultural development is quite well known
and has often been described; but Mathewson cuts a good deal deeper than
the usual accounts by analyzing the specific attitude toward human experience that emerges from the theories of the radicals. Dobrolyubov's famous article "What Is Oblomovism?" focused on the character type of the
alienated gentry-landowner intellectual, "the superfluous man," as he had
been portrayed in Russian literature from Pushkin to Herzen, Turgenev,
or Goncharov; and the fiery young critic violently attacked the paralysis of
will exhibited by all such admired prototypes, who rejected the prevailing
barbaric mores of Russian life in their heart and their conscience but were
incapable of translating any of their cherished values into determined social
action. He called for the portrayal of a Russian "new man," who would
possess the same qualities of moral strength and total selfless dedication to
a social cause as Turgenev's Bulgarian nationalist Insarov in *On the Eve*.
Chernyshevsky obligingly complied by depicting such all-conquering
"new men" in his absurd but enormously successful novel *What Is to Be
Done?* (one of Lenin's favorite books); and the Russian radical ideal of
character thus became defined in terms that predetermine that of the exemplary Bolshevik. "The points of similarity," Mathewson writes, "are a
total mobilization of personal resources in the fulfilment of a single purpose, always a public one, the unquestioning rejection of the private pur-
suits of ordinary man, and a willingness to endure any sacrifice" (55). In
his *Aesthetic Relations of Art to Reality*, Chernyshevsky also decided that
poetry's "great significance" is that it "distributes an enormous amount of
information among the mass of readers"; and he decreed that tragedy was
simply out of date because nobody could any longer take seriously the
primitive Greek view of fate.

It is little wonder that the writers who constitute the glory of Russian
literature were aghast at such attempts to narrow the human horizon of
their art (not to mention of life itself); and they responded immediately.
Tolstoy, fresh from the triumph of his *Sevastopol Sketches*, spoke out in
1858; Turgenev's famous article, "Hamlet and Don Quixote" is also a
more veiled response to the radical critics. (Turgenev's work, incidentally,
was one of the chief targets for the attack of the radicals, despite his known
sympathy with their general social aims; and this played its part in the genesis of *Fathers and Sons*.) Turgenev argued that both the fanatical man of
action (Don Quixote) and the "superfluous man" paralyzed by indecision
(Hamlet) were equally sympathetic and equally tragic figures, each representing certain human values that transcended their immediate situation.
But the radicals would of course have none of this; they refused to consider

the revolutionary tragic because, after all, he had to be triumphant; nor
would they concede that the weak-willed Hamlet should not simply be
despised. It is unfortunate that Mathewson does not also include Dostoevsky's contribution to this controversy, which is contained in an article directed against Dobrolyubov in 1860. This is perhaps the most incisive and
effective refutation made at the time of the radicals' position, and it has still
not lost its value as a defense of the autonomy of art, of its right not to turn
away from "life" but to handle it in total freedom.

How does classical Marxism fit into this picture? The chapters that
Mathewson devotes to answering this question are among the most valuable in the book, and should be required reading for all those concerned
with the problems of a Marxist aesthetic. In the first place, one does not
find in Marx and Engels any of the desire to harness literature exclusively
to a social task that is so characteristic of the Russian tradition. Second, the
ultimate aim of classical Marxism is to create a world in which the human
potential expressed in the great art of the past would be liberated and made
a part of the daily life of all. However chimerical and Utopian such an
ambition may seem, there can be no doubt that the image of man in German Marxism does possess a strong aesthetic component. Indeed, as Herbert Marcuse has pointed out in *Eros and Civilization*, it owes a good deal
to Schiller's *Letters on the Aesthetic Education of Mankind*. But there is,
nonetheless, a considerable difference between the Communist man in the
presumed paradisial world of the future, and what Mathewson calls the
"interim man" of the present period of transition. Destined by the laws of
history to participate in the class struggle, this "interim man" is truly "free,"
according to Engels, only to recognize the "necessity" to join in the fray.
It is this aspect of Marxism, never developed explicitly in the canonical
texts, which then became fused in Russian thought with the image of the
revolutionary "new man" first elaborated by the radicals of the 1860s.

Just as Lenin grafted the Russian conspiratorial tradition on to the original Marxist idea of a huge mass movement sweeping away a tiny handful
of capitalists (and he did so in a pamphlet titled, after Chernyshevsky's
novel, *What Is to Be Done?*), so too he broke with the relative tolerance and
humanist respect for literature still exhibited in classical Marxism. Since, in
the Russian tradition, no aspect of human life could (or should) be exempt
from politics, Lenin's famous article "Party Organization and Party Literature" proclaimed the obligation of the artist to subordinate himself to the
demands of the Communist Party. To be sure, this article was written in
1905 and refers only to those artists who had chosen freely to ally themselves with the party; others were still allowed to exist independently
(though Lenin speaks of this so-called "bourgeois freedom" with uncon-
cealed contempt, and labels it "a masked dependence on the money-bag").
Once the Revolution triumphed and the Communists came to power,

however, the dictates laid down in Lenin's article naturally became the law of the land. "In the one-Party state today," Mathewson explains, "the writer still has the 'freedom' to refuse to accept controls, but it is a freedom that leads only to silence or obloquy." (Or, one can now add, if no longer to complete silence, then to a dangerous duel with the authorities, which may lead to prison, exile, or expulsion.)

The assertion of party control over literature was not made all at once after victory had been won; there were far more important matters to attend to. In the early 1920s, literature was still relatively free to go its own way, and writers like Konstantin Fedin, Veniamin Kaverin, and Yuri Olesha were able to produce works of considerable artistic stature in which the human difficulties of adjusting to the new revolutionary situation were honestly explored. But Mathewson concentrates on a series of other novels (most of lesser artistic value, but including Babel's *Red Cavalry* and Sholokhov's *Quiet Don*) that manifest various degrees of tension between the Communist ideal of character and the ordinary fallibilities of unregenerate human nature. Both in the literary discussions of the time and in the work being produced, the degree to which artists could deviate from the ideal standard of Bolshevik virtue—a standard ultimately deriving from the Russian radical tradition—became narrower and narrower. While a gifted writer like Leonid Leonov, for example, could still come close to some sort of tragic statement in his *Road to the Ocean* (1935), his *Russian Forest* (1953) degenerates into patriotic kitsch. Ever since Zhdanov's speech at the First Writers' Congress in 1934, where the doctrine of Socialist Realism was initially promulgated, Russian literature has been under tight Party control and obliged to meet official specifications. In a 1946 speech reasserting this doctrine, and making it even more stringent, the same Zhdanov mentioned Belinsky, Chernyshevsky, and Dobrolyubov nineteen times, Lenin seven times, Stalin six times—and Marx not at all.

Stalin's death in 1953 inaugurated a new period in Russian history, and the slight loosening of the iron grip of the police state allowed once again for the appearance of a genuine literature—even if mainly in *samizdat*, or smuggled abroad—among the interstices. Mathewson devotes his final section to this "Dissident Vision," giving most attention to Pasternak and Solzhenitsyn. The perspective already attained enables him to give a sensitive reading of *Dr. Zhivago*, much less ambitious than some of the more esoteric interpretations but far more persuasive in its fidelity to the human and historical experience that the characters undergo. The movement of the book is from Zhivago's acceptance of the Bolshevik Revolution as a cleansing and purifying force to a growing awareness of how a total identification with a social cause perverts the ultimate springs of morality and destroys man's humanity. Zhivago's life is a desperate struggle to escape the fanaticism of ideology, and to preserve a realm of privacy in which he can commune with nature and the great eternal verities of human destiny. Pasternak's "Christianity" is precisely the assertion of such a spiritual realm, which guarantees the inestimable value of the individual against the claims of the world and justifies his right to inviolability. Nowhere else in modern literature can one find such a paean of celebration to the simple joys of private life; and "a thirst for plain human decency," as Mathewson remarks acutely, "lies close to the centre of Zhivago's complaint, and deep in this dissident literature." It is curious, all the same, that he fails to notice how Zhivago revives and glorifies the superannuated "superfluous man" of the nineteenth century, and that nothing is made of Pasternak's invocation of Hamlet in this connection.

Pasternak is still a survivor of the pre-Revolutionary Silver Age of Russian Symbolism, who can bring to bear a highly sophisticated literary sensibility, steeped in all the richness of late nineteenth-century Russian culture, to his treatment of the present. Solzhenitsyn is purely a product of the Soviet period, and his work has some of the elemental strength and crudity of the world from which he comes. Mathewson's chapters on *The First Circle, Cancer Ward*, and *August, 1914* are very useful in probing beneath the political surface of these works, which overflow with such a plethora of material, to get at the underlying motifs that give each its individual unity. Particularly good is his analysis of how, in *The First Circle*, Solzhenitsyn rings constant ironic variations on the Marxist-Leninist dogma that social being determines consciousness; this motif functions "much as Ivan's rational arrogance and intellectual skepticism do in *The Brothers Karamazov*, spreading to the far corners of the novel, animating dramatic conflicts, provoking arguments, influencing important decisions, appearing and reappearing to shape the documentary matter of the novel." In *Cancer Ward*, perhaps Solzhenitsyn's most satisfactory long novel, it is the problem of evil that is uppermost—the evil of illness and death, which no social system can mitigate, and the gratuitous evil contained in men themselves as exemplified by the senseless blinding of a monkey in a zoo. Only "morality" in the old sense can cope with such forces; and Solzhenitsyn's book is a passionate assertion of the necessity to establish (or reestablish) a moral foundation for society that would break with the pseudo-scientific doctrines that permitted and justified the monstrous perversities of Stalinism.

In conclusion, Mathewson comments on the sense of "old-fashionedness" that many Western readers feel as they turn the pages of dissident Soviet writers. Most commentators attribute this common reaction to a lack of technical refinement in the Soviet dissidents, their neglect of the experiments in novelistic form associated with such names as Henry James, Proust, and Joyce. Mathewson, however, suggests that it is caused by Russian cultural isolation "in Stalin's Fourth Rome," and says:

These writers are fighting an anachronistic battle from the nineteenth century against the extension of scientistic systems to areas of experience not susceptible to scientific reduction, against the closing of systems around not-yet-known or unknowable areas of experience. . . . Only Russian writers, it appears, are still required to do battle with these venerable enemies of human wholeness. (354)

These remarks seem to me unimpeachable as far as they go; but they raise a question that deserves further discussion. There is, perhaps, a slight touch of complacency in such an observation, which is scarcely warranted by the present situation of Western culture; and there may be some things we can profitably learn from this dissident literature despite its air of fighting battles that, for us, have long since become dusty history.

For one thing, it is not really self-evident that these battles have definitely been won. Who can truly say that pseudo-scientific rationalism, whether Marxist or otherwise, has lost its appeal and no longer plays any role in the West? And even more important, a state-imposed ideology of this type is not the only form in which "human wholeness" may be threatened. It can also be destroyed by an anarchic neoprimitivism that dissolves man into his impulses, complexes, and sensations just as surely as Marxism-Leninism petrifies him into a social automaton. In this sense, the clear and even strident call in Soviet dissident literature for a morality based on respect for human dignity and on man as primarily a *moral* being is far from irrelevant to our own concerns. At a moment when the Western avant-garde, under the influence of the latest post-Existentialist French thought, is busily engaged in turning the word *humanism* into a term of opprobrium, it is good to be reminded of what may be lost when the values that the word represents are so flippantly denigrated and decried. Some of the resonance in the West of this Soviet dissident literature, despite its lack of formal sophistication, may well be attributed not only to its obvious political significance but also to its response to a genuine spiritual need that our own literature has ceased to satisfy.

CHAPTER SEVEN

Russian Populism

FRANCO VENTURI's *Roots of Revolution*, originally published in Italy in 1952 as *Il Populismo Russo*, is certainly familiar to all Slavists everywhere in the world. It became an instant classic upon publication, equally appreciated both in Russia and the West; and its translation into English in 1961 only served to spread its well-deserved reputation even more widely. For anyone interested in the Russian history and culture of the last century— the century whose agitations paved the way for the Russian Revolution— it has become not only recommended but obligatory reading.[1]

In fact, Venturi has written far more than a history of the Populist and Socialist movements in mid-nineteenth-century Russia. He has also written a history—the most ample and detailed to date, synthesizing a vast amount of scattered Russian documentation—of the political ideas of these movements. And as everyone who has studied the subject is aware, a history of left-wing ideas in Russia is almost a history of Russian culture *tout court*. This is particularly true of the period between 1848 and 1881, which is covered in Venturi's book. The genesis of radical Populism is intimately linked to Slavophile ideas; hence Venturi is naturally forced to include them in his purview, though he does not give them an independent chapter. Also, he takes full advantage of the publication of tsarist archives by Soviet scholars, and refers constantly to the official documents in which the tsars and their advisers discuss the problems posed by peasant unrest and radical agitation. The result is a masterly and balanced panorama of the beginnings of a movement destined to have a profound effect on the future of the entire world.

Within the limits of a brief essay, it is impossible to give an adequate idea of the richness of material that *Roots of Revolution* contains. Beginning with Herzen and Bakunin, whose intellectual evolution is skillfully blended with biography and sociopolitical history, Venturi continues with wide-ranging chapters on all the various groups and movements contributing to the formation of Russian radicalism. Detailed attention is given to the Petrashevtsy in the mid-forties, Chernyshevsky, Dobrolyubov, and the "new people" of the sixties, to the Nihilists influenced by Pisarev and Zaitsev, and to such diverse figures as the Russian Jacobins Nechaev and Tkachev, as well as the "back-to-the-people" movement of the early seventies. There

---

[1] Franco Venturi, *Roots of Revolution*, trans. Frances Haskell (New York, 1961).

are detailed histories, culled from the memoirs of survivors, of all the terrorist groups and their activities; and the book culminates with the assassination of Alexander II. The ample quotations make the work almost an encyclopedia of its subject. And Venturi writes not only with a fine sense for the human drama of the events he narrates but also for the broader European context of Russian radicalism, whose widely scattered representatives in exile came into firsthand contact with all the variegated stirrings of radicalism in the West.

Approaching his subject with a calm impartiality of judgment that cannot be too highly praised, Venturi manages to combine sympathy for the heroism and self-sacrificing ardor of the radicals with a lucid understanding of the impossible dilemmas confronting the tsarist régime. Caught between a nobility defending its economic interests, a peasantry living in the Dark Ages, and an intelligentsia inspired by a fanatical and quite unjustified belief in the innate political virtues of this same peasantry, all official efforts at reform and improvement were hamstrung from the very start. Dependent on a corrupt bureaucracy for the enforcement of his policies, Alexander II was like the Chinese emperor of Kafka's stories whose messengers never arrived—and even when they did, had to speak to a population that could not understand their language.

Far more than the England of Disraeli, Russia was divided into "two nations"—not the bourgeoisie and the proletariat but the educated classes and the peasantry. And while the radical intelligentsia always spoke in the name of the people, they had as little actual relation to them as the nobles whose stewards came up yearly from the country to hand over the proceeds from the estates. The anguish of this problem is reflected both in Dostoevsky and Tolstoy, as well as in the isolation that drove the populists of the seventies along the path of systematic terror. Perhaps the greatest single example of Lenin's political genius was to have accepted this fact and, in the teeth of all the Marxist dogma to the contrary, to have made it the basis of Bolshevik party organization.

One impression that emerges very sharply from Venturi's history is the substantial and paradoxical identity of Russian political opinion underneath the seeming divergence of bitter opposition. The sources of populism were originally Slavophile and even reactionary. The *mir* and the *obshchina*, which the Populists saw as the embryo of future Russian Socialism, were first noticed and praised by the Slavophiles and by the Prussian Baron Haxthausen, who regarded these institutions as Russia's guarantee against the revolutionary ferment of a dispossessed proletariat. Both Slavophiles and Populist Socialists united against all attempts to belittle the peasant commune by the small handful of free-trade liberals who wished to encourage industry and create a mobile working force. The Slavophiles regarded the commune as possessing a unique moral and religious value, as primitive Christianity in action; the Populist Socialists saw it as the nucleus of the Utopia of the future; both shared the conviction that it made Russia morally superior to the egotistic individualism of the West.

For this reason, none of the political categories that are usually applied to Russia—Westernizer or Slavophile, radical or revolutionary—quite fits the Russian political picture. These categories are derived by analogy from Western ideas of Utopian Socialism or conservative nationalism; but the Russian situation contains configurations that have no Western counterpart at all. The Slavophiles supported both an absolute monarch and the complete autonomy of the democratically administered peasant commune; far from glorifying the state, the early Slavophiles accepted it only as a necessary evil. The Populists were in favor of political liberty and individual freedom to an extent bordering on anarchy; but they idealized the patriarchal peasant commune in which the very idea of individualism (in the Western sense) had not yet even begun to take root. One of the greatest merits of Venturi's patient thoroughness is to help us to grasp the special metamorphoses and permutations that a Western idea such as "socialism" underwent in being transplanted to Russian soil. Only by a careful study of such permutations can we hope to understand some of the enigmas of what used to be called "the Russian soul."

Sir Isaiah Berlin, whose services to Slavic scholarship are well known, provides a lengthy preface to Venturi's volume. Written with all of Sir Isaiah's torrential eloquence, admirable erudition, and penetrating discernment, it is much more an extremely valuable supplement to Venturi than merely an introduction to its contents. It is as if Sir Isaiah had felt a certain lacuna in the book for all its excellencies—the lack of a *critical* confrontation with all the ideas and historical events presented with such lavish knowledge; and so, instead of an introduction, Sir Isaiah has actually penned a conclusion, one that brilliantly defines the fateful antinomies faced by the Populists and shows to what an astonishing extent their experience still remains relevant to the problems of the twentieth century.

Venturi's book itself contains no such considerations because (as he has explained in the illuminating introduction written for a second Italian edition in 1972) his work had been begun while he was attaché to the Italian embassy in Moscow between 1947 and 1950; and it was inspired and shaped by a desire to bring back to life a whole segment of the Russian revolutionary tradition that had been, if not forgotten, then treated with a notable lack of enthusiasm or comprehension. The Populists of the end of the century had been the most determined opponents of the Marxists, competing with them for the allegiance of the intelligentsia and for that fraction of the people who would listen to their revolutionary message. The memories of this fratricidal struggle, in which Lenin himself had taken part, were still very much alive; and if the Populists were spoken of at all, "in 1946 even in the best of cases the impassioned discussion had become severe erudition, the [Populist] heritage was reduced to a few phrases of Lenin, always endlessly repeated, and the most complete silence had fallen on those revolutionaries, like the men of the *Narodnaya Volya* (The People's Will), who with more intensity than the others had tried to bring together thought and action."[2] As a result of this situation, Venturi felt obliged to resurrect the past with as much amplitude as possible, quoting copiously from hard-to-find documents, and subordinating analysis to the exposition of ideas and events that had been largely forgotten.

It is probably for this reason that Sir Isaiah's introduction so sharply picks out the main ideological outlines of this epic of revolutionary struggle, among whose enthralling details it is all too easy for the reader to lose sight of the whole. This "whole," to be sure, exists only in a very loose and amorphous sense, and the groups of which the Populists were composed, as Sir Isaiah writes, "tended to differ both about ends and means." Indeed, there is some question whether any such movement as Russian "Populism" existed at all, and Richard Pipes has pointed out that the term *narodnie-hestvo* (Populism) began to be used only in the mid-seventies to designate the young men and women who were "going-to-the-people" to find out about the real needs and desires of the peasantry.[3] Whether this designation should be used to take in the entire sweep of the history of the radical intelligentsia from the 1820s up to the assassination of Alexander II remains an open question; but Sir Isaiah agrees with Venturi that all these groups "held certain fundamental beliefs in common, and possessed a sufficient moral and political solidarity to entitle them to be called a single movement." All, at any rate, were united in looking "on the government and social structure of their country as a moral and political monstrosity—obsolete, barbarous, stupid and odious—and dedicated their lives to its total destruction" (viii).

Sir Isaiah accurately stresses the dominating influence of Alexander Herzen in creating Populist ideology, with its unshakable conviction that the peasant *mir* (assembly of elders) and the *obshchina* (commune) provided the basis for a truly just and democratic social order. But while inspired by deep moral and ethical convictions and by a burning need for social justice, the Populists were confronted by a socioeconomic and political situation that posed agonizing dilemmas the moment they tried to put their ideas into practice. Should they agitate among the peasants to bring on an immediate revolution, no matter what the costs or consequences, or wait un-

---

[2] Franco Venturi, *Il Populismo russo*, 3 vols. (Torino, 1972), 1:ix. This introduction, which contains a survey of all the work done in Russia and elsewhere on Russian Populism since the first edition, is itself of great value and should be translated.

[3] Richard Pipes, "Narodnichestvo: A Semantic Inquiry," *Slavic Review* 23, no. 3 (September 1964):441ff.

til the people were capable of understanding their own situation and could use their freedom to the best advantage? The first option might lead to a new tyranny of the intelligentsia over the ignorant people, a tyranny perhaps even worse than the old; the second might allow the horrors of capitalism to develop, and to the creation of a bourgeoisie and professional middle class who would support the old régime, or even worse, create a parliamentary democracy clever enough to stave off Socialist revolution entirely by palliatives and concessions. And what of the state? How would the communal forms of government so rapturously glorified by the Populists be combined with a state that, exactly like the Slavophiles, they believed was "intrinsically evil" in its nature as power (though the Slavophiles were willing to accept it for Christian reasons). Would the revolutionaries abolish the state entirely, or use it as an instrument to transform the people, even against their will, for the benefit of their future well-being?

Russian Populism thus actually divides into two broad streams, and was racked by a continual quarrel between the Russian Jacobins, who wanted to rule at any price, and the gradualists or moderates with qualms about coercing the ignorant people. These dilemmas, as Sir Isaiah justly notes, are still very much alive in the modern world, especially among Third World countries with largely peasant populations exposed, as was Russia in the nineteenth century, to the perils of industrial development. The main issue debated by the Populists was whether the harmful social consequences of capitalism could be avoided while, at the same time, its evident economic benefits could be acquired. This question is very far from having been resolved; and its challenge gives a new pertinence and relevance to what may seem, at first sight, only the history of an unsuccessful and long-dead movement. For the example of Russia would indicate that the dictatorship of the proletariat, even if it ameliorates some of the injustices so sarcastically vituperated by Karl Marx, brings others in its wake that even the long-suffering Russian population has finally found intolerable (now that, thanks to Gorbachev, it has at last been able to express some of its discontents). This dictatorship, of course, was justified in the name of history; and the basis of Sir Isaiah's evident sympathy for the Populists, aside from the personal heroism that so many of them exhibited, is surely that unlike the Marxists they never attempted to justify their actions by an appeal to his own *bête noir* of historical inevitability. "Neither [Chernyshevsky] nor Lavrov, not even the most ruthlessly Jacobin among the proponents of terror and violence, ever took cover behind the inevitable direction of history as a justification of what would otherwise have been patently unjust or brutal" (xxv).

This preservation of a moral sense, according to Sir Isaiah, is what firmly distinguishes the Populists from the Marxists. Others have also made this same distinction, most memorably Albert Camus, whose play *Les Justes* dramatizes precisely the moral sensitivity even of Populist terrorists of the late nineteenth century. If one reads this along with Jean-Paul Sartre's *Les Main Sales*, which portrays an East European Communist functionary at work half a century later, the contrast could not be more strikingly expressed. But perhaps, in making his point, Sir Isaiah draws too sharp a line between the two, and refuses to see, as Dostoevsky had seen, all those elements in Populist thought—particularly, in the 1860s, its thoroughgoing Utilitarianism— which paved the way for, and could later so easily be utilized, to form what came to be known as the implacable Bolshevik character. As Sir Isaiah writes, "The Populist did indeed virtually invent the conception of the party as a group of professional conspirators with no private lives, obeying a total discipline—the core of the 'hard' professionals as against mere sympathizers and fellow-travelers" (xxv). It is not for nothing, after all, that Lenin first defined the tasks of such a party of professional revolutionaries in his pamphlet *What Is to Be Done?*—whose title is taken from Chernyshevsky's famous novel, the still-revered bible of Russian radicalism, in which the ideal revolutionary Rakhmetov was first depicted in all the splendor of his disciplined devotion to the cause.

It is one of the many ironies of modern Russian history that while the Marxists won the ideological war they waged against the Populists, and became the leaders of the radical Left in Russia at the turn of the century, it was ultimately the view of the Russian Jacobins that prevailed when matters came to a head. Lenin and the Bolsheviks took power when they had the chance, and accepted in practice the Jacobin view that a Russian Communist revolution could and should take place *before* a full-fledged capitalism had taken root. And Lenin also "transformed the cells of dedicated revolutionaries—perhaps the most original contribution of Populism to revolutionary practice—into the hierarchy of centralized political power, which the Populists steadily and firmly denounced." Bolshevism thus "borrowed the technique of its rival and adapted it with conspicuous success to serve the precise purpose which it had been invented to resist" (xxx). But could this have taken place so easily if the gap between the two was as yawning as Sir Isaiah would lead us to believe, and would no doubt like to believe himself? Dostoevsky was able to foresee quite clearly how the moral yearnings of the Populists could be transformed into a reign of terror; and this was not because he possessed an imagination of evil, or an uncanny gift of prophecy. It was because he could sense in the doctrines of the Russian Jacobins the very possibilities that Lenin was later to exploit with the mastery of a great political tactician.

CHAPTER EIGHT

From Gogol to the Gulag

1

SINCE THERE is no work on Pushkin among the volumes I am considering, it is appropriate to begin this survey of books on Russian literature with Henri Troyat's life of Gogol.[1] For Gogol, along with Pushkin, is one of the founding fathers of modern Russian literature, the initiator of one of its two main traditions. It was customary, in Russian criticism of the last century, to distinguish between a Pushkin and a Gogol tradition; and the radical critics of the 1860s used this distinction for purposes of historical periodization. The advent of the Gogol period in the 1840s, superseding the dominance of Pushkin's influence, meant, according to Nikolay Chernyshevsky, the welcome replacement of a sterile poetic aestheticism by a prose literature oriented toward the social problems of the day. Later, however, the terms were used less narrowly; the Pushkin tradition became identified with such writers as Turgenev, Goncharov, and Tolstoy, who depicted Russian upper-class life with some of Pushkin's calm objectivity and poeticization of the personal, the ordinary, and the everyday (the great example here being *Eugene Onegin*). The Gogol tradition, on the other hand, which included such writers as Saltykov-Shchedrin, Leskov, and—the greatest of all—Dostoevsky, used exaggeration, caricature, melodrama, and fantasy, descended into the social depths, and focused on the unusual and eccentric rather than the average or commonplace.

Henri Troyat's life of Gogol has the virtues and defects of the other biographies written by this prolific Franco-Russian novelist. A very popular writer in his own country, who turns out middle-brow *roman fleuves* that have earned him a seat in the Académie Française, Troyat is covering Russian literature with the same steady thoroughness. After Pushkin, Lermontov, Dostoevsky, and Tolstoy, it is now the turn of Gogol. Troyat's books are always informed by a thorough knowledge of the Russian sources, a novelist's eye for effective detail, and a great deal of expository skill. Honest journeyman's work, they stick quite close to the facts, speculate within the bounds of common sense, and are always easy and enjoyable to read. They do not, however, go very deep, and are likely to disappoint anyone

---

[1] Henri Troyat, *Gogol: The Biography of a Divided Soul*, trans. Nancy Amphoux (London, 1974).

interested in the writer not so much as a personality but as a literary creator.

The picture Troyat paints of Gogol does full justice to this truly astonishing and bewildering character. Gogol was at once a provincial from the
Ukraine who never felt at home in Petersburg; a mythomaniac convinced
from his earliest years that he had been sent by God to fulfill a great moral
mission; a sponger who shamelessly exploited his wealthy admirers while
preaching the virtues of poverty to his mother and sisters whenever they
asked *him* for money; a sensual glutton who apparently never touched a
woman; a moralist who proclaimed that the highest Christian virtues could
only be realized in serf-ridden Russia; a writer whose very success filled
him with despair because his best work was interpreted as an exposure of
the moral-social monstrosity of Russian life rather than as a call to individual moral regeneration. His death seems to have been caused, not by a
mortal illness, but by a religious crisis whose source was his inability to
write a continuation of *Dead Souls* in which his famous scoundrel, Chichikov, would be redeemed and become a "positive" moral hero. Troyat gives
sensible descriptions and plot summaries of Gogol's work that can be recommended as an introduction; but it is impossible to understand from him
how such a silly, capricious, hypocritical, conceited, totally irresponsible
human being could have changed the entire course of Russian literature,
and continue to inspire writers like Mikhail Bulgakov and Andrey Siniav-
sky (Abram Tertz).

Gogol's best work is a brilliant combination of Romantic fantasy with a
grotesque depiction of the eternal absurdities and stupidities of human nature in their particular Russian and early nineteenth-century incarnation.
A comic genius of the first rank, Gogol had a wonderful eye for the trivial,
the ordinary, the commonplace, the mediocre, the pretentiously conventional—for everything that Flaubert summed up in the word *bêtise*, and
which the Russians call *poshlost*. Vladimir Nabokov, whose brilliant little
study of Gogol is indispensable, defines *poshlost* in a series of examples, one
of which effectively brings its meaning home in American terms:

> "Open the first magazine at hand and you are sure to find something of the
> following kind: a radio set (or a car, or a refrigerator, or table silver—anything
> will do) has just come to the family: Mother clasps her hands in dazed delight,
> the children crowd around, all agog. Junior and his dog strain up to the edge of
> the table where the Idol is enthroned; even Grandma of the beaming wrinkles
> peeps out somewhere in the background (forgetful, we presume, of the terrific
> row she has had that very morning with her daughter-in-law); and somewhat
> apart, his thumbs gleefully inserted in the armpits of his waistcoat, legs a-straddle
> and eyes a-twinkle, stands triumphant Pop, the Proud Donor.[2]

---

[2] Vladimir Nabokov, *Nikolai Gogol* (Norfolk, Conn., 1944), 66.

Gogol not only satirizes a world of this kind on the level of a comedy of manners, but presents it with such overwhelming force that, so to speak, it acquires a metaphysical dimension, taking on tragicomic overtones as the reader begins to feel human existence itself swamped in this morass of meaninglessness and absurdity. The effect is the famous "laughter through tears" conventionally (but nonetheless aptly) used to characterize Gogol's art, and which, with some adjustment to the bleaker and harsher mood of the present, could just as well be used for Beckett.

There has been a continual quarrel in Russian criticism over the nature of Gogol's work. Depending on whether one stresses the social implications of his depictions of *poshlost* or focuses on the existential ennui emanating from a world in which diabolic temptation takes on such comfortably familiar and trivial forms, it is possible to see him either as a "realist" or as a creator of Romantic grotesques. Historically, at any rate, his sharp vignettes of Russian—and particularly of Petersburg—life (the latter in such stories as *Nevsky Prospect* and *The Overcoat*) gave rise to a group of writers known as the Natural School, who began with local-color sketches of Petersburg types. Turgenev, Dostoevsky, and Goncharov all served their apprenticeship in this movement, which proved to be the fertile soil out of which came the luxuriant growth of the Russian realistic novel. And if this movement took Gogol's work (or rather, its "realistic" aspects) as a model, it was not only because Russian literature was ripe for such a development; it was also because the most powerful critical voice of the time, V. G. Belinsky, was urging young Russian writers to follow precisely this path.

2

The book on Belinsky by Victor Terras is a first-rate work, a major contribution to the understanding of a critic who dominated most of Russian intellectual life throughout the nineteenth century whether for good or ill, and who has since become one of the pillars of Soviet Russian culture.[3] Indeed, one of the best features of Terras's book is that he sets the study of Belinsky's ideas in the context of the critic's continuing influence today— an influence enforced by the authority of the Communist Party—and deals both with Belinsky's precursors and successors (as well as their opponents, the Russian Formalists) up through the 1930s. The book thus fully justifies the promise of its title.

Belinsky grew up in a period when Russian culture was completely dominated by German Idealism, and his early essays reveal the strong influence of Schelling and then Hegel. There has been somewhat the same sort of quarrel in Russia over Belinsky's "originality" as there has been over Cole-

[3] Victor Terras, *Belinskij and Russian Literary Criticism* (Madison, Wis., 1974).

ridge in English. Was he simply a secondhand purveyor of ideas or, even worse, a plagiarist? Belinsky's opponents, even during his lifetime, made insinuations of this kind; and as Belinsky freely acknowledged himself (unlike Coleridge in some instances), he *was* heavily indebted to his German sources. But just as in the case of Coleridge, his importance is not as an original thinker; it is as a critic capable, in Terras's words, of using "the tools placed into his hands by others independently, intelligently and creatively." Belinsky's box score in spotting and evaluating new talent in Russia is remarkably high; there is not a single important writer of his time whose early work he did not single out for praise; and his literary flair more than compensated for his triteness as a theoretician or his deficiencies as a stylist. (D. S. Mirsky, whom Terras does not quote, once called Belinsky's language "long-winded, vulgar and untidy, . . . altogether the worst Russian written by a writer of anything like his importance.")[4] Belinsky's style, filled with passion and vigor, certainly lacks elegance; but he most often wrote in haste to meet a looming deadline, and he inveighed bitterly against the poverty that forced him to drive his pen mercilessly like a tired and stumbling steed.

Organized thematically rather than chronologically, Terras's chapters give us various cross-sections through the body of Belinsky's work. This procedure involves a certain amount of repetitiveness, but has the merit of highlighting essential topics and providing a very clear and lucid picture of Belinsky's ideas on key issues. As a disciple of the Idealists, Belinsky's thought was typically Romantic and "organic." A work of art was a living totality, not an inert mechanism, a product of imagination and genius rather than of fancy and skillful adherence to some set of preconceived rules. The vital unity of the work of art expressed, as a microcosm, the organic unity and harmony—or at least the aspiration to harmony—of the macrocosm to which it belonged, the universe as a whole. Art was given an exalted status as one of the forms (the other two being religion and philosophy) through which the Absolute (or God) becomes manifest in time and space; true art is thus always an expression of the deepest meanings of the period in which it is created. At the same time, however, art should be free to follow its own dictates, unhindered by rules and prescriptions, whether aesthetic or moral; it was too important a function of the human spirit to be tampered with arbitrarily.

The aesthetics of German Idealism thus maintained a precarious balance between an exalted view of art as a carrier of the highest meanings and the need to guarantee its autonomy so that it could function freely. This view is more or less the one that Belinsky accepted all through his life, and to which he remained nominally faithful up to the very end. But Terras re-

[4] D. S. Mirsky, *Pushkin* (New York, 1963), 237.

turns again and again to the problem posed by his conversion to Utopian Socialism in the 1840s, which gradually led him to value only that kind of literature directly relevant to bringing about humanitarian and progressive social reform. In this last phase, marked by the rise of the Natural School in response to his urgings, Belinsky gives literature an explicitly "utilitarian" function that was to have fatal consequences in the future, even though he himself avoided its worst excesses. "Belinsky," as Terras says, "was saved from flagrant misjudgment of any work of Russian literature by his natural aesthetic sense and genuine love of art." But his tendency to give art a socially utilitarian role makes it quite easy for the Soviet Russians to use his enormous prestige and genuine critical merits to buttress Lenin's view that literature should be subordinate to the control of the Communist Party.

Particularly valuable in Terras's book is the last chapter, "Belinsky's Heritage," which traces the development of Russian criticism up to the 1930s. The most influential current was that of the radicals of the 1860s, Chernyshevsky, Dobrolyubov, and Pisarev—who began where Belinsky's last phase ended. They saw art exclusively in Utilitarian terms and refused to accord it any other importance; Pisarev called for the elimination of art entirely as a waste of time and a diversion of resources that could be used for more important social purposes. The other aspect of Belinsky, his Romantic reverence for art, was preserved by Dostoevsky, by the latter's important friend Apollon Grigoriev (the best Russian critic of the midcentury), and revived by the Russian Symbolists in the early 1890s. All these combated the social-utilitarian conception of art in the name of a religious or metaphysical irrationalism deriving ultimately from Belinsky and his Idealist sources. And Belinsky's "organic" view, which always links art with "life" or society, has dominated Russian criticism in one or another mutation ever since. It was only the Russian Formalists who attacked this "organic" synthesis of German Idealism, and reversed it by stressing the importance of form over content.

Art for them was no longer the expression of "life" but, as Victor Shklovsky wrote, it is "the ontology of his literary form [that] determines the writer's consciousness." This approach provided a needed corrective to the exclusive emphasis on "meaning" (whether social or philosophical) so typical of Russian criticism; and it is valuable as a reminder that art does not express "life" directly but through a medium that has its own intrinsic requirements and history. The Formalists unquestionably offer extremely valuable and original insights into the history of literary forms in general, and the formal aspects of Russian literature in particular; but their effort to reduce the creative impulse entirely to a concern with form was perverse and anachronistic. It took one of the dominating tendencies of contemporary literature (particularly of Russian Futurism) and assumed it to be true for all the art of the past as well.

Terras remarks, with a good deal of justice, that "most of what has been new, original, and stimulating" in Russian criticism of the past half century has come from opponents of the Belinsky tradition (meaning the Formalists). But while it is natural to sympathize with the revolt of the Formalists, one should also remember that their extremism is a product of peculiar conditions. Russian criticism has never been truly "literary" in the Western sense because it has always been used as a way of carrying on social-political arguments in Aesopian language. No doubt this is why the Formalists felt impelled to cut off their own concerns so sharply from "life"; but it would be unfortunate if the limitations of their position, itself a product of the "life" of their culture, were simply taken as dogma by their admirers or followers in the more liberal countries of the West. There is no real need to sacrifice either the relation of art to the "life" of society, or the right of the aesthetic domain to enjoy its relative autonomy.

3

If Belinsky had no other claim to fame, he would still glory in the distinction of having been the first important voice to hail the genius of Dostoevsky. It was Belinsky who signaled to the world that, with the publication of *Poor Folk* in 1845, a new literary star had risen on the horizon of Russian literature. A few years later, to be sure, Belinsky changed his mind because Dostoevsky's work had not been going in the direction that he would have preferred; but Belinsky's about-face has been more or less forgotten, while his early words of excited praise live on as foreshadowing a fame whose proportions surpass even what he might have expected. The present cluster of books about Dostoevsky is an accurate indication of the interest he continues to evoke everywhere, and the fascination that his work never fails to exert. For the study of Dostoevsky is not—or at least, not only—an academic pursuit; his novels continue to be a commentary of genius on the moral-social issues that still agitate the modern consciousness. The triumph of Marxism-Leninism in Russia, and the spread of the same doctrine, in various mutations, to most of the rest of the world, has kept Dostoevsky's novels alive as a vital ferment in modern culture. If readers of Dostoevsky have no difficulty in recognizing his characters and themes in their daily newspapers, it is because Dostoevsky foresaw, in the Russia of his day, the ultimate implications of that moral justification of violence and terror that began to appear among the Russian radicals of his own time and that continue to inspire those of our own.

The three volumes called *The Unpublished Dostoevsky* contain translations of Dostoevsky's notebooks covering the span of all his post-Siberian years

(1860–1881).[5] Part of the material originally included in these note-books—the notes for his five major novels—were published separately in Russian years ago and, in English translation, more recently by the University of Chicago Press. The present volumes gives us the remainder of this important document, published in the Soviet Union only in 1971 and, until that time, unavailable to Western scholars. They turned out to have few revelations for those familiar with the body of Dostoevsky's work, but are nonetheless an extremely valuable addition to the Dostoevsky canon. Dostoevsky's notebooks are a disorderly mass of jottings of all kinds, set down helter-skelter on the spur of the moment; about a quarter of the pages are simply lists of numbers, addresses, and names relating either to Dostoevsky's personal affairs or to the business of the various publications he edited (*Time, Epoch, The Citizen*). Volume 1, however, does supply the text of his important entry while sitting at the bier of his first wife—an entry that contains the clearest statement of his religious convictions, and indicates all the complexity of his relation to the question of faith. We also find in them the notes for an uncompleted essay on "Socialism and Christianity," as well as those for a proposed rewriting of *The Double* that was never undertaken.

There is no room here to discuss the wealth of material in these volumes in any detail; but they should succeed in setting right certain misconceptions still current, particularly in Western criticism of Dostoevsky. Such criticism has been so fascinated by Dostoevsky's psychology that it has tended to interpret his work purely as a reflection of his own inner emotive conflicts. Or, alternatively, it has followed the lead of such émigré Russian philosophers as Berdyaev and Shestov, who have discussed Dostoevsky's work in terms of philosophical antinomies or existential dilemmas. What becomes glaringly clear from the notebooks, however, is the extent to which Dostoevsky was immersed in the agitated hurly-burly of the Russian cultural life of his time, and the intimate connection of his work with the polemics that he carried on in his journalism all through his later career. If Dostoevsky's books are the greatest dramatizations in modern literature of the clash of competing moral-social ideologies, it was not because he brooded over his Oedipus complex or pondered in solitude the enigmas of free will and determinism or of reason and faith. It was because he was passionately plunged into the merciless ideological warfare of Russia in the 1860s and 1870s, and was able to project its issues both in terms of his own inner conflicts and with a brilliant grasp of their larger significance. Dostoevsky's genius enabled him to turn these internecine Russian quarrels into great literature of universal import; but if we are ever to under-

[5] *The Unpublished Dostoevsky*, ed. Carl Proffer, trans. by various hands, 3 vols. (Ann Arbor, Mich., 1976).

stand his books properly, we must go back to study the sociocultural context out of which they came and try to grasp the process of transformation responsible for their birth. Otherwise we shall never understand who Dostoevsky was and what he was really aiming at.

The Unpublished Dostoevsky is issued by the Ardis Press in Michigan, a small, independent enterprise specializing in the publication of Russian literature both in the original and in translation. Ardis is doing such useful work in making Russian texts available in this country that one hesitates to criticize the often poor quality of their translations and the irritating sloppiness of editing and proofreading. All the same, it is unfortunate that such deficiencies add to the difficulties of the unfamiliar work they specialize in, and thus defeat their own purpose of bringing Russian literature to a wider audience. Nonetheless, Ardis publications have now become indispensable; and they are to be commended for publishing not only poetry, novels, and such scholarly material as Dostoevsky's notebooks but also important works of Russian criticism. Two of these works, by Leonid Grossman and Mikhail Bakhtin, are landmarks in the history of Dostoevsky criticism in Russia.

Grossman is one of the pioneers of Dostoevsky scholarship, the author of numerous books and essays on the subject, and the compiler of the most reliable day-to-day chronicle of Dostoevsky's life. He is here represented by two early essays, one first published in 1913 and the other in 1916 (the dates of first publication should have been given in the translation), whose conclusions have long been accepted and assimilated in Dostoevsky scholarship.[6] The first, on Balzac and Dostoevsky, is an eye-opening exploration of the relation between the two writers. It was Grossman who first analyzed the history of this relationship, pointed out the traces of *Eugénie Grandet* in *Mr. Prokharchin* and *The Idiot*, and, most important of all, remarked that *Le Père Goriot* "is an essential prolegomenon for the study of *Crime and Punishment*." He noted the evident similarities in structure between the two books, and that Rastignac is tempted by a variation of the Superman philosophy preached by the arch-criminal Vautrin. Rastignac too, in order to aid his family (particularly his sisters), raises the question of whether murder is justifiable for this purpose; and his friend Bianchon tells him that, to act successfully in this fashion, "you must be Alexander [the Great] or go to prison." Grossman perceptively points out, however, that in Dostoevsky "the problem of personal will is complicated by the altruistic motif and made into a profound moral problem." He also argues—less convincingly—that the source of Raskolnikov's "philosophical system" may be found in Balzac; but there is no genuine altruism in Balzac, only familial self-interest and a glorification of the ruthless Napoleonic

---

[6] Leonid Grossman *Balzac and Dostoevsky* (Ann Arbor, Mich., 1973).

"great man." The clash between altruism and personal will that we find in Raskolnikov grows, rather, out of the theories of the Russian radicals in the 1860s.

In his second essay, "Composition in Dostoevsky's Novels," Grossman laid the foundation for all future serious study of Dostoevsky's poetics. Dostoevsky's novels differed so greatly from the European tradition of his time, and from the more easily assimilable works of Turgenev and Tolstoy, that Western criticism at first took them as the products of an immense but untutored and greatly flawed talent. Grossman shows, however, that the notion of Dostoevsky as an uneducated barbarian of genius is simply ridiculous. Dostoevsky was very widely read and intensely interested in the problems of his craft; but he went his own way and solved these problems in a completely independent manner. He read and admired the writers of the popular tradition of the "adventure novel"—the English Gothic, the French *roman-feuilleton*, the Russian historical novel of the 1830s descended from Scott—with its compulsive readability, its social and topical significance, its lavish use of spectacular action, intrigue, and a mystery plot. The essential structural features of this genre, as Grossman demonstrates, are employed in Dostoevsky's major works. But of course he uses this subliterary form to dramatize the most profound moral-philosophical themes, and raises the exciting but superficial melodrama of the adventure novel to the level of genuine tragedy. "Dostoevsky's novel," writes Grossman, "is a philosophical dialogue expanded into an epic of adventure; it is the *Phaedo* put at the center of the *Mysteries of Paris*, a mixture of Plato and Eugène Sue." Saint Augustine might have been a more appropriate name than Plato in this context; but the formulation is strikingly apt all the same.

This view of Dostoevsky seems to me incontestable and definitive; but it is challenged in Mikhail Bakhtin's *Problems of Dostoevsky's Poetics*.[7] The first edition of this text appeared in 1929 and was instantly recognized as of major importance; but its author vanished from sight in the 1930s, only to surface again in the 1960s when a new and enlarged edition of his study was published. Bakhtin, who died in 1975, is probably the most important critical influence in Soviet Russia at the present time, and his ideas about the novel have attained somewhat the same canonical status that those of Henry James and Percy Lubbock enjoyed for so long in Anglo-American criticism. Indeed, there is more than a little similarity between Bakhtin and these predecessors in English—apparently without direct familiarity, though Bakhtin was well read in Western criticism. In any case, his views are expressed in relation to Russian literature; and his prestige derives, not

[7] Mikhail Bakhtin, *Problems of Dostoevsky's Poetics*, trans. R. William Rotsel (Ann Arbor, Mich., 1973). Rotsel's translation, now out of print, was almost unreadable, and has been replaced by that of Caryl Emerson. See 7.

only from his genuine abilities as a critic, but also because he initiated for Russia somewhat the same sort of technical discussion of the novel as James and Lubbock did in English.

Bakhtin's most famous idea is that Dostoevsky invented a new type of novel, which he calls "polyphonic," wholly unlike anything that can be found before. Previously, all novels were "homophonic," that is, always controlled by the dominating consciousness of the author or by a hero acting as the author's surrogate. In Dostoevsky, however, there is only a polyphony of individual "voices," each of whom speaks entirely for himself and out of his own point of view, with no controlling authorial consciousness to link them to any homophonic unity. Rather, according to Bakhtin, "the essence of polyphony is precisely the fact that the voices remain independent and, as such, are combined in a unity of a higher order than in homophony." A major weakness of Bakhtin's position is that he never offers any convincing analysis of this higher polyphonic unity that he postulates. And indeed, if we take seriously what he says about the independence of each of the individual voices, it is difficult to see how such a unity is possible.

Bakhtin criticizes Grossman's conception of the Dostoevskian novel because, in his view, it remains on the surface and does not penetrate to the deep source of Dostoevsky's technical originality. "If Grossman had made the connection between Dostoevsky's compositional principle—the unification of utterly heterogeneous and incompatible materials—and the plurality of consciousness-centers which are not reduced to a common denominator, he would have arrived at the artistic key to Dostoevsky's novels—polyphony." Bakhtin, as we see, does not reject Grossman but rather assimilates him to his own perspective; and Bakhtin goes even further in grounding his observations about Dostoevsky's polyphony in a more general theory. Dostoevsky's polyphony itself, he argues, is ultimately based on an anthropology—an intuition of man as free, unique and unpredictable, hence impossible to understand except within his own point of view and equally impossible to categorize and define in any fixed and immutable fashion. There is a definite Existentialist ring about many of Bahkin's formulations that must have sounded (and probably still do sound) strange and heretical to orthodox Marxist ears. "The consciousness of others cannot be contemplated and analyzed and defined like objects or things—one must *relate dialogically* to them." "For the [polyphonic] author the hero is not 'he' and not 'I' but a full-valued 'thou,' that is, another full-fledged 'I' ('Thou art')." One cannot help wondering whether Bakhtin ever read Martin Buber, some of whose major works came out in the early 1920s. There is some evidence (a quotation from Georg Simmel, for example) that Bakhtin was keeping up with avant-garde German culture.[8]

---

[8] These sentences were written before very much was known of Bakhtin's antecedents, and

This is not the place to explore all the questions raised by Bakhtin's fascinating book, especially those introduced into his second edition by a large new chapter containing ideas fully developed only in his next book, *Rabelais and His World*.[9] My own opinion coincides with that of numerous critics (there is an extensive literature on Bakhtin, mainly in Russian and Czech), who are greatly impressed by the penetration and power of his numerous insights into essential aspects of Dostoevsky's art, but who cannot accept his theory of the polyphonic novel. Indeed, Bakhtin himself does not seem to be absolutely certain about his position on the crucial issue of authorial control. For while he constantly stresses the "freedom" of Dostoevsky's characters from any authorial violation of their integrity, he also writes that Dostoevsky's characters are not "removed from the author's intention entirely, but simply from his monological field of vision, the elimination of which is part and parcel of Dostoevsky's plan." This makes the distinction between polyphony and homophony much less radical, and seems to be identical with the Jamesian campaign against intrusive narrators whose point of view is not part of the dramatic structure. Dostoevsky *did* move in the direction of eliminating any overtly authoritative narrator, and, like the stream-of-consciousness writers later, he dissolves and internalizes the objective world into the consciousness of one or another character. But this is far less epoch making and decisively innovative than Bakhtin would have us believe; nor does it initiate an entirely new era in the history of the novel.

The best part of the book is the last chapter, "The Word in Dostoevsky," which remains unchanged from the first edition. Here Bakhtin utilizes his insight into Dostoevsky's "dialogical" grasp of character to show how his language reflects and expresses this fundamental trait of his world. Dostoevsky's language rarely possesses an unequivocal relation to what it signifies; the point of view of the signifier is always affected and deflected by an awareness of other points of view relating to what is being signified. Hence Dostoevsky's "word" is never "objective," but always (or most often) uttered with reference to another consciousness, whether explicitly or

---

I leave them uncorrected as examples of a first reaction. These speculations have of course since been amply confirmed. See 19, esp. n. 3.

[9] For whatever it may be worth, and because the chronology of Bakhtin's intellectual evolution still poses numerous problems, it may be useful to record a rumor that reached me at the time I was writing this essay. In conversation with an American Slavist greatly interested in Bakhtin, and who had recently returned from the Soviet Union, I made some remarks about what seemed to me the rather lopsided inclusion of this new chapter; and he responded with the following explanation, which he had heard during his Russian visit.

Bakhtin, it would seem, had been very eager to get the main ideas developed in his Rabelais book into print, and was by no means convinced that it would ever be published. When his book on Dostoevsky was cleared for a second edition, and he was certain it would again become available, he decided to tack on a new chapter (making the necessary adjustments) so that at least some of his more recent conceptions would become known to the public.

by implication. Bakhtin constructs an elaborate typology of such "utterances" in Dostoevsky, which he illustrates with illuminating examples; and this allows him to clarify Dostoevsky's frequent use of parody, as well as the way in which characters blend together and mutually illuminate each other. No critic before Bakhtin has analyzed this aspect of Dostoevsky with anywhere near his delicacy and precision. If only for this chapter, Bakhtin fully deserves the high reputation he enjoys in Russia (though one suspects that his popularity there is also aided by the potentially subversive implications of his emphasis on the inviolable freedom of the personality).

4

Another writer raised to fame by Belinsky is Ivan Goncharov, whose first novel, *A Common Story*, appeared in 1847; his second and much more famous work, *Oblomov*, created a type that became an important cultural symbol. There is very little critical literature on Goncharov in English, and Milton Ehre's book fills a long-felt need.[10] He has provided a serious and solid monograph, very well informed, well written, and exhibiting the critical finesse of someone who has absorbed the work of the Russian Formalists as well as the Anglo-American concern with the novel as an art form.

Goncharov was a shy, retiring, quite timid human being, who spent most of his life as a high civil servant (he served for many years as a censor of literature), and who, after a certain point, definitely suffered from mild paranoia. At one time a very good friend of Turgenev's, he later accused his fellow novelist of stealing some of his still-unpublished ideas and using them himself, as well as passing them along to Flaubert, George Sand, the Goncourts, and others. Ehre paints a discerning portrait of Goncharov as a split personality, constantly subject to surges of emotional impulse against which he guarded himself by irony and a deflating skepticism. This conflict appears in his novels as the clash between Romanticism and Idealism on the one hand, and "practicality" in some prosaic and down-to-earth guise on the other.

A Common Story takes a young provincial nourished on Romantic sentimentalism to Petersburg, where he is sobered by his experiences and by the advice of his disillusioned, hardworking uncle, a bureaucrat in charge of one of the government's industrial enterprises. Most of the book is composed of conversations between these two main characters, and becomes so schematic, as Ehre well notes, that it seems more a stage comedy of manners than a novel. Comparing it with Balzac's *Les Illusions perdues*, he points out the lack of density in the social texture, the relative emptiness of the background, the absence even of scenic description. Nonetheless, the

[10] Milton Ehre, *Oblomov and His Creator* (Princeton, N.J., 1973).

book was greeted as an important contribution to the campaign then being waged by Belinsky against the last vestiges of Romanticism, and in favor of materialism and a rational, scientifically positive approach to the problems of man and society. Even though Goncharov has often been accused of *meshchantsvo* (a word whose connotations resemble those of Gogolian *poshlost*, though the emphasis is more social than personal) because he seems to favor his "practical" protagonists, his attitude is much more ambiguous than appears at first sight. For when young Peter Aduev finally turns into a perfect replica of his supposedly exemplary uncle, he is suddenly made aware of how narrow, stifling, and humanly unsatisfying this sort of life is—a life without sentiment or feeling, one that has sacrificed all "higher things" to the bitch-goddess of material success.

Only suggested at the end of his first novel, this theme is given a striking embodiment in *Oblomov*, where the central character—a monster of sluggishness and inactivity, scarcely capable of the effort of getting out of bed—is nonetheless inspired by sublime visions of great moral elevation and touching purity. By contrast, his friend the Russian-German Andrey Stolz again represents, on a somewhat higher level of culture, the values of practicality, efficiency, and European "progress." The novel is the story of Oblomov's unsuccessful efforts to come to terms with "reality," that is, to assume some personal responsibility in life by marriage, and to shoulder his social responsibility as a large landowner. But while Oblomov fails despite Stolz's prodding and guidance, his dreams, like those of Don Quixote, retain their splendor. And though Stolz is successful in everything he undertakes, even winning the girl with whom Oblomov was in love, his perfectly ordered existence is undermined by a gnawing emptiness against which he can only take refuge in Stoic resolution. Oblomov may be defeated, but a world without some of the values that he represents is not worth living in.

Ehre's lengthy "reading" of *Oblomov* is extremely alert to every nuance of the text; but for my taste its categories remain too much on the level of psychic generality and critical theory, too far removed from the specific sociocultural significance of Goncharov's work. Russian criticism, to be sure, has amply dwelt on Goncharov from this point of view; and no doubt Ehre, who is thoroughly familiar with its results, wanted to do something different. But most of his readers would not be acquainted with such criticism, and it would have been helpful if he had presented some of its results rather than merely alluding to them in footnotes. Someone ignorant of the Russian background, and who knows only what Ehre tells him, would have difficulty understanding why *Oblomov* aroused all the excitement that it did, and why the name became a symbol around which battles were fought concerning the meaning and value of Russian life. Indeed, such battles have by no means ceased being waged, and Goncharov's symbols have lost none of their relevance. Solzhenitsyn's Colonel Vorotyntsev in *August 1914*, who wishes to instill some of the efficiency of the German military into the Russian army, is only the most recent incarnation of this perennial Russian theme.

Edward Crankshaw's book on Tolstoy is the final volume on my list dealing with another writer who, at least by the calendar, also belongs to the generation of the 1840s.[11] But Tolstoy is never referred to in this way because he cannot be pigeonholed in any convenient fashion; he is simply too large and independent a figure to be defined in any terms except those of his own creation. And indeed, his life as a wealthy aristocrat, descended from one of the oldest and most distinguished families of the ancient nobility, remained quite separate from the schools, movements, and groupings into which his literary contemporaries flocked for self-protection and mutual sustenance. Crankshaw's volume, lavishly illustrated with photographs and reproductions, is more a coffee-table item than either a biography or a critical monograph. But as a journalist and historian with an intimate knowledge of Russian life and history, he provides a text of unusual quality. Sharp and incisive in its judgments, written simply but with telling precision, Crankshaw's sketch offers a provocative and rather hostile view of Tolstoy's career as man and writer.

A number of years ago, a small book was published in France by an émigré Russian woman of letters, Nina Gourfinkel, called *Tolstoi sans Tolstoisme*. The idea was to free the image of Tolstoy from the cloying hagiographic adoration of his admirers and followers and to attempt to see the man as he really was. The same impulse inspires Crankshaw's portrait, and leads to a similarly iconoclastic result. Neither Gourfinkel nor Crankshaw is interested in any cheap debunking, any Stracheyan sneer; but with due reverence for Tolstoy's overpowering genius, it is still legitimate to examine his actions and behavior with the same severe and relentless moral scrutiny that he never failed to apply to others. Measured by such a standard, Tolstoy emerges as a mass of contradictions, totally unable to live up to his own moral precepts but forever trying to impose them on others; a monster of egoism in relation to his family; always—even when (or particularly when) he donned peasant clothes—an incarnation of the arrogant, overweening Russian *barin*, possessed of absolute power and accustomed to being instantly obeyed. Tolstoy's grandeur was to have elevated this attitude into a cosmic challenge; but for him other human beings were only insignificant pawns in his magnificent duel with destiny. "Sainthood cannot be achieved by precept," Crankshaw writes sharply. "Splendid as some of his conceptions were, they were nullified by his behavior. A man is as good as his actions, and Tolstoy's actions were too often simply bad."

---

[11] Edward Crankshaw, *Tolstoy: The Making of a Novelist* (New York, 1974).

What Crankshaw has to say about Tolstoy's works, as with everything he says, is acute and interesting; but his real subject is Tolstoy the man rather than the artist. It is thus all the more interesting to see how neatly one of his remarks dovetails with an observation of Bakhtin's. Precisely because of Tolstoy's refusal to acknowledge any limitations to his own Godlike powers, Crankshaw finds that the fictional world he created lacks a sense of "mystery." This perception exactly coincides with the terms of Bakhtin's distinction between Dostoevsky and Tolstoy. "A dialogical relationship to his heroes is foreign to Tolstoy. He does not (and fundamentally cannot) extend his point of view via-à-vis the hero to the hero's own consciousness. . . . The external world in which the story's characters live and die [Tolstoy's *Three Deaths*] is *the world of the author*, an objective world in relation to the characters' consciousness. Everything in it is perceived and depicted within the author's all-embracing and omniscient field of vision." Crankshaw and Bakhtin thus supplement each other very revealingly; and it is only by combining the two approaches that we can get a truly three-dimensional view of Tolstoy—or, for that matter, of any other writer.

5

In the last section of this chronicle, we turn to the contemporary writer who, leaping over the hiatus caused by the decimations of Stalinism, has demonstrated the continuing vitality of Russian literature. Once again a commanding voice—that of Alexander Solzhenitsyn—has emerged from Russia to bring the world a spiritual message flowing from the ascetic heart of Russian Christianity. It was this moral-cultural essence that Dostoevsky, like Solzhenitsyn, discovered in the purifying martyrdom of captivity, and that Tolstoy, after indulging in the pleasures of the senses to the full, returned to in old age with a fanaticism (at least in theory) surpassing that of either of the others. For discussion here we have only a small sampling—a play, *Candle in the Wind*, and the *Letter to the Soviet Leaders*—of the flood of works that have been pouring in recent years from Solzhenitsyn's pen. In addition, there is an excellent anthology of Western critical comment on this exemplary figure who, like Tolstoy again, has successfully opposed the power of the pen against the might of a tyrannical and oppressive state. This volume also includes the text of Solzhenitsyn's *Lenten Letter* (which attacks the servility of the Russian Church to a régime officially encouraging atheism), as well as of his speech accepting the Nobel Prize.[12]

[12] Alexander Solzhenitsyn, *Candle in the Wind*, trans. Keith Armes and Arthur Hudgins (Minneapolis, Minn., 1960); Alexander I. Solzhenitsyn, *Letter to the Soviet Leaders*, trans. Hilary Sternberg (New York, 1974); *Aleksandr Solzhenitsyn: Critical Essays*, ed. John B. Dun-

Solzhenitsyn's worldwide importance is primarily as a mighty moral force, a relentless witness fearlessly denouncing the monstrous hypocrisy of Soviet claims to have achieved not only a just, but a practically ideal, society. His stature in the internal history of Russian literature, however, is less well understood. As Father Alexander Schmeeman points out, he is the first writer of major proportions to have emerged from the torments of Russia since the Revolution. All the others—Blok, Mandelstam, Pasternak, Akhmatova—were really surviving refugees from the great Silver Age that began in the 1890s. All were to some extent enthralled (one can see this very well in *Dr. Zhivago*) "by the romance of the revolution. . . . Chaos and blood was still seen by many as that 'primeval chaos' from which, they believed, something would be born, would grow and would blossom." Solzhenitsyn is the first great voice to have come to maturity totally in the post-Revolutionary period, and to have known no other physical or spiritual reality. As a result, he is "the first *national* writer of the Soviet period of Russian literature," one who is so completely immersed in Soviet reality that he is "uniquely capable of *revealing* that world from within, of creatively *explaining* it, and finally of *overcoming* it."

This excellent observation helps to define the nature of Solzhenitsyn's work and some of the reactions to it in the West. His books, impressive and compelling as they are, nonetheless inevitably seem "old-fashioned" to tastes schooled on Joyce, Proust, and Kafka; and this is because, as the émigré Polish poet and man of letters Czeslaw Milosz points out, "the Western reader is living at the end of the twentieth century, Solzhenitsyn is a writer of the nineteenth." Milosz hastens to add, however, that this should not be taken as a judgment of value since "to maintain that that which bears a later date is better would be absurd."

Solzhenitsyn came to maturity in a world dominated by the theory of "Socialist Realism" (a codification based on achievements of nineteenth-century Russian literature), and he still creates within its conventions. But Solzhenitsyn had been taught that "realism" demands the "truth," and it was "truth" that became the hero of his works—to paraphrase what Tolstoy once said about his own *Sevastopol Sketches*. It is bitterly ironic, as Irving Howe remarks, that Georg Lukács—who spent his life inventing subtle philosophical rationalizations for blind obedience to the dictates of the Communist Party—should have finally hailed Solzhenitsyn as the genuine fulfillment of the demand for a literature of "Socialist Realism." Nothing could be farther from the abject works that usually go by that name than Solzhenitsyn's novels; but Solzhenitsyn does expose them and their creators (for example, his contemptuous portrait of the corrupt and time-serv-

---

lop, Richard Haugh, and Alexis Klimoff (Belmont, Mass., 1973). The critics I cite are all included in this volume.

ing writer Galakhov in *The First Circle*, the winner of a Stalin Prize for Literature) within the framework of their own presuppositions.

It would be a mistake, however, to attribute the "old-fashioned" quality of Solzhenitsyn's novels to only an external factor such as enforced cultural isolation. Such a view implicitly assumes that, if Solzhenitsyn had had the opportunity, he would have utilized the experiments of Modernism; but this seems to me very doubtful. Technique, after all, when it is not just arbitrarily adopted to keep up with fashion, always translates a vision of the world; and Solzhenitsyn's "vision" is diametrically opposed to that of most modern literature. Here again Milosz is helpful and perceptive. For the experiments of modernism, he notes, are based on a sense of the relativism of moral values and of characters as "nothing more than drifting receptacles of perceptions and reflexes." But Solzhenitsyn's fundamental theme is precisely the *affirmation* of character, the ability to survive in a nightmare world where moral character is the only safeguard of human dignity and the very conception of humanity itself as something precious and valuable. To a Western world that sees its image reflected in the wistful nihilism of Beckett's metaphysical clowns and basket cases, Solzhenitsyn is indeed "old-fashioned"; but literature, after all, is not (or should not conceive itself to be) in competition with haute couture, and Solzhenitsyn's technique renders a "vision" that one hopes transcends the modes of the moment. (It is instructive that, when Solzhenitsyn experiments with modernism in *August 1914*, where he uses some of Dos Passos's techniques in *USA*, he does so precisely to translate delusory mass consciousness and experiences of confusion, defeat, and despair.)

Solzhenitsyn's vision of life is approached from many angles in the anthology—all of them illuminating—but most penetratingly, it seems to me, in an impressive piece by Terence Des Pres, "The Heroism of Survival." Solzhenitsyn's values come both from his experiences as a front-line officer fighting a war in whose purpose he believed, and then from his cruel years in a concentration camp. In each case he was inevitably confronted with the ultimate questions of human existence; and he learned that simply to survive as a human being under such circumstances—not to sink into animality—was itself a feat of heroism. But for Solzhenitsyn, survival in this sense also meant a transvaluation of values, a process of purification by which the very meaning of life itself became transformed. "From this experience," Des Pres writes, "comes a special integrity and clarity of vision, and more, something close to what we speak of as the religious experience, that unique liberation and concentrated fulfillment of the saint—of those who, having passed in pain beyond family, possessions and self-will, find themselves face-to-face, in joy and in peace, with the numinous power of life itself." It is this transformation that causes Gleb Nerzhin, the unjustly imprisoned hero of *The First Circle*, to exclaim: "Thank God for prison! It gave me the chance to think." This is Solzhenitsyn's updated version of the kenotic tradition, which, as G. P. Fedotov has shown, distinguishes Russian Christianity among all others and takes the sufferings of the humiliated Christ as its model and ideal.[13] Both Tolstoy and Dostoevsky drew on the same source, though Solzhenitsyn, despite obvious resemblances, differs from these predecessors in stressing the steeling of moral character that the experience of suffering brings in its wake.

The "survivor" in Solzhenitsyn thus always feels himself in total opposition to the trivial, workaday world of "the others"—those who live in abasement and subjection to the powers that be. This opposition is dramatized in *Candle in the Wind*, not a very good play but interesting for what it reveals about the author. Here a "survivor" (a returned prisoner) finds himself living in the midst of a materialistic and hedonistic future world resembling that of *A Clockwork Orange* (without the sadism)—a world that has lost all sense of moral value in the frantic scramble for pleasure and power. For someone who has learned to what depths of degradation men can sink if they aim only to satisfy their physical and material needs, such a world is intolerable. And Solzhenitsyn, in pillorying the blatant materialism fostered by Marxist ideology in his own country, also strikes at that universal belief in the beneficence of "science" and technological progress that is more or less the new religion of mankind the world over. In his *Letter to the Soviet Leaders*, he urges them to abandon this belief both in the interests of preserving that Western civilization of which Russia is a part, and—more specifically—in the interests of Russia herself. Solzhenitsyn's ideas, which very much resemble (in tenor if not in detail) those the Southern Agrarians used to propound in this country, have naturally been denounced as "reactionary"; but since so much of the radical New Left here and elsewhere has joined in the same repudiation of mindless technology, it is difficult to know what these old-fashioned labels mean anymore.

Solzhenitsyn's works, in the words of the German novelist and fellow Nobel Prize winner Heinrich Böll, have "the sweep of Tolstoy and the spirit of Dostoevsky, thus synthesizing the two minds which were thought to be antithetical both in the nineteenth century and in present-day literary criticism." The very fact that such comparisons can be made without a sense of incongruity (what other contemporary novelist anywhere could bear their weight?) indicates Solzhenitsyn's stature, which has only increased with the publication of his explosive *Gulag Archipelago*. Russia has once again produced, even against its will, a writer who truly fulfills the Belinskian requirement that literature be *both* a free creation of the spirit and a powerful expression of the life of its society.

[13] See the reference to Fedotov in Chapter 2, n. 8.

PART THREE

Dostoevsky

CHAPTER NINE

Freud's Case History of Dostoevsky

1

IT IS well known that the discovery of the importance of Dostoevsky's work in Western Europe, and the acceptance of his novels as an astonishing harbinger of the crisis of values that has haunted Western culture for the past half century, coincided with the development of psychoanalysis and the growth of its influence. Dostoevsky's novels—whose main characters so often wrestle with repressed aspects of their personality, and whose psychology, in most cases, is so emotionally ambivalent—could not help but attract the attention of Freud himself and the growing army of his disciples, who were only too happy to cull examples from the latest cultural idol with which to illustrate and garnish their speculations.

Dostoevsky's works proved to be a gold mine for psychoanalysts because, as Freud remarked, "He [Dostoevsky] cannot be understood without psychoanalysis—i.e., he isn't in need of it because he illustrates it himself in every character and every sentence." These words come from a letter that Freud wrote to Stefan Zweig in 1920,[1] and they show that, even at this relatively early date, Freud had already become fascinated with the Russian novelist. This interaction between psychoanalysis and Dostoevsky scholarship in Germany was crowned by Freud's notable essay, "Dostoevsky and Parricide," first printed in 1928 as the preface to a volume in the famous German edition of Dostoevsky's works—the Piper edition—containing some of the material in Dostoevsky's notebooks and letters relating to *The Brothers Karamazov*.

Freud's article was translated into English the very next year and published in a journal called *The Realist*.[2] Ever since then it has occupied a prominent place in much of the writing outside of Russia devoted to the study of Dostoevsky's work. There was, to be sure, some expression of dissent in Freud's inner circle at the time his article appeared. Theodore Reik answered it in the second issue of *Imago*, protesting against what he considered the rather philistine view of Dostoevsky implicit in Freud's remarks. Freud criticizes Dostoevsky for the "compromise with morality"

[1] *Letters of Sigmund Freud*, selected and ed. Ernst L. Freud, trans. Tania and James Stern (New York, 1960), no. 191, 331–33.

[2] This essay can be found in Sigmund Freud, *Complete Works*, trans. James Strachey (1961), 21:175–94. The letter to Theodor Reik that I mention is also included (195–96).

inherent in the belief that "a man who has gone through the depths of sin can reach the highest summits of morality"; and Reik countered that Freud seems to place a stamp of unconditional approval on the dullest conformist to the ethical code of society in preference to Dostoevsky. Freud parried in an exchange of private letters that indicated he did not wish to become seriously engaged in arguing the matter. On the one hand, he said that he accepted Reik's "subjective psychological view of ethics"; but, on the other, he maintained that "I should not wish to deny the excellent Philistine a certificate of good ethical conduct, even though it has cost him little self-discipline." He added that his paper on Dostoevsky was just a "triviality," which he did not think warranted any more extensive consideration.[3]

Reik's article did not arouse any public interest in debating Freud's point of view; and with the exception of another article by E. H. Carr in 1930, which raised questions about Freud's acceptance of one factual point[4]—we shall return to this matter later—there has been very little critical discussion of the text. Philip Rieff has remarked in passing on Freud's "facile identification" of the novelist's later support of tsarism with his attitude toward his father.[5] Fritz Schmidl, in 1965, traced Freud's evident hostility toward Dostoevsky to the fact that, at the time he was analyzing the great defender of the need for religious faith, he was also at work on *The Future of an Illusion*. For the most part, however, Freud's article has been hailed as a classic work, the most extended psychoanalytic exploration of a major literary figure by the founder of psychoanalysis, and a canonical text for the psycho-historical investigations that have emerged under the influence of the theories of this school.

It so happens that my own work on Dostoevsky led me to review all the available source material concerning Dostoevsky's life, and particularly the material relating to his early years on which Freud naturally focuses. In the course of doing so, I became aware of disturbing discrepancies between this material and the account of Dostoevsky that Freud gives—an account I had long accepted as being reliable in its data, even if, as is often the case with psychoanalysis, the conclusions drawn from such data could only be highly conjectural. As a result my curiosity was aroused, and I decided to see if I could pin down my uneasiness about Freud's article with some precision. How reliable is Freud on the purely factual level, so far as this can be established? What are his sources, and how did he use them? These are questions it seemed to me worth trying to answer in the interest of historical truth.

[3] Reik's essay and Freud's reply are discussed in Fritz Schmidl, "Freud and Dostoevsky," *Journal of the American Psychoanalytic Association* 13 (July 1965):518–32.

[4] E. H. Carr, "Was Dostoevsky an Epileptic?" *Slavonic and East European Journal* 9 (December 1930):424–31.

[5] Philip Rieff, *Freud: The Mind of the Moralist* (New York, 1961), 152.

2

Freud's knowledge of Dostoevsky is revealed in the letter to Stefan Zweig already quoted (October 19, 1920), thanking his friend for having sent him a copy of his book *Three Masters*. This work contains a biographical study of Dostoevsky, along with two others on Balzac and Dickens (actually, Zweig's long essay is an expressionistic rhapsody very short on "facts" and information and very long on overheated lyricism). Declaring himself quite satisfied with Zweig's treatment of both the English and French author, Freud adds, however, that "the confounded Russian Dostoevsky" is another story. "Here," Freud remarks, "one feels gaps and unsolved riddles"; and he then proceeds "to produce some material" to solve these riddles "as it comes to my layman's mind." Freud means, of course, that he is a "layman" as a literary critic or historian; but far from disqualifying him from venturing an opinion about Dostoevsky, he thinks that in this instance quite the opposite is true. "It is also possible that here the psychopathologist, whose property Dostoevsky must inevitably remain, has some advantage." (One suspects that Freud may have felt piqued and challenged by Zweig's remark that "not the psychologists, men of science though they be, have laid bare the deep recesses of the modern soul, but the men of genius who overstepped all frontiers.")[6]

Zweig's portrait of Dostoevsky as a mad Russian genius—the Rasputin of literature, as it were—laid stress on epilepsy as a key to his enigmatic character; but Freud objects to the notion that Dostoevsky was a true epileptic. "Epilepsy is an organic brain disease independent of the psychic constitution," he writes, "and as a rule associated with the deterioration and retrogression of the mental performance." True epilepsy, in Freud's view, always leads to mental degeneration (or almost always; the great scientist Helmholtz is cited as the single known counterexample). What is generally considered epilepsy in men of genius, according to Freud—who is here polemicizing with the then-influential theory of Cesare Lombroso—are always "straight cases of hysteria." So-called epileptic geniuses thus fall within the province of psychiatry rather than medicine, since "hysteria springs from *the psychic constitution itself* [italics added] and is an expression of the same organic basic power which produces the genius of an artist." As a result, Freud says, "I feel that the whole case of D. could have been built on his hysteria."

Freud is not, however, content with attributing Dostoevsky's genius solely to an innately hysterical psychic constitution. For he assured Zweig that, important though Dostoevsky's "constitution" may be as a cause of hysteria, "it is nevertheless interesting that the other factor to which our

[6] Stefan Zweig, *Master Builders* (New York, 1939), 202–3.

theory [psychoanalysis] attaches importance can also be demonstrated in this case." This "other factor" turns out to be a severe punishment for some childhood offense. "Somewhere in a biography of D.," Freud writes, "I was shown a passage which traced back the later affliction of the man to the boy's having been punished by his father under very serious circumstances—I vaguely remember the word 'tragic,' am I right? Out of 'discretion,' of course, the author didn't say what it was all about."

Freud, though, knows very well what it was "all about"—it was about the classic threat of punishment for masturbation, which creates a castration complex. He does not, to be sure, say so explicitly; but he remarks that Zweig, as the author of *Erste Erlebnisse*—a volume of short stories dealing with the sexual awakening of children and adolescents—would certainly know what he was alluding to. "It was this childhood scene . . . which gave to the later scene before the execution the traumatic power to repeat itself as an attack, and D.'s whole life is dominated by his two-fold attitude to the father-tsar-authority, by voluptuous masochistic submission on the one hand, and by outraged rebellion against it on the other. Masochism includes a sense of guilt which surges toward 'redemption.' "

This is Freud's original sketch of his analysis of Dostoevsky; and a number of points in it call for comment. First, the question of whether Dostoevsky's epilepsy was "organic" or "psychic" in character. I am not competent to utter a word about the rightness or wrongness of Freud's views from a medical point of view; but there is one fact of Dostoevsky's biography that Freud does not mention either now or later, and that has some relevance to this question. In May 1878 Dostoevsky's three-year-old son Aleksey died suddenly because of a severe and unexpected epileptic attack lasting three hours and ten minutes. It would thus appear that epilepsy ran in Dostoevsky's family, and that the child had probably inherited it from his father. This creates a strong presumption that Dostoevsky's epilepsy was organic in origin and not primarily hysterical. But since Freud, as we know, was an unrepentant Lamarckian, who continued to believe in the inheritance of acquired characteristics long after this view was generally abandoned, he might well have argued that the epilepsy originated with the writer nonetheless.

Second, there is the reference to the passage that Freud once saw in a biography. This can only refer to a tantalizing footnote in the official biography (1882) by Orest Miller and Nikolay Strakhov.[7] In the section written by Miller, he remarks that, according to a well-informed source, there was "a very particular piece of evidence about the illness of Feodor Mikhailovich which relates to his earliest youth and connects it with a tragic event in their [the Dostoevskys'] family life." Freud, as we have seen,

---

[7] Orest Miller and Nikolay Strakhov, *Biografia, Pisma i Zametki iz Zapisnoi Knizhi F. M. Dostoevskogo* (St. Petersburg, 1883), 141.

immediately transforms this into a reference to a castrating incident by a tyrannical father, even though there is nothing about either "punishment" or "father" in the passage. Moreover, Dostoevsky scholars agree that the footnote, in all probability, contains an allusion to the presumed murder of Dostoevsky's father in the spring of 1839, when Dostoevsky, a student at the Academy of Engineers, was eighteen years old and by no means the "child" Freud thinks him to have been.[8] To be sure, Freud could not have known about the murder when he wrote his letter; the event became public knowledge only with the appearance in 1921 of the memoirs of Dostoevsky's daughter Lyubov.

Freud's ignorance of the murder is also important in interpreting the final sentence quoted from his letter. At this point, he could only have assumed that Dostoevsky's first epileptic attack occurred in the 1850s while he was in prison camp. By "the later scene before the execution," Freud is presumably referring to the mock execution ceremony arranged by Nicholas I. Dostoevsky was led to believe that he and his companions under arrest in 1849 were going to be shot by a firing squad; but about a half hour later they learned their true sentences of exile and hard labor. Freud links Dostoevsky's previous punishment by his father as a boy with this later "scene," and seems to mean that the psychic pressure induced by this repetition of his childhood trauma finally brought on epilepsy shortly thereafter in Siberia. In this way, Dostoevsky's alternating pattern between masochistic submission and outraged rebellion became established for the remainder of his life.

Here we have Freud's first stab at working out a case history for Dostoevsky; and one cannot help admiring the ingenuity with which he does so. Even without knowing anything about the murder of Dostoevsky's father, he manages to interpret his epilepsy as a symptom of an unresolved conflict between submission and revolt.

3

Eight years later, Freud has learned about the murder and the family story connected with it. "According to family traditions," Lyubov Dostoevsky wrote in her book, "it was on learning of the death of his father that Dos-

[8] Up until quite recently, it had been taken for granted that Dostoevsky's father really *had* been murdered by his peasants. Additional research in local archives, however, has cast some doubt on whether any such murder actually occurred. It was not previously known that the death had been carefully investigated by the local authorities, and that two doctors had certified the cause as being the apoplexy from which Dr. Dostoevsky had long suffered. A neighbor, who wished to purchase the property, spread the rumor of the murder, and this was presumably accepted by the absent Dostoevsky family. For more information, see my *Dostoevsky: The Seeds of Revolt, 1821–1949* (Princeton, N.J., 1976), 86–87. The archival material is discussed in G. Fedorov, "K biografii F. M. Dostoevskogo," *Literaturnaya Gazeta* 25 (June 18, 1975):7.

toevsky had his first attack of epilepsy."⁹ This new information now becomes the center of Freud's interpretation; the "scene" before the firing squad is mentioned tangentially, but it no longer plays a determining role in *causing* the epilepsy.

Freud's article is considerably expanded over the causal remarks he makes in his letter, and it contains a much fuller treatment of his point of view. This is not the place to discuss all the implications of that point of view—not only the implication pointed out by Reik, but such an excursion into ethnopsychology as the remark that Dostoevsky's "compromise with morality" was "a characteristically Russian trait" that can also be seen in Ivan the Terrible, as well as in the behavior "of the barbarians of the great migrations, who murdered and did penance for it, till penance became an actual technique for enabling murder to be done." I do not wish to quarrel with Freud's opinions or ideas, but to limit myself solely to the facts he adduces to support his argument. This argument begins, as it did in the letter, with a much lengthier discussion of whether Dostoevsky's epilepsy was "organic" or "affective." Freud is much more cautious in writing for publication, and admits that "we know too little in this instance to make any confident diagnosis." But he nonetheless concludes that it is "extremely probable" Dostoevsky's disease was of the second type.

Freud's analysis of Dostoevsky's psychic constitution is also much more detailed, but a good bit of it has nothing in particular to do with Dostoevsky at all—or only as much as with any other male member of the human race. For as background Freud outlines his theory of the Oedipus complex and the inevitable "ambivalence" of the relation of every boy to his father because of a desire for the mother; when this desire is repressed by the threat of castration, it leads to the creation of an unconscious sense of guilt.

Such a "normal process" of psychic development, however, is complicated when the constitution of the child in question contains a strong factor of bisexuality. In such instances, the boy wishes to *replace* the mother as an object of his father's love; but this also involves castration (for how otherwise become a woman?), and so this desire is repressed as well. According to Freud, this latter type of repression leads to a "pathogenic intensification" that is "one of the pre-conditions or reinforcements of neurosis." Freud finds such a strong feminine attitude of latent homosexuality in Dostoevsky, and cites as proof "the important part played by male friendships in his life . . . his strangely tender attitude towards rivals in love . . . his remarkable understanding of situations which are explicable only by repressed homosexuality, as many examples from his novels show" (184).

These statements are so unspecific that it is difficult to know to what

⁹ Cited in Carr, "Was Dostoevsky an Epileptic?" 428.

they refer; but they seem to me very questionable all the same. Freud is probably thinking of the intense male friendships of Dostoevsky's late adolescence with Ivan Berezhetsky, a fellow student at the Academy of Engineers; with the slightly older Ivan Shidlovsky, both a friend and father figure, at the same period of his life; and perhaps, a few years later, the strong but very short-lived attachment he felt for Turgenev. But all these friendships were very brief, and not at all typical. There are no male friendships in Dostoevsky's life comparable in length and emotional importance to Freud's own intimacies with, for example, Wilhelm Fliess and Josef Breuer. Dostoevsky's relations with women—his two wives, his mistress Apollinaria Suslova, and several others whom he courted or with whom he flirted—were of much greater significance all through his maturity. His later friendships with men, so far as one can judge from the evidence, did not involve any deep emotional ties (with the single exception of his friendship with his older brother, Mikhail), and were based rather on common intellectual interests or ideological convictions.

The same is true about Dostoevsky's attitude toward rivals in love. Presumably, Freud is referring here to Dostoevsky's effort to obtain a promotion for a young man competing with him for the hand of the widow in Siberia who later became his first wife. His reason for doing so was that, if she did reject him and marry his rival, he did not wish her to live in misery. At the same time, it should be pointed out that he was doing everything in his power to dissuade Madame Isaev from entering on what he thought would be a disastrous marriage and to persuade her to choose him instead.

Also, there are numerous illustrations, both in his letters and in the memoirs of his (much younger) second wife, of his pathological jealousy toward possible rivals. Freud has thus taken the one incident in Siberia and blown it up out of all proportion in relation to other material. It is true that examples of this type of behavior can be found in Dostoevsky's novels, particularly in *The Insulted and Injured*; but such "tenderness" was a literary and cultural cliché of the period. It is far more important both in the life of the revolutionary Nikolay Chernyshevsky, and in his novel *What Is to Be Done?* (entirely based on the theme of how rational it was to give way to a rival in love), than anything we can find in Dostoevsky.

4

Freud, in any event, sees Dostoevsky's character pattern shaped by the combination of his Oedipal ambivalence and a strong bisexual disposition, later becoming transformed into a sadistic superego (the repressed hatred of the father) and a masochistic ego (the repressed wish to become the mother). The severity of a conflict between the two, Freud remarks, depends on "the accidental factor" of "whether the father, who is feared in any case, is also especially violent in reality. This was true in Dostoevsky's case, and we can trace back the fact of his extraordinary sense of guilt and of his masochistic conduct of life to a specially strong feminine component" (185). What "violence" means in a Freudian context is not very clear; but if we take the word in the ordinary sense, as implying physical brutality, then Freud's statement is unsubstantiated. The only evidence we have, given in the memoirs of Dostoevsky's younger brother, Andrey, portrays the elder Dostoevsky as irritable, quick-tempered, and despotic; but he disapproved of the corporal punishment of children and never struck his own. Indeed, he sent them all to private schools (though he could scarcely afford the luxury) to avoid the possibility of their being beaten for disciplinary purposes.

Freud's conviction that Dr. Dostoevsky was "especially violent in reality," however, unquestionably goes back to the notion expressed in his letter that Dostoevsky had undergone some "tragic" punishment as a child. This is no longer stated directly as a fact; but Freud cites, in a long footnote, the passage that first established it in his mind, as well as additional material seeming to confirm it. "Of special interest," he writes, "is the information that in the novelist's childhood 'something terrible, unforgettable and agonizing' happened to which the first signs of his illness were to be traced" (181).

Freud's quotation is taken from an article by Aleksey Suvorin, written shortly after Dostoevsky's death and also assumed by Dostoevsky scholarship to allude to the murder of his father. This is followed by the quotation from Miller already given, which Freud has now succeeded in locating. And he remarks, using almost the same wording as his letter, that "biographers and scientific research workers cannot feel grateful for [Miller's] discretion" in refusing to specify the "tragic event." This footnote is appended to an assertion that the first symptoms of Dostoevsky's illness appeared in childhood, long before the murder of his father; the references are evidently meant to document some "event" that brought on these first symptoms. Freud, in other words, persists in interpreting this material exactly as he had done before knowing anything about the murder of the father at all. Perhaps he simply did not make the connection, or was misled by the loose use of the word *childhood*; perhaps he stubbornly stuck to his own view despite the weight of opinion, as he did on so many other questions.

To be sure, to have given up his belief in the existence of a specially severe childhood "trauma" in Dostoevsky's life would have been fatal to his theory; he could not have abandoned it without seeing his entire case history collapse. For he wished to show that the presumed coincidence between the murder of the father and the first epileptic attack was only the culmination of an inner process that had begun a long while before, and that had been triggered by the violence of the father acting on Dostoevsky's innately and strongly bisexual constitution. This had led to the appearance of symptoms in Dostoevsky's childhood, foreshadowing the later disease, but not as yet in themselves epileptic. And Freud finds these symptoms confirmed in some other material.

"We have one *certain* starting point," he writes (my italics); we know the meaning of the first attacks from which Dostoevsky suffered in his early years long before the incidence of the "epilepsy." These attacks had the significance of death; they were heralded by a fear of death and consisted of lethargic, somnolent states. The illness first came over him, while he was still a boy, in the form of a sudden, groundless melancholy, a feeling, as he later told his friend Soloviev, as though he were going to die on the spot. And there in fact followed a state exactly similar to real death. His brother Andrey tells us that even when he was quite young, Feodor used to leave little notes about before he went to sleep, saying that he was afraid he might fall into this deathlike sleep during the night and therefore begged that his burial should be postponed for five days. Such symptoms, Freud says, show an identification with a person one wishes dead; and for a boy, "this other person is usually his father . . . and . . . the attack is thus a self-punishment for a death-wish against a hated father" (182–83).

If such symptoms are really the only "certain" starting point for Freud's diagnosis of Dostoevsky, then his conclusions can only be said to rest on very "uncertain" premises. For if we turn to the sources, we see that there is no evidence whatever relating such symptoms to Dostoevsky's childhood. He did speak to his friend Vsevolod Soloviev about a fear of death; but he dates it very precisely at a much later time. "My nerves have been unsettled since my youth," he told Soloviev in 1873. "Just about two years before Siberia, at the period of my various literary difficulties and quarrels, I was overcome by some sort of strange and unbearably torturing nervous illness . . . it often seemed to me that I was dying, and really—actual death came and then went away.[10] There is nothing else available that would place such nervous attacks any farther back in Dostoevsky's life than 1846–1847; and they coincide, as we know, with a severe nervous disorder documented in his letters of the time.

Freud's dating is equally mistaken with regard to Dostoevsky's fear of lethargic sleep. Andrey Dostoevsky does not refer to any such symptom in his memoirs dealing with his own childhood and that of his brother. He mentions it in an article he wrote in 1881 to the Russian newspaper *New Times*—an article whose aim was to deny that Dostoevsky suffered from

[10] Soloviev's article is reprinted in *F. M. Dostoevsky v Vospominaniakh Sovremennikov*, ed. A. S. Dolinin, 2 vols. (Moscow, 1964), 2:191.

anything resembling epilepsy as a child. In the course of doing so, he remarks that he had seen his brother "from 1843 to April 1849" almost every week, and that he had never heard about any such childhood illness even though they often talked about matters of health. "True," he writes, "*within this period of time* (I do not now recall the exact year) he [Feodor] was quite irritable and, it seemed, suffered from some sort of nervous illness" (italics added). The reference to lethargic sleep and the notes follows this sentence, and unmistakably places them *only* within this time span; they also probably began in 1846–1847.[11]

It is quite likely that the secondhand German sources on which Freud relied only quoted snippets from the Russian material and did not date the information they gave very precisely; his mistakes about these "preliminary symptoms"may thus well have been inadvertent. But there was one issue on which he knew that his own ideas were in conflict with most of the available evidence, and where he continues to maintain them all the same. The issue, quite simply, is whether, if Dostoevsky's epilepsy began in 1839 on hearing of his father's death, there is any reason to believe that it ceased or became less severe during his years in Siberia. This is a very important question for Freud because its answer provides a crucial test for his theory.

If it is true that Dostoevsky's first epileptic attack occurred when he learned about the murder of his father, then this onset of the acute phase of the disease can be interpreted as the expression of a particularly harsh need for self-punishment. He had been repressing a hatred of his father supposedly indicated by his earlier symptoms; and "it is a dangerous thing if reality fulfills such repressed wishes. The phantasy has become reality and all defensive measures are thereupon reinforced" (186).

As a result, Dostoevsky's self-punishment "had become terrible, like his father's frightful death itself" (186). When this internal punishment was replaced by the external punishment of a sentence to exile and hard labor for rebellion against the father figure of the tsar, the pressure of internal conflict should have been relieved. This is why "it would be very much to the point if it could be established that they [his epileptic attacks] ceased completely during his exile in Siberia; but other accounts contradict this" (181–82). A few pages later, he reiterates: "If it proved to be the case that Dostoevsky was free from his seizures in Siberia, that would merely substantiate the view that his seizures were his punishment" (186).

Now, it is regrettably awkward for Freud's whole thesis that, according to *all* the evidence *except* the family tradition, Dostoevsky's epilepsy *began* in Siberia; the only possible proof of Freud's argument thus turns out to be a counterproof. To circumvent this difficulty, he tries to undermine the

[11] The relevant citation from Andrew's article is given in *Literaturnoe Nasledstvo* 86 (Moscow 1973):550.

embarrassing evidence without openly contradicting it. "Most of the accounts," he writes in a footnote, "including Dostoevsky's own . . . assert . . . that the illness only assumed its final, epileptic character during the Siberian exile. Unfortunately there is reason to distrust the autobiographical statements of neurotics. Experience shows that their memory introduces falsifications, which are designed to interrupt disagreeable causal connections" (182).

Freud here clearly imagines Dostoevsky in the role of one of his own patients, asked to recount the past and naturally distorting it under the influence of repression. The evidence about Dostoevsky's illness in Siberia does not, however, at all depend on the *memory of a remote past*, as Freud implies. It derives from Dostoevsky's *letters* of the early 1850s, immediately after his release from prison, which mention the outbreak of the disease just a year or two earlier and still indicate uncertainty about whether or not the attacks are genuinely epileptic.

It is scarcely credible to imagine that, in the feverish letters he poured out to his family on being released from prison camp—letters in which he tried to tell them everything important that had happened to him in the four-year interim—Dostoevsky should have spoken about epileptic symptoms that had not occurred, or mentioned as a distressing novelty an illness with which he had long been familiar. Moreover, people who knew Dostoevsky well both before and after Siberia all speak of his epilepsy as a new development of these Siberian years. There is not a single scrap of evidence of any kind to support Freud's position.

Nevertheless, even though his epilepsy probably began (or at least worsened) in Siberia, Dostoevsky's health did improve there in some respects. The symptoms of his "nervous illness" of the 1840s (fear of death, hallucinations, dizziness, hypochondria, and the like) were all alleviated, probably by the hard physical labor he was forced to perform at the camp. In later life, he often mentioned this general improvement of his physical condition; but such statements do not in any way contradict what he says about his epilepsy. Indeed, references to both are often made together— for example, in his letters on being released from prison.

Freud, we may assume, was probably aware of the distinction between the two kinds of illness; but he tends to confuse them for the purposes of his argument. For while in one place he admits that "it cannot be proved that Dostoevsky's epileptic attacks abated in Siberia" (a statement implying, of course, that some evidence less than "proof" leads him to think this may have been so), elsewhere he remarks that "it appears certain that Dostoevsky's detention in the Siberian prison markedly altered his pathological condition" (182). This last statement is true of Dostoevsky's "nervous illness"; but to a reader unfamiliar with all the details of Dostoevsky's biography, and warned by Freud not to trust the declarations of a neurotic, it certainly creates the presumption that Freud has some good reason besides theoretical necessity for believing Dostoevsky's *epilepsy* to have let up in Siberia.

5

There is still one other matter that needs discussion, though here I can be very brief because the question has been fully explored by E. H. Carr. Freud, as we have seen, accepts the family tradition that Dostoevsky's first attack of epilepsy was caused by hearing about his father's murder. How much credence should be given to this rumor?

Carr surveyed all the existing material in his 1930 article (nothing additional has come to light since), and found the rumor reflected in the three sources already mentioned: the article of Suvorin, the footnote of Miller, and the explicit assertion of Lyubov Dostoevsky. None of these people had any firsthand knowledge; nor did their presumed original source, Dostoevsky's second wife, Anna Grigorievna. There is no supporting evidence at all by anyone who knew Dostoevsky at the time (1839), even though a number of such people wrote reminiscences when Dostoevsky's epilepsy was known to all the world, and to have revealed the date of his first attack would not have been an indiscretion.

To supplement Carr's view, I may add that there is no mention of any such attack in the letter Dostoevsky wrote to his brother Mikhail in August 1839 expressing grief at his father's death. We should also remember that Dostoevsky was then sharing common quarters with a hundred other student-engineers, and could scarcely have concealed a severe epileptic attack even if he had wished to do so. It thus seems reasonable to accept Carr's summary and conclusion: "The evidence is at best pure hearsay; it contradicts all our other information, written as well as verbal; and it is probable that a story so poorly attested would not have been taken seriously if it had not happened to fit in so well with the hypothesis of the psycho-analysts."[12]

There still remains the question of why such a story should have been spread about by Dostoevsky's second wife if it were not true. Carr supplies a complicated answer that I do not need to discuss; in my opinion it may well have been just a mistake. A year before the murder of Dr. Dostoevsky, in the spring of 1838, Feodor learned that he was not to be promoted at the Academy of Engineers and wrote home to tell his father the bad news. The letter brought on an apoplectic stroke, and the stricken doctor had to be bled in order to relieve his condition. Feodor himself, as a result of all this, fell ill and spent some time in the academy hospital.

My own view is that Dostoevsky, reminiscing about these events with

---

[12] Carr, "Was Dostoevsky an Epileptic?" 429.

his wife, probably spoke of having fallen ill because of something that had happened to his father, and that this became intertwined with what he may have told her about the murder, which occurred at approximately the same time. Obsessed as she was with his epilepsy, she naturally took the illness her husband mentioned to have been the onset of the disease that haunted her life as well has his; and the shocking horror of the murder overshadowed all the other surrounding events of that remote period. This innocent falsification was destined to have an astonishing career when it became the center of the case history Freud constructed, out of such fragmentary and questionable data, to deal with the enigma of Dostoevsky.

CHAPTER TEN

The Background of *Crime and Punishment*

THE ITALIAN novelist Alberto Moravia once said, in a rather sensational article called "The Marx-Dostoevsky Duel," that *Crime and Punishment* "will for a long time remain as an indispensable key to understanding what has happened in Russia and Europe during the last fifty years." Why? Because, he explained, "although [Raskolnikov] had not read Marx and regarded himself as a superman beyond good and evil, [he] was already, in embryo, a people's commissar; and, in fact, the first people's commissars came out of that same class of the intelligentsia to which Raskolnikov belonged, and possessed his identical ideas—the same thirst for social justice, the same terrible ideological consistency, the same inflexibility in action. And Raskolnikov's dilemma is the very same one that confronts the people's commissars and Stalin: 'Is it right for the good of humanity to kill the old usurer (read: liquidate the bourgeoisie)?' "—or, to update Moravia's example a bit, eliminate the kulaks (wealthy peasant farmers)?[1]

This view of Dostoevsky's great novel, written in the same year and under the immediate impact of Khrushchev's denunciation of the crimes of Stalin (1956), may at first sight seem only a clever literary illustration of a political argument, not something that should be taken seriously as a commentary on Dostoevsky's work. What, after all, does Raskolnikov really have to do with political revolution? His crime is depicted as a totally individual act divorced from any larger movement; and though he is quite aware of the Socialist theories of the student radicals of his time, he emphatically *dissociates* himself from them. Besides, Raskolnikov is anything but a people's commissar, and if he does have a "thirst for social justice," he certainly cannot be said to have "ideological consistency" (actually, he wavers all the time), or "inflexibility in action" (he commits his murder in a sort of waking trance).

Despite such particular objections that could be made to Moravia's remarks, his general point is, all the same, very well taken. There is a connection between the people's commissars, Stalin, and Raskolnikov, and Moravia's intuition has hit on something fundamental, even if it is less univocal and direct than his words suggest. Raskolnikov is not so much a people's commissar as he is Dostoevsky's remarkable prevision of how such

[1] The relevant passages of Moravia's article can be most conveniently found in the W. W. Norton edition of *Crime and Punishment*, translated by Jessie Coulson and edited by George Gibian, with a large sampling of critical material (see 642–45).

a human type eventually would come to be born and of what its arrival on the historical scene might presage for Russia—and now has come to mean for the world. *Crime and Punishment* was meant to warn against what Dostoevsky considered to be this misshapen birth and, if possible, to abort its existence; the value of Moravia's observations is that they point to this dimension of the book, which is often overlooked or not taken with sufficient seriousness. But, as we shall see, it is precisely from such an attempt to grapple with the moral implications of the social and cultural realities of his day that Dostoevsky produced a work whose timeliness increases rather than diminishes with the years, and whose artistic power has scarcely been matched since it was first published in 1866.

1

Crime and Punishment is the first of Dostoevsky's important novels, and the one in which his genius can perhaps be felt in its purest and most limpid form. He began to write it five years after returning from his exile in Siberia (1850–1860), four years of which he had spent in a work camp, and just after the failure of the second of the two literary political journals that he edited with his older brother, Mikhail, during the early 1860s. The novel was written in a period of great personal distress, at a time when Dostoevsky's personal life had suddenly collapsed around him and he was desperately searching to establish it on a new footing. His first wife—whom Dostoevsky had once called a "knight in female clothing," and some of whose character traits appear in Katerina Ivanovna Marmeladova—had died of tuberculosis in April 1864 after a long and heartrending death agony. Mikhail, with whom he worked in close association and harmony, suddenly expired a few months later. And although Dostoevsky had labored like a galley slave to keep their journal *Epoch* (*Epokha*) afloat even after his brother's demise, his efforts proved unavailing and left him saddled with a huge debt.

Hounded by creditors in St. Petersburg, he longed to obtain some peace and quiet by taking a trip to Europe. Residence in Europe had in the past afforded him some relief from his epilepsy, and he also looked forward to a reunion with his ex-mistress, the young writer Apollinaria Suslova, to whom he was still passionately attached. He had remained in correspondence with her and had not yet surrendered the hope of winning her back. Dostoevsky thus scurried around in the spring of 1865 trying to raise the necessary funds for such a journey, and managed to obtain a loan from the Literary Fund established to help needy intellectuals and students (Dostoevsky served as recording secretary of this organization between 1863 and 1865). He also approached several periodicals with the idea for a new novel.

In a letter to A. A. Kraevsky, the editor of a journal called *Notes of the Fatherland*, Dostoevsky described his new idea: "My novel is called *The Drunkards*, and will be related to the present question of drunkenness. It will take up not only this question, but represent all its offshoots, particularly with images of the family, the education of children under such conditions, etc., etc." He added that it would be at least three hundred pages in length, perhaps more; and he requested an advance of three thousand rubles at a rate considerably lower than usual for an author of his stature. Despite this surrender of authorial pride to dire necessity, his offer was turned down. As a result, Dostoevsky was forced to appeal to a cutthroat publisher named F. T. Stellovsky, who paid him the sum requested in return for permission to publish a three-volume edition of Dostoevsky's works; in addition, Dostoevsky promised to supply Stellovsky with a new work of at least novella size by November 1, 1866. If the writer failed to fulfill his contract, Stellovsky obtained the right to publish all of Dostoevsky's future works without compensation for a period of nine years.

Whether the project of *The Drunkards* had advanced further than the few sentences of Dostoevsky's letter cannot be determined; the perfunctory tone of his remarks leads one to believe that at best he may have made a few preliminary jottings. Moreover, these remarks suggest he was thinking of a type of social-problem novel he would scarcely have been interested in writing at this stage of his career. But perhaps he spoke of it in such terms only to stress its possible journalistic appeal to a skeptical editor, and because, twenty years before, Kraevsky had published such early works of Dostoevsky's as *Poor Folk* and *An Honest Thief* in which drunkards had been portrayed with penetrating and touching sympathy. Scholars agree, however, that whatever notes Dostoevsky may have accumulated for this novel were eventually employed in the subplot involving the Marmeladov family of *Crime and Punishment*.

Stellovsky's contract enabled Dostoevsky to go abroad after distributing most of his funds to creditors, his stepson Pasha, and the numerous family of his late brother. Stopping off at Wiesbaden, where he hoped to replenish his pocket by gambling, he promptly lost what little he had left. Unable to pay his hotel bill, he was literally imprisoned in this German spa for two months while waiting for funds that would allow him to renew his journey. Some image of his state of mind may be gathered from this extract of a letter to Apollinaria Suslova, who had left Wiesbaden shortly before, after paying him a visit:

My affairs are terrible *nec [sic] plus ultra*; it is impossible to go any further. Beyond, there must be another zone of misfortune and filthiness of which I still have no knowledge. . . . I am still living without meals, and this is already the third day that I live on morning and evening tea—and it's curious! I do not really wish to eat. The worst is that they snip away at me and sometimes refuse me a candle in the evening (especially) when some bit of the previous one is left over, even the smallest fragment. But I leave the hotel every day at three o'clock and only return at six, so as not to give the impression that I do not dine at all.[2]

It was during this period of personal humiliation and intense inner rage, when he could certainly feel boiling within himself all the hatred of a Raskolnikov against the injustices of the world, that we catch our first glimpse of the idea for a story that eventually became his novel.

In a letter to his friend A. P. Milyukov, Dostoevsky asks him to make the rounds of the journals and try to obtain an advance on a story. Nothing specific is said about its nature, except that, as Dostoevsky assures his correspondent, "people will pay attention to it, talk about it . . . nothing of this kind has yet been written among us; I guarantee its originality, yes, and also its power to grip the reader." None of the Petersburg journals were interested, however, and Dostoevsky was reluctantly forced to write to an old enemy, Mikhail Katkov, the powerful editor of what had recently become a conservative journal, *The Russian Messenger*. Katkov was also the publisher of Turgenev and Tolstoy, but luckily, at this particular moment, neither had recently supplied him with any new manuscript, and he accepted Dostoevsky's proposal. A copy of a rough draft of Dostoevsky's letter, found among the novelist's papers, provides our first substantial view of his new conception.

He describes it as the "psychological report of a crime," which is committed by "a young man, expelled from the university, petty bourgeois in origin and living in the midst of the direst poverty." Falling under the influence of "the strange, 'unfinished' ideas that float in the atmosphere," he "decides to break out of his disgusting position at one stroke" by killing an old pawnbroker.

[She is] stupid and ailing, greedy . . . is evil and eats up other lives, torturing a younger sister who had become her servant. 'She is good for nothing.' 'Why should she live?' 'Is she at all useful for anything?' These questions befuddle the young man. He decides to kill her in order to bring happiness to his mother living in the provinces, rescue his sister, a paid companion in the household of a landowner, from the lascivious advances of the head of the gentry family—advances that threaten her ruin—finish his studies, go abroad, and then all his life be upright, staunch, unbendable in fulfilling his 'humane obligations to mankind,' which would ultimately 'smooth out' his crime, if one can really call a crime this action against a deaf, stupid, evil, sickly old woman who does not herself know why she is on earth and who perhaps would die herself within a month.

[2] *Selected Letters of Fyodor Dostoevsky*, ed. Joseph Frank and David I. Goldstein, trans. Andrew McAndrew (New Brunswick, N.J., 1987), 219.

Dostoevsky also indicates how he plans to resolve the action of the story. A month passes, "no one suspects or can suspect him," but "here is where the entire psychological process of the crime is unfolded. Insoluble problems confront the murderer, unsuspected and unexpected feelings torment his heart. Heavenly truth, earthly law take their toll, and he finishes by *being forced* to denounce himself." What impels him to do so is "the feeling of isolation and separation from mankind which he felt right after completing the crime," and which has continued to torture him. Finally, "the criminal himself decides to accept suffering in order to atone for his deed." Dostoevsky also remarks that newspaper accounts of various recent crimes committed by educated members of the young generation have convinced him "that my *subject* is not at all eccentric," and he instances two examples of murders perpetrated by university students after cool calculation and reflection (*Selected Letters*, 221–23).

2

It may well have been such reports in the press, to which he always paid the closest attention, that had initially stimulated Dostoevsky's imagination and given him the idea for a story that could be written quickly and be eminently salable. But if he seized on the latest sensation in this way, it was because he had long been preoccupied with the question of crime and conscience and because, as a result of the attempt of the Russian radicals of the 1860s to establish morality on new and more "rational" foundations, such questions had taken on a burning actuality.

Dostoevsky's years in the prison camp had brought him into firsthand contact with a terrifyingly extensive diapason of human experience, and he had glimpsed the awful possibility of a world in which the categories of good and evil had simply ceased to control behavior. He was very much struck, for example, as he wrote in his prison memoirs, *Notes from the House of the Dead*, by the lack of any manifest signs of "inner anguish or suffering" among the peasant convicts, almost all of whom were murderers. But he also noted that "almost all of the convicts raved and talked in their sleep," and that what they raved about usually had some connection with their violent past. Nor did any of the peasants reject the moral law by which they had been judged; during the Easter services, they all fell to their knees and asked forgiveness from Christ.

The person who most truly terrified Dostoevsky was not a peasant at all but a clever, handsome, well-educated member of the upper class named Pavel Aristov, who was, Dostoevsky wrote, "the most revolting example of the depths to which a man can sink and degenerate, and the extent to which he can destroy moral feeling in himself without difficulty or repentance." Aristov was a spy and informer who had landed in prison for having falsely accused various people of plotting against the government, and then financing his debauches with the money obtained from the secret police to entrap others. Dostoevsky saw such degeneration as an ever-present possibility when moral standards collapsed or were destroyed; and prison camp persuaded him that this was far more likely to occur among the educated élite than among the people. When the character of Svidrigaïlov, Raskolnikov's completely cynical alter ego, first makes his appearance among the early notes for *Crime and Punishment*, he is designated by the name: Aristov.

But in *House of the Dead* Dostoevsky also mentions another type of educated personality, whom he does not identify with any of his fellow prisoners; we may plausibly take him to be an imaginary projection of Dostoevsky himself, brooding over the revolutionary enthusiasms of his youth. (These, we might recall, had included the plan to incite a peasant revolution in which blood would have been amply spilled.) Such a personality was quite different from a peasant criminal, who might be guilty of a savage murder but "never once . . . reflects upon the crime he has committed . . . and even considers himself to be in the right." The other type of wrongdoer is "an educated man with a conscience, with awareness, heart. The pain in his heart will be enough to do away with him, long before any punishment is inflicted upon him. Far more mercilessly, far more pitilessly than the sternest law, he condemns himself for his crime." Here is the prototype of the character Dostoevsky places at the center of the story he was offering to Katkov.

Dostoevsky's fascination with the theme of crime and the problem of conscience unquestionably arose from such firsthand impressions and reflections, mingled with his immersion in the works of such writers as Shakespeare, Schiller, Pushkin, Hugo, Balzac, and Dickens, where such issues time and again are given powerful embodiment. But his preoccupation came into especially sharp focus because of the agitated climate of Russian sociocultural thought during the 1860s. The radicals were pressing for a revolution and, firmly believing one would occur in the very near future, were at the same time engaged in reshaping the whole notion of what constituted morality. Influenced by the Utilitarian doctrines of Jeremy Bentham and John Stuart Mill, which Karl Marx considered to be a middle-class apologia for capitalist selfishness, the leading Russian radical thinker Nikolay Chernyshevsky proclaimed that "rational egoism" was far preferable to the old idea of conscience propagated by the Christian faith. Human nature was "egotistic," and men preferred whatever was to their own advantage; the notion of self-sacrifice was harmful nonsense; but by the use of reason men would learn that their greatest advantage consisted in identifying their personal interests with the greatest happiness of the greatest number. Such ideas, with their naive belief in the power of rational reflection to control and dominate all the explosive potentials of the human psyche, seemed the sheerest and most dangerous illusion to the post-Siberian Dostoevsky. And his major works of the early 1860s (*The Insulted and Injured, House of the Dead, Winter Notes on Summer Impressions*, and *Notes from Underground*) all attempted to reveal the limitations and perils of such a doctrine.

Indeed, if we look for some general formula to characterize Dostoevsky's works after the ordeal of his exile, we can describe them as a dialectical amalgam of what he had learned during that racking time of observation and self-scrutiny applied to the theories of the radical intelligentsia that he encountered on his return. Impressions gathered during this Siberian period—including, of course, the searching analysis to which he subjected his own past—are obviously contained in all of his later works. But these are never presented simply in and for themselves (even in his *Notes from the House of the Dead*, written in the form of journalistic sketches); they are always oriented by the moral implications of the philosophical doctrines of the radical intelligentsia. The combination of, and tension between, these two elements gives Dostoevsky's work both its outstanding human depth and its intellectual and philosophical stature. He measured the possible consequences of radical ideology against those ineluctable verities of human nature whose existence had so strongly impressed itself upon him in Siberia. And he did so by imaginatively projecting the realization of such radical theories *in action*, dramatizing them with the incomparable gift for psychological portraiture that he had displayed from his very earliest work.

3

What began as just a lengthy short story dealing with "the psychological account of a crime" did not remain in that format for very long. Dostoevsky's notebooks contain a draft of this initial conception, which concentrates on the desperate anguish and intense loneliness—the sense of total alienation from humanity—that the narrator experiences after his crime. Written in the first person, the story resembles a self-exposing confession such as *Notes from Underground* much more than it does the novel we know. This version breaks off at the point where the character begins to express resentment, defiance, and rage as well as to experience dejection and despair, and one has the impression that the character itself grew beyond the boundaries of Dostoevsky's initial idea. Once he began to see his character as *both* rebellious and inwardly suffering, it was no longer possible for Dostoevsky to keep him within the narrow confines of his original plan.

It was probably at this stage of composition that Dostoevsky decided to fuse the story with his earlier project *The Drunkards* and introduced the

Marmeladov family, especially Sonya, to aid in the process of bringing about Raskolnikov's voluntary surrender. The "psychological account of a crime" thus widened to become the first of Dostoevsky's novel-tragedies of ideas, a work incorporating a broad social canvas with, at its center, a protagonist who murders under the influence of the fashionable radical ideas of the moment. But as the scope of the work continued to grow under Dostoevsky's hands, he became increasingly troubled by the technical problem posed by his first-person narrator. Such a choice had come naturally with his early inspiration; but as the story turned into a novel, this narrative stance proved increasingly difficult to sustain.

Raskolnikov's state of mind, for example, necessarily had to be represented as continually chaotic and confused by the shock of his crime; there are moments when he is scarcely aware of what he is doing, yet he is also required to function as a reliable narrator in these drafts, which show him rather implausibly transcribing long speeches by the other characters and sharply noting their expressions and gestures. Since Dostoevsky determinedly wished to maintain his stress on the moral struggle taking place in Raskolnikov's consciousness, he tried various alternatives to solve his dilemma. One was to imagine Raskolnikov sitting down to write only after completing his prison term, and thus contemplating everything as recollected in tranquillity; but finally Dostoevsky decided to shift to the third-person form. This is the event that he mentions in a letter to Baron Wrangel (February 1866), in which he confides to his friend that at the end of November, although a good deal had already been written and was ready, "a new form, a new plan swept me away, and I began again from scratch."

In opting for this new form, however, Dostoevsky still did not wish to surrender the advantages derived from viewing the world largely as projected through Raskolnikov's sensibility; and his notebooks show how carefully he thought about preserving this vantage point. "Narration from the point of view of the author," he jots down, a "sort of invisible and omniscient being, who does not leave him [the character] for a moment, even with the words: 'All that was done completely by chance.' " Dostoevsky thus cautions himself to stay as close to Raskolnikov as possible and, even when commenting on the action, to retain his focus exclusively on that character. Brilliantly original for its time, this technique enabled Dostoevsky to conserve most of the psychological intimacy of the first person while freeing himself from its limitations. It also turned him into a precursor of such writers as Henry James and Joseph Conrad in their experiments with perspective and point of view, though Conrad's bitterly anti-Russian animus probably did not allow him to acknowledge how much he had learned from Dostoevsky. (That he knew *Crime and Punishment* by heart is clear to any reader of *Under Western Eyes*.)

By this time, as well, the initial motivation that Dostoevsky, in his letter to Katkov, had given Raskolnikov for the crime had also considerably expanded in scope. Raskolnikov's desire to aid his family is no longer dominant, but has become linked with, and only part of, a much larger framework. Just two years before, Suslova had set down in her notebook a remark that Dostoevsky had made when they were together in Turin. "As we were having dinner, he said, looking at a little girl who was doing her lessons: 'Well, imagine, there you have a little girl like her with an old man, and suddenly some Napoleon says: "I want this city destroyed." It has always been that way in the world.' " Napoleon as the incarnation of absolute, ruthless, despotic power had long haunted the Russian imagination, and Dostoevsky was familiar with many literary sources, including his beloved Pushkin, where Napoleon's image is used as the symbol of a will-to-power uncontrolled by moral considerations of any kind. But this Napoleonic complex of Russian culture, as it might be called, had just recently taken a new lease on life and become linked, not with the awesome emperor whose figure looms over so much of European Romanticism, but with the Russian *raznochinets* of the 1860s—the intellectuals of the new generation who were Dostoevsky's chief concern.

This came about as the result of an internal development within radical ideology itself. In the years just prior to the writing of *Crime and Punishment*, a new variety of this ideology began to exercise a growing influence on the Russian sociocultural scene. Essentially, it was an offshoot of the doctrine of "rational egoism" already mentioned; but it placed a stronger accent than had Chernyshevsky on individual self-fulfillment, on enjoying the satisfactions of life in the here and now rather than postponing them for some indefinite future of communal social bliss. This new branch of radicalism was linked with the name of Dmitry I. Pisarev, and Dostoevsky dramatizes the two currents with his contrasting portraits of Raskolnikov and the bumbling but essentially well-meaning Utopian Socialist Lebezyatnikov. "Why was that fool Razumikhin abusing the socialists?" Raskolnikov asks himself. "They are industrious, commercial people; 'the happiness of all' is what they care about. No, life is only given to me once and I shall never have it again; . . . I want to live myself, or else better not live at all."

This is only one of the ways through which Pisarev's ideas enter into Dostoevsky's creation of his central figure. Far more significant are some utterances of Pisarev in a famous essay-review of Turgenev's *Fathers and Children*, in which he defended that book—a work also greatly admired by Dostoevsky—against its detractors in the radical camp to which Pisarev himself belonged. The character Bazarov, according to Pisarev, was the exemplar of the new radical hero of the time, and Pisarev glorified him in terms going far beyond Turgenev's skeptical, alternatively admiring and undermining portrayal. Indeed, Pisarev elevated Bazarov, a radical Russian intellectual of lowly birth, almost to the level of a Nietzschean Superman standing beyond good and evil. "Neither over him, nor outside him, nor inside him," he declared, "does [Bazarov] recognize any regulator, any moral law, any principle." In addition, "nothing except personal taste prevents him from murdering or robbing . . . [or] causes him to make discoveries in the field of science and social existence." Bazarov is thus declared to be psychologically immune to moral scruples of any kind; and a common crime is placed on exactly the same footing as outstanding intellectual achievement or important transformations of social life.

Transpositions of such ideas run throughout Raskolnikov's frenzied soliloquies; and if we look anywhere for the origin of Raskolnikov's fateful article *On Crime*, then it is to Pisarev that we must again turn (though he has been generally neglected in this connection). Pisarev draws a clear distinction, as does Raskolnikov, between two types of people—the mass, who live a "customary, dreamily tranquil, vegetative existence," and a small minority of "other people" who live and work on their behalf. These "other people" are "eternally alien to [the mass], eternally regarding it with contempt, and at the same time eternally working to increase the amenities of its life." The mass, writes Pisarev, "does not make discoveries or commit crimes"; but these "other people" most emphatically do, in the name of the mass and for their benefit, and they unquestionably possess the *right* to transgress the moral law that Raskolnikov claims for his "extraordinary people."

Such views, in my opinion, became embodied in the creation of Raskolnikov as we know him in the novel. The "strange, 'unfinished' ideas" that Raskolnikov "completes" are no longer simply those of the all-pervasive Utilitarianism of the early 1860s in Russia, ideas that earlier had been combined with the type of naively Utopian humanitarianism Dostoevsky mocks with the figure of Lebezyatnikov. Rather, it is Bazarov, in the monumentally proto-Nietzschean image popularized by Pisarev, who had come to represent the ultimate realization of Utilitarian heroism; and it is these consequences that Dostoevsky found himself envisaging as he feverishly worked on his scenarios. "Now Pisarev has gone further," he had confided to his notebooks in 1862; and among the drafts of a speech by the oily lawyer and capitalist Luzhin—who wished to marry Raskolnikov's sister, and specifically attacks a morality of charity and compassion—appear unmistakable references to Pisarev, which Dostoevsky later eliminated. It is highly significant as well that Raskolnikov recognizes in Luzhin's words a reformulation of the same doctrines that had led him to murder.[3]

[3] For more information on the relation of this article to *Crime and Punishment*, see my *Dostoevsky: The Stir of Liberation, 1860–1865* (Princeton, N.J., 1986), chap. 12, esp. 172–78. The article itself can be found in D. I. Pisarev, *Literaturnaya Kritika*, 3 vols. (Leningrad, 1981), 1:235, 233.

4

Crime and Punishment, then, arose from Dostoevsky's efforts to dramatize the moral dangers that he sensed lurking in the ideology of Russian Nihilism—dangers not so much for society as a whole, though these certainly existed—but those primarily threatening the young Nihilists themselves. He knew very well that the impulses inspiring the average Russian radical were generous and self-sacrificing, and that they were moved by the noblest feelings—sympathy, altruism, love—whatever they might believe about the impregnable rationality of their "egoism." When about half of Dostoevsky's novel had been written and published, the first attempt on the life of the tsar was made by an ex-student who bears more than one resemblance to Raskolnikov; and even though Dostoevsky was horrified by the deed, he wrote a remarkable letter to Katkov in which he *protests* against the general vilification of the younger generation that had ensued:

> And among us Russians, our poor little defenseless boys and girls, we still have our own, eternally present *basic* point on which Socialism will long continue to be founded, that is, their enthusiasm for the good and their purity of heart. There are countless rogues and scoundrels among them. But all these high school pupils, these students, of whom I have seen so many, have become Nihilists so purely, so unselfishly, in the name of honor, truth and genuine usefulness. You know they are helpless against these stupidities [radical ideology] and take them for perfection. (*Selected Letters*, 228–30)

This was the frame of mind in which Dostoevsky was working on his novel, whose aim, if we define it in the perspective of his period, was to reveal to the radicals themselves the *true* implications of their deepest convictions and the total contradiction between its moral-emotive sources and the cruel deeds that their doctrine explicitly justified. Dostoevsky set himself the task of portraying this conflict in the form of a self-awakening, the gradual discovery by Raskolnikov *himself* of the unholy mixture of incompatibles in his ideology. This is why Raskolnikov seems to have one motive for his crime at the beginning (the desire to aid his family and then devote himself to good works) and another when he makes his famous confession to Sonya (the desire to prove to himself "whether I can step over barriers or not . . . whether I am a trembling creature or whether I have the right").

Many critics have pointed to this seeming duality of motive as a weakness in the novel, an artistic failure on Dostoevsky's part to project a unified character. A close reading will show, however, that all through the first part Dostoevsky carefully prepares the reader for Raskolnikov's final self-discovery. He indicates how, whenever Raskolnikov falls under the sway of his "ideas," his character becomes transformed from one of human responsiveness and compassion to arrogant superciliousness, contempt, and indifference to the suffering of others. The whole point of the novel is to reveal this inner dialectic: the impossibility of combining the feelings that impel Raskolnikov to conceive of himself as a benefactor of humanity with those required to put into practice the idea that he can blithely disregard the moral law. Raskolnikov fails to realize his ambition of entering the ranks of "Napoleons" precisely because he cannot totally suppress the workings of his moral conscience—a conscience that has become so grotesquely twisted by the radical ideology of the 1860s that it can justify murder.

Mikhail Bakhtin, one of the best Soviet Russian commentators on Dostoevsky, has remarked of Raskolnikov that "it is enough for a person to appear in his field of vision to become for him instantly an embodied solution to his own personal question";[4] and Dostoevsky skillfully weaves together this underlying ideological structure with the action of his internalized detective story plot. The drunken Marmeladov confronts Raskolnikov's fashionable Utilitarianism, his belief in the all-powerful workings of "reason," with the intense religious pathos of the helpless reprobate who hopes for the miracle of a pardon from Christ just because he is so painfully aware that he is the *least* worthy to receive it. And accomplishing an artistic miracle of his own, Dostoevsky manages to raise the all-pitying love of Marmeladov's self-sacrificing prostitute daughter Sonya far above the level of a sentimental cliché. No greater contrast can be imagined than the one between the values by which *they* live and those that Raskolnikov tries to put into practice; and the juxtaposition between the two constitutes the heart of the book.

The values of the Marmeladovs, it should be stressed, are not the pious platitudes of the official church (Dostoevsky bitingly sweeps *these* aside in Katerina Ivanovna's sarcastically despairing dialogue with the priest come to administer the last rites to her dying husband). They are, rather, the eschatological ethics of primitive Christianity, with its dominating stress on the supreme importance of all-forgiving and self-sacrificing love, the credo of the Sermon on the Mount and the crucified Christ that Saint Paul knew was "foolishness for the Greeks." Dostoevsky passionately believed that such an ethos existed at the heart of Russian peasant life, and he represents this folk aspect through the character of the *raskolnik* (religious schismatic) Nikolay, the house painter wrongly accused of the crime but ready to confess out of a sense of his own sinfulness so as to take on "suffering" as a means of atonement. This contrast between the genuine *raskolnik* of the people and the false *raskolnik* newly produced by the intelligentsia is a crucial part of Dostoevsky's ideological subtext.

Other characters are also related to Raskolnikov beneath the level of the

---

[4] See my discussion of this phrase in Chapter 2, "The Voices of Mikhail Bakhtin," 31–32.

plot action. The good-hearted and ebullient Razumikhin (whose name contains the Russian word for "reason," *razum*, as if to indicate Dostoevsky's view of how this faculty should be personified) is Dostoevsky's image of the young Russians he would have liked to see replacing the negative and embittered radicals like Raskolnikov. Razumikhin has a "broad" Russian nature; he flings himself into the sea of life and enjoys coping with its adversities—the very opposite of his friend Raskolnikov—and allows himself all sorts of indulgences without losing sight of moral principle. Luzhin and Svidrigaïlov both represent Raskolnikov's Utilitarian "egoism" reduced either to a rationale for bourgeois money grubbing or to aristocratic debauchery and sensuality touched with world-weariness. Nor should one forget the brilliant investigating magistrate Porfiry Petrovich, who understands so well the innermost recesses of Raskolnikov's twisted psyche and who really wishes to save him from madness and despair. He may perhaps be seen as a father figure, who represents the chastened Dostoevsky contemplating with sympathy and sadness a reincarnation of his own youthful revolutionary delusions and impetuosities.

It is when Raskolnikov recognizes his own inescapable identification with these two debasing alternatives of his ideology, and recoils in horror, that he finally turns to Sonya. His surrender, however, is more an admission of personal weakness than an abandonment of his ideas. But these also finally give way when, in the much-criticized and much-misunderstood Epilogue, he suddenly dreams of a world in which *everyone* becomes infected with the virus of believing themselves to be "extraordinary people" whose remarkable intelligence allows them absolute, uncontrolled authority; the result is unending mutual slaughter and social chaos, a literal realization of the Hobbesian state of nature with its war of all against all. Only when Raskolnikov imaginatively "finishes" his own convictions in this way does he allow himself to envisage also accepting Sonya's beliefs, though in truth they have been shown to be alive in his heart and soul all through the book.

5

This introduction has been largely concerned with providing information about the origins of Dostoevsky's superb novel and locating it in the sociocultural context of his time. But the true sign of genius is the ability to begin from the tensions and problems of one's own world, wherever and whenever it may be, or from one's personal experiences, and use these for creations that never lose their ability to speak to the future because they illuminate certain permanent aspects of the human condition. Such creators, as William Blake wrote, possess the capacity "To see a World in a Grain of Sand / And a Heaven in a Wild Flower." Out of the acute social instability and rather jejune radical doctrines of Russia in the 1860s (judged, that is, against any larger philosophical horizon), Dostoevsky managed to produce the greatest depiction of a conscience in conflict with itself since *Macbeth*. So long as the injunction "Thou shalt not kill" continues to be a part of the Judeo-Christian moral code, Raskolnikov's anguish will speak directly to the sensibility of any reader who intuitively believes with Sonya that human life is (or ought to be) sacred. The confrontations between Sonya and Raskolnikov, which dramatize, with such agonizing sublimity, the clash between the ideals of justice and love, raise some of the deepest issues of a Western culture whose double heritage derives from both Greco-Roman civilization and Christian faith. Such passages soar to heights that can only be compared with Aeschylus's *Eumenides*, Sophocles' *Antigone*, and Shakespeare's *Measure for Measure* in their tragic grasp of the most profound moral-philosophical dilemmas.

But if Dostoevsky's novel raises such "eternal" questions, it also grasps them in a form that is both peculiarly modern (taking that word to mean the stretch of history since the French Revolution) and remarkably contemporary. As the percipient Porfiry Petrovich tells Raskolnikov, "This is a fantasic, gloomy business, a modern case, an incident of today when the heart of man is troubled. . . . Here we have bookish dreams, a heart unhinged by theories." Or as another ex-radical, Wordsworth, had written somewhat earlier in *The Prelude* about the French Revolution:

> This was the time, when, all things tending fast
> To depravation, speculative schemes—
> That promised to abstract the hopes of Man
> Out of his feelings, to be fixed thenceforth
> For ever in a purer element—
> Found ready welcome. Tempting region that
> For Zeal to enter and refresh herself,
> Where passions had the privilege to work,
> And never hear the sound of their own names. (Book XI)

Wordsworth's last two lines penetrate to the core of *Crime and Punishment*, and define in advance exactly what Raskolnikov will discover about himself.

Dostoevsky's novels, and *Crime and Punishment* most of all, address us with such astonishing immediacy because they were created in a world whose problems are still very specifically our own, and in which the situations that Dostoevsky created and imagined (hoping they would not come true) have now turned into quotidian reality. We can now see to what extent Moravia was speaking the truth, and in what way *Crime and Punishment* is relevant to the history of the past fifty years. For if Raskolnikov had not read Marx, he *had* read Chernyshevsky and Pisarev, whose ideas, much more than those of Marx, provided the people's commissars with their education.

What is historically called Russian Nihilism was haughtily regarded elsewhere, in the late nineteenth century, as a peculiar aberration of the Russian soul. But it has now, for reasons it would be fascinating to explore—a central one surely being the Bolshevik revolution—become a much more widespread and worldwide phenomenon. The notion of benefiting humanity and eliminating injustice by virtuous violence has never been more widely accepted; terrorism, no longer even against selected individuals but against populations, has become a fact of daily life and is justified by the most exalted motives. Those who sympathize with the grievances of its perpetrators may well say, as similar people said in Dostoevsky's day, that his novel offers no real solution to the social problems it so movingly presents. This is incontestably true; but Dostoevsky's aim was not to add still another solution to those already in existence. It was, rather, to insist that *any* solution would turn out to be inhuman and morally unendurable if it lost sight of the values of compassion and love that inspire Sonya—the values that, because they continue to remain alive in one part of Raskolnikov's sensibility, enable her to rescue him as well.

CHAPTER ELEVEN

The Devils and the Nechaev Affair

1

THE RELATION between history and the novel has always been a complex one, and it has often been difficult to make a sharp and clear-cut distinction between the two. History recounts the past, whether remote or immediate, in a way that makes a factual claim to truth; the novel manifestly is a work of fiction. But it is also one of the oldest conventions of the novel form for an author to pretend that his story is actually a work of history, a fragment of the past accidentally preserved and presented for the delectation and perhaps instruction of posterity. How many manuscripts have been discovered long abandoned and moldering in attics or accumulating dust in some antique desk drawer! How many English novels of the eighteenth century offer themselves as *A True History* of—whatever the subject may happen to be! How many French novels of the same period contain the word *Mémoires* in their titles! Even when the claim to historical validity was no longer made so overtly, it nonetheless, as Henry James well saw, existed as an implicit premise of the novelistic enterprise. "All painters of manners and fashions, if we will, are historians," he wrote, "even when they least don the uniform: Fielding, Dickens, Thackeray, George Eliot, Hawthorne among ourselves."[1] The role of the novelist is mainly that of a "historian" whether he or she will or no, and even when novelists no longer feel it necessary to improve their somewhat questionable moral and aesthetic status by donning the more imposing and dignified mantle of Clio.

This aspect of the novel only highlights the "formal realism" that Ian Watt, in his classic *Rise of the Novel*, has so well analyzed as the basis of the genre; and it has invariably given rise to quarrels over the validity of the images of social life created by novelists. Such quarrels no longer agitate modern criticism because, for one thing, we have become much more conscious of the extent to which *any* account either of the past or the present is invariably an arbitrary presentation governed by the conventions of a literary genre and subject to manipulation and selective presentation. The claim of history itself to "truth" in any objectively verifiable sense has become increasingly dubious and relativized; and in the absence of a generally accepted standard for such "truth," the novelists who deal with the social realities of the past or present are not measured by any criterion

[1] Henry James, *Notes on Novelists* (New York, 1914), 113.

outside their own creative purposes. If they are studied or analyzed in terms of the world they represent, it is in order to understand the conditions that led to the formation of the point of view expressed in their books or to assist in its clarification. Such an approach, of course, contains an implicit presupposition that the world of their creations corresponds *in some broad sense* to the actual contours of the world they have depicted; but they are rarely evaluated any longer according to criteria judging the accuracy or legitimacy of such a depiction.

Quarrels over this latter question are much more likely to arise among the contemporaries of a novelist than among those who study his or her work as a phenomenon of the past. As the world of the work recedes into the distance, as the moral or social questions raised by the novelist lose the sharpness of edge naturally felt by the first readers, it is much easier to view such creations dispassionately and aesthetically. But it sometimes happens that the novelist will touch on matters that are still alive for the present of later readers; and then the same arguments, deriving from the much-ridiculed notion of verisimilitude (the sense of conformity to something "real"), tend to be perpetuated, or, if momentarily lapsing, continually to resurface.

A good example is the never-ending argument over Dickens's treatment of the trade unions in *Hard Times*. Critics still fault him for his hostile portrait of the trade union organizer Slackbridge, who comes down from London to whip up the starving coal miners on strike in Coketown; and they have accused Dickens of a gross failure to grasp the importance of the trade union movement of his day. No one objects to his wildly satirical depictions of the sadistic school system, the bureaucratic futilities of the Circumlocution Office, the heartless procrastinations of the Court of Chancery, and the like; these are no longer living problems for mid-twentieth-century English readers or critics. They can, as a result, savor the fierce grotesquerie that Dickens lavishes on the portrayal of such institutions; but the trade union movement is another matter.

Somewhat the same problem arises in the case of Dostoevsky and *The Devils* (which has also been translated into English as *The Possessed*).[2] Everyone knows that Sergey Nechaev, or more exactly, the Nechaev affair—the murder of a student named Ivan Ivanov in Moscow in 1868, a murder instigated by Nechaev and committed by him along with others in his small revolutionary group—furnished Dostoevsky with the main threads of action in his novel. On its publication, Dostoevsky was immediately accused of falsifying and distorting the Russian revolutionary movement in his "novel-pamphlet" (as he called it in a letter during an early stage of

---

[2] Fyodor Dostoevsky, *The Possessed*, trans. Constance Garnett (New York, 1936). My quotations are taken from this version of the text.

composition). The charge has of course continued to be repeated in Soviet Russian criticism; a typical example may be taken from a perfectly respectable book whose second edition appeared in 1971. "*The Devils* is Dostoevsky's artistic failure," wrote M. Gus, ". . . because the idea was false and in contradiction to actual life developing historically in Russia."[3] Even an admirer of the book such as Irving Howe sees it as an at least partly tendentious attack that can only be considered a caricature, and he remarks regretfully of one episode that "for once—it does not happen very often—Dostoevsky the novelist has been tripped by Dostoevsky the ideologue."[4]

Such comments squarely raise the question of how accurately and conscientiously Dostoevsky used his source material. Is his novel, for all its brilliance, really only a malicious slander on the heroic struggles of the Russian revolutionary movement? How valid is this opinion, so very widespread both in Russian and Western criticism? This is the question that this essay will attempt to answer.

2

Now *The Devils*, to be sure, is a work of art and neither literal history nor reportage (as, for example, *The House of the Dead*); nor did Dostoevsky ever pretend that it had any claim to truth other than as a creation of his imagination.

> Several of our critics have observed that in my novel I used the plot of the well-known Nechaev affair. But they hastened to add that my book did not contain any actual portraits or a literal reproduction of the Nechaev history—having taken an event, I tried only to clarify its possibility in our society, and precisely as a social event, not as an anecdote, not as a description of a particular occurrence in Moscow. All this, I may observe, is quite correct. In my novel I have not handled the well-known Nechaev and his victim Ivanov in any personal way.[5]

It is true that in a letter to the Crown Prince Alexander Alexandrovich, accompanying a presentation copy of the book (February 10, 1873), Dostoevsky referred to it as "almost a historical study";[6] but the qualification is indicative of his caution. His notion of "history," moreover, had always involved the idea of its imaginative extrapolation—as when he wrote that the narrator of *Notes from Underground* "not only may, but positively must,

[3] M. Gus, *Idei i Obrazi F. M. Dostoevskogo* (Moscow, 1962), 356.

[4] Irving Howe, "The Politics of Salvation," reprinted in Dostoevsky, *A Collection of Critical Essays*, ed. René Wellek (Englewood Cliffs, N.J., 1987), 62, 64.

[5] Fyodor Dostoevsky, *Diary of a Writer* (Santa Barbara and Salt Lake City, 1979), 142.

[6] *Selected Letters of Fyodor Dostoevsky*, ed. Joseph Frank and David I. Goldstein, trans. Andrew McAndrew (New Brunswick, N.J., 1987), 369.

exist in our society, given the circumstances under which our society was in general formed."

In the light of these admissions, one can see how relatively easy it has been to convict Dostoevsky of historical falsification, distortion, and even defamation of the revolutionary movement in *The Devils*. Moreover, since the book was admittedly inspired by his detestation of the doctrines of Russian Nihilism—whose final noxious consequences he saw embodied in the actions of Nechaev and his group—it is scarcely surprising that sympathizers with the radicals at the time (not to mention their latter-day descendants) should have attacked the book on these grounds. If one replies to these attacks by the argument that Dostoevsky never intended his work to be a documentary account of the Nechaev affair, it can be legitimately retorted that he opens himself to such criticism by having drawn so extensively on the well-known history for his narrative. Such a retort is unquestionably telling; but, at the same time, it raises the larger issue of the relation of novels as a whole to the "reality" they employ as their source.

It is perfectly obvious that no novel, in view of the inevitable stylization involved in the creation of any work of art, is immune to the type of criticism leveled against Dostoevsky. No novel, when stringently compared to its sources, can escape the indictment of distortion or falsification in some way. Indeed, it was this very conviction of the inevitable betrayal of history by art that persuaded so great a historical novelist as Alessandro Manzoni to abandon the form.[7] But so radical a resolution of the problem has not been generally accepted, and critics have contented themselves, in relation to such writers as Scott and Balzac, with demanding only a general conformation to the contours of historical reality rather than an unattainable accuracy in every detail of interpretation and every trait of character. As long as the novelist revealed essential aspects of the period or the event he was dealing with, and did not violate the limits of historical verisimilitude and psychological probability, the question of accuracy in the strict sense became comparatively irrelevant. Nobody criticizes Scott because *Ivanhoe* does not conform in every respect to our present knowledge of the Middle Ages, or *The Talisman* to the latest results of researches about the Crusades. No one bothers to attack Balzac because the characters of *Les Illusions perdues*, based on well-known nineteenth century French literary and cultural celebrities, are reflected through the distorting prism of Balzac's magnifying imagination. Nobody thinks it a major criticism of *War and Peace* that so impressive and powerful a personality as Napoleon is turned into a pathetic and self-indulgent little puppet.

All this is merely to argue that what has become true for Scott, Balzac,

---

[7] See Alessandro Manzoni, *On the Historical Novel*, trans. Sandra Bermann (Lincoln, Neb., 1984). This is a translation, with a valuable introduction by the translator, of Manzoni's *Del Romanzo Storico* (1850). Manzoni wrote one of the finest of all historical novels, *I Promessi Sposi* (The Betrothed).

and Tolstoy should also begin to be the case for Dostoevsky. It is time to stop dwelling on the inevitable discrepancies between the historical record and the novel, and to pose the question of "accuracy" in the broad sense that has become customary for other works of the same genre. Is there anything in *The Devils* that unconscionably violates historical verisimilitude and psychological and moral probability when compared to the materials that Dostoevsky employed?

3

At first sight, no example one could choose would seem to be more detrimental to Dostoevsky than that of Peter Verkhovensky. Peter plays the role in the novel taken by Nechaev in actuality; and we know that Dostoevsky treated this character with the utmost freedom. In a letter to Katkov (October 20, 1870), Dostoevsky remarks that he had no special knowledge of the case other than public accounts, and would not have used such special knowledge even if he had had it. "Even if I did know, I would not start in to copy. I take only the accomplished fact. My fantasy may diverge in the greatest degree from what actually occurred and my Peter Verkhovensky may not at all resemble Nechaev, but I believe that the impression in my mind will form the image of the kind of character, the type, which corresponds to this crime."[8] Indeed, Dostoevsky's notes reveal that the conception of Peter Verkhovensky changed, in the course of composition, from that of a passionate, romantic figure à la Lermontov to one who resembles, at least externally, the fast-talking, ingratiating impostor of Gogol's *Revizor*. Here, if anywhere, one would suppose that Dostoevsky's bitter enmity toward the radicals would carry him past the bounds of the permissible manipulation of his materials.

To judge this question, we are fortunate in possessing a real-life portrait of Nechaev in action painted by no less a pen than that of Bakunin himself—a witness who knew Nechaev intimately, and whose judgment would not be affected by any a priori prejudices. The letter was written by Bakunin to a friend in Switzerland (July 24, 1870) to warn him against Bakunin's erstwhile protégé. The letter appears to be so little known, and is so vivid and fascinating, that it is worth quoting in extenso. "My dear friend," Bakunin writes,[9]

> I have just learned that Nechaev has called on you and that you hastened to give him the address of our friends (M and his wife). I conclude that the two letters by which O and I warned you, and begged you to turn him away, arrived

[8] *Selected Letters of Fyodor Dostoevsky*, 340.

[9] *Correspondence de Michel Bakounine, 1860–1874*, ed. M. Dragomanov, trans. Marie Stromberg (Paris, 1896). Most of the letters were originally written in Russian, but Bakunin wrote this one directly in French. The translation into English is my own.

too late; and, without any exaggeration, I consider the result of this delay a veritable misfortune. It may seem strange to you that we advise you to turn away a man to whom we have given letters of recommendation addressed to you and written in the warmest terms. But those letters date from the month of May; and since then we have been obliged to admit the existence of matters so grave that they have forced us to break all our relations with N. And, at the risk of appearing inconsistent and light-headed in your eyes, we have thought it our sacred duty to warn you and to put you on your guard against him. Now I shall try to explain briefly the reasons for the change.

It remains perfectly true that N is the man most persecuted by the Russian government, which has covered the continent of Europe with a cloud of spies seeking him in all countries; it has asked for his extradition from both Germany and Switzerland. It is equally true that N is one of the most active and energetic men I have ever met. When it is a question of serving what he calls the cause, he does not hesitate; nothing stops him, and he is as merciless with himself as with all the others. This is the principal quality that attracted me, and that impelled me to seek an alliance with him for a good while. Some people assert that he is simply a crook—but this is a lie! He is a devoted fanatic, but, at the same time, a very dangerous fanatic, whose alliance cannot but be harmful for everybody. And here is why: at first he was part of a secret committee that really existed in Russia. The committee no longer exists; all its members have been arrested. N remains alone, and alone he constitutes what he calls the Committee. His organization in Russia having been decimated, he is trying to create a new one abroad. All this would be perfectly natural, legitimate, very useful—but the methods he uses are detestable. Very much struck by the catastrophe that has destroyed the secret organization in Russia, he has gradually succeeded in convincing himself that, to found a serious and indestructible organization, one must take as a foundation the tactics of Machiavelli and totally adopt the system of the Jesuits—violence as the body, falsehood as the soul.

Truth, mutual confidence, serious and strict solidarity exist only among a dozen individuals who form a *sanctum sanctorum* of the Society. All the rest must serve as a blind instrument, and as exploitable material in the hands of the dozen who are really united. It is allowed—and even ordered—to deceive all the others, to compromise them, to rob them, and even, if need be, to get rid of them—they are conspiratorial fodder. For example: you have received N, thanks to our letter of recommendation, you have partly given him your confidence, you have recommended him to your friends. . . . Here he is, transplanted in your world— and what will he do? First he will tell you a pack of lies to increase your sympathy and your confidence; but he will not stop there. The tepid sympathies of men who are devoted to the revolutionary cause only in part, and who, besides this cause, have other human interests such as love, friendship, family, social relations—these sympathies are not, in his eyes, a sufficient foundation, and in the name of the cause he will try to get a hold on you completely without your knowledge. To do this, he will spy on you and try to get possession of all your secrets; and in your absence, being alone in your room, he will open all your drawers and read all your correspondence. If a letter seems interesting to him, that is, compromising from any·point of view either for yourself or one of your friends, he will steal it and preserve it carefully as a document either against you or your friends. He has done this with O, with Tata, and with other friends—and when, at a general meeting, we accused him of this, he had the nerve to say—"Well, yes, that's our system. We consider as our enemies all those who are not with us *completely* and we have the duty to deceive and to compromise them." This means all those who are not convinced of their system, and have not agreed to apply it to themselves.

If you have presented him to a friend, his first concern will be to sow discord between the both of you by gossip and intrigue—in a word, to cause a quarrel. Your friend has a wife, a daughter; he will try to seduce them, to make them pregnant, in order to tear them away from official morality and to throw them into a forced revolutionary protest against society.

All personal ties, all friendship, all [gap in text] are considered by them as an evil, which they have the right to destroy because all this constitutes a force that, being outside the secret organization, diminishes the sole force of this latter. Don't tell me that I exaggerate: all this has been amply unraveled and proven. Seeing himself exposed, poor N is still so naive, so childish, despite his systematic perversity, that he thought it possible to convert me—he went so far as to implore me to develop this theory in a Russian journal that he proposed to establish. He has betrayed the confidence of us all, he has stolen our letters, compromised us terribly, in a word, behaved like a villain. His only excuse is his fanaticism! He is terribly ambitious without knowing it, because he has ended by identifying the cause of the revolution with himself—but he is not an egoist in the usual sense of the word because he risks his life terribly, and leads the existence of a martyr full of privations and incredible activity. . . . His last project was nothing less than to set up a band of thieves and brigands in Switzerland, naturally with the aim of acquiring some revolutionary capital. I saved him by persuading him to leave Switzerland because he would certainly have been discovered, he and his gang, in a few weeks; he would have been lost, and all of us lost with him. . . .

Persuade M that the safety of his family demands that he break with them completely. He must keep N away from his family. Their system, their joy, is to seduce and corrupt young girls; in this way they control the whole family. I'm very sorry that they learned the address of M because *they would be capable of denouncing him* [italics in text]. Didn't they dare admit to me openly, in the presence of a witness, that the denunciation of a member—devoted or only partly devoted—is one of the means whose usage they consider quite legitimate and sometimes useful? To get possession of the secrets of a person or his family, so as to hold them in the palm of their hand, is their principal means. I'm so frightened at their knowing M's address that I beg him to change his lodgings secretly, so that they won't discover him.

After perusing such a document, it is difficult to have much patience with those numerous critics who have so insouciantly accused Dostoevsky of willful slander and distortion. It is true that Dostoevsky does not show Peter Verkhovensky leading "the existence of a martyr full of privations"; but, as we shall see in a moment, this is because Dostoevsky allowed Peter to realize certain conspiratorial possibilities of which Nechaev dreamed but could not himself put into practice. Nor does Dostoevsky fail to indicate in Peter—through of course not very prominently—what Bakunin, in another letter (November 2, 1872), called Nechaev's "genuine ache for the people's age-long suffering." " 'Listen' [Peter says to Stavrogin]. 'I've seen a child six years old leading home his drunken mother, while she swore at him with foul words. Do you suppose I am glad of that? When it's in our hands, maybe we'll mend things' " (428).

But Nechaev's "ache" for the people's sufferings did not excuse his misdeeds even in the eyes of most of his revolutionary comrades; and there is not a single action of Peter Verkhovensky that Nechaev did not perform, or would not have performed if given the chance.

4

Just as Dostoevsky, in my opinion, does not transgress the bounds of verisimilitude in his portrait of Peter Verkhovensky, neither does he do so in the entire political intrigue of the book. To be sure, he does not limit himself to the actual proportions and dimensions of the events leading up to the murder of Ivanov (this would have given him only a tale of petty and futile agitation among a handful of students), any more than he tried to give a photographic picture of the purely private personality and character of Nechaev. True to his method of "fantastic realism," however, Dostoevsky based his political plot on a dramatic actualization of the tactics and aims of the Nechaev movement.

What Dostoevsky meant by this much-misunderstood term "fantastic realism" was that, in every case, his imagination began to operate on what he sensed to be the moral and psychic dilemmas of Russian life caused by the predominance among the educated class of "radical"—that is, progressive—Western European ideas and convictions in their Russian guise. His work was "realistic" because it started from this controlling historical-social ideological framework and used it as a guide in the operation of his artistic intuition. But it was also "fantastic" in the sense of allowing itself complete freedom to dramatize the ultimate and most extreme human consequences of such ideas in action, and to potentiate them in forms that rarely if ever appeared elsewhere with such sharply delineated typicality.

What distinguishes *The Devils* from his other works, however, is that, as it were, so much of Dostoevsky's usual imaginative labors was already performed for him in advance.

For the imagination displayed in the Bakunin-Nechaev propaganda (the part of the two men in the composition of these documents is still a matter of dispute) matched and even surpassed Dostoevsky's own in its implacable logic; it coldly drew all the bloodcurdling conclusions that, as Dostoevsky had predicted earlier in the 1860s, would be the inevitable outcome of a morality of Utilitarian egoism allied to the purpose of provoking a violent revolution. And thus, in *The Devils*, Dostoevsky had merely to give artistic life to what he found already expressed as the aims and ambitions of the Nechaev movement—not its "history" in the strict sense, but its myth of itself, the fantastic self-image that it tried to create for the world. Dostoevsky gathered this self-image primarily from two sources: the famous (or infamous) *Catechism of a Revolutionary*—a small book written in code and printed in Latin script—which contained the precepts of what Bakunin called Nechaev's "system"; and the Bakunin-Nechaev propaganda issued in the spring and summer of 1869. Let us see in a little more detail what use Dostoevsky made of this material.

The power of Peter Verkhovensky in *The Devils* is based on his claim to be the representative of a secret, worldwide, revolutionary organization situated vaguely in Europe, and which he had contacted in Switzerland. Nechaev in fact carried credentials attesting that he was representative no. 2771 of the "Russian Section of the World Revolutionary Alliance"; and these credentials, signed by Bakunin, were also stamped with the seal of the "Central Committee" of a "European Revolutionary Alliance." Neither of these organizations existed anywhere except in the vast reaches of Bakunin's conspiratorial imagination. It is doubtful whether Nechaev—who had presented himself to Bakunin as the representative of an equally fictitious revolutionary committee of Russian students—really placed much faith in the power or efficacity of these bodies. But he was perfectly content to use the aura of Bakunin's prestige, and the looming shadow of these all-powerful organizations, to impress his dupes in Moscow. To reinforce his authority, he once arrived at a meeting of his group with a stranger (an inoffensive visiting student from Petersburg) whom he introduced as a member of the "Central Committee," and who sat silently all through the session taking notes. Present at the meeting at Virginsky's in *The Devils* is also "a young artillery officer who . . . scarcely taking any part in the conversation, continually made notes in his notebook" (399). Peter Verkhovensky, however, supplements him by the more glamorous Stavrogin, whom he instructs to come to the meeting as "one of the original members from abroad, who knows the most important secrets—that's your role" (393).

Nechaev's career almost from the very start is marked by a systematic use of falsehood and deceit, not only against the enemies of his cause but also toward his allies and followers. Such a policy was consciously affirmed as a principle in the *Catechism*, which states that "the degree of friendship, of devotion, and of other obligations toward . . . a comrade is measured only by his degree of utility in the practical work of revolutionary pan-destruction." Peter Verkhovensky only reveals the "secrets" of his activity—namely, that there really are no "secrets," and that he is acting entirely on his own—to Stavrogin, who is the key to his revolutionary plan; all the rest of his followers he considers "raw material," who are to be used and manipulated as he sees fit for the good of the cause. Such manipulation was foreseen in the paragraph of the *Catechism* devoted to "revolutionary chatterers" (a perfect description of the group at Virginsky's), who were to be "pushed and involved without ceasing into political and dangerous manifestations, whose result will be to make the majority disappear, while some among them will become revolutionaries."

It is in accordance with this ruthless application of the principle of utility that Nechaev disposed of Ivanov; and Dostoevsky's interpretation of the crime, whose motives continue to remain obscure, in no way violates the evidence. Whether Nechaev really believed that Ivanov would betray the underground group, or whether, as Dostoevsky was convinced, he wished to gain a hold on his followers by involving them in a crime against a troublesome dissident, still remains a mystery to this day. The Old Bolshevik and one-time editor of *Izvestia* Yuri Steklov, in his massive biography of Bakunin, has carefully reviewed all the material on this point; and he comes to the same conclusion as Dostoevsky.

To silence Ivanov, Steklov writes, Nechaev had the choice either of abandoning his dictatorial methods, or "carrying to its extreme logical conclusion his characteristic system of terror and deceit, kill Ivanov, and in this way intimidate the remaining members of his organization by linking them together in a bloody crime. Nechaev chose the second path, along which he was impelled by the logic of his chosen method of action on the one hand and, on the other, by his stubborn fanaticism and confidence in his great mission."[10]

Verkhovensky arrives in the provincial town where the novel is set as the companion of the aristocratic Stavrogin, and also as an intimate of the equally wealthy Drozdov family. He has learned the secret of Stavrogin's perverse marriage to Marya Lebyadkina, and also of Liza Tushin's infatuation with Stavrogin. Whether by intimidation or by catering to Stavro-

[10] Yuri Steklov, *Mikhail Aleksandrovich Bakunin, Ego zhizn i deyatelnost*, 4 vols. (Moscow, 1916–1927), 3:491–92. A copy of the *Catechism of the Revolutionary* is transcribed by Steklov (468–73). All my quotations from the Bakunin-Nechaev propaganda are also found in Steklov's chapters (418–550).

gin's lusts, he hopes to use this knowledge to gain a hold over Stavrogin and exploit him for revolutionary purposes. Such maneuvers are completely in conformity with the doctrines of the *Catechism*, which recognize that "with the aim of implacable destruction a revolutionary may, and often must, live in the midst of society pretending to be quite different from what he really is." And the aim of this disguise is, as with Peter Verkhovensky, to gain power over "the great number of highly placed animals who, by their position, are rich and have relations." Such dupes "must be exploited in every possible way, circumvented, confused, and, by acquiring their dirty secrets, be turned into our slaves. In this manner their power, their relations, their influence, and their riches will become an inexhaustible treasure and an invaluable aid in our various enterprises."

The same tactics are used by Peter Verkhovensky to gain control over the von Lembkes, whom he also exploits for his revolutionary aims. Through Stavrogin, Peter obtains a letter of introduction to Yulia Mikhailovna from "a very important old lady in Petersburg, whose husband was one of the most distinguished old dignitaries in the capital." Peter himself is rumored to have gained the approbation of certain mysterious and powerful government personages by having repented of his past sins and "mentioned certain names" (215). It would have been perfectly consistent for Nechaev to have sacrificed one or two comrades for the purpose of infiltrating the higher spheres; indeed such betrayal, as he admitted to Bakunin, was part of his "system."

Once entrenched in Yulia Mikhailovna's good graces, Peter encourages the giddy lady, who liked to flirt with "liberal" ideas, into believing that, with his help, she could scale the dizziest social heights and save Russia from disaster at the same time. "To discover the plot, to receive the gratitude of the government, to enter on a brilliant career, to influence the young 'by kindness,' and to restrain them from extremes—all these dreams existed side by side in her fantastic brain" (352). Revolutionaries, the *Catechism* declares, should conspire with liberals "on the basis of their own program, pretending to follow them blindly" but actually compromising them so that they can be "used to provoke disturbances in the State." Peter takes over Yulia Mikhailovna's innocent liberal "fête" for the benefit of the governesses of the province in exact accordance with these instructions, and turns it into a riotous manifestation of protest against the government.

Peter's strategy with the dim-witted and bewildered Russo-German von Lembke, over whom he gains a hold both through Yulia Mikhailovna and through flattering his literary vanity, is directed toward attaining the same goal by different means. With him, Peter plays the agent provocateur; he spurs von Lembke on to harsh suppression of signs of unrest among the Shpigulin workers, and taxes von Lembke with being "too soft" and "liberal" in the performance of his gubernatorial duties. "But this has to be handled in the good old way," Peter jovially tells the hesitant von Lembke. "They ought to be flogged, every one of them; that would be the end of it." Peter's metamorphosis into an advocate of the "good old days" is justified by a passage in the *Catechism* requiring the revolutionary "to aid the growth of every calamity and every evil, which must, at last, exhaust the patience of the people and force them into a general uprising." It can also be linked to two of the Bakunin-Nechaev pamphlets supposedly issued by the "Descendants of Rurik and the Noble's Revolutionary Committee." These pamphlets preached the most outrageously reactionary sentiments, and were intended to stir up right-wing, oligarchical opposition to tsarist autocracy; they also probaby suggested Peter's friendship with the retired Colonel Gaganov—who challenges Stavrogin to a duel—and who resigned from the army partly because he "suddenly felt himself personally insulted by the proclamation" of the liberation of the serfs. Gaganov is described, significantly, as a person who "belonged to that strange section of the nobility, still surviving in Russia, who set an extreme value on their pure and ancient lineage" (that is, "the descendants of Rurik").

5

Sources and parallels for every other political-ideological feature of *The Devils*, even those that seem the most extravagant and the least credible, can also be found either in the Bakunin-Nechaev propaganda or in other easily identifiable material linked with the radical agitation of the 1860s.

Peter Verkhovensky's use of Fedka the convict as the executing arm of the revolution brings to life (rather feebly, it is true) the advice given in the *Catechism* for the revolutionaries to unite "with the fierce world of the bandits," who are "the sole and genuine revolutionaries in Russia." Coupled with this Romantic glorification of the fearsome bandit of Russian folklore, the propaganda is also filled with bloodcurdling exhortations and apocalyptic images of total destruction.

> We must dedicate ourselves to wholehearted destruction, continuous, unflagging, unslackening, until none of the existing social forms remain to be destroyed. . . .
> "Poison, the knife, the noose. . . . The revolution sanctifies everything in this battle."

Peter Verkhovensky only echoes such passages when he cries: " 'We shall proclaim destruction . . . why? why? well, because it is such a fascinating little idea! . . . Every scurvy "group" will be of use. I'll find you fellows so eager in these groups that they'll be glad to shoot and will be grateful for the honor. . . . There's going to be such an upheaval as the world has never seen before' " (428).

Nothing is more striking, in this Bakunin-Nechaev propaganda, than its total negativism, the complete absence of any positive aim or goal that would justify the horrors it contemplates. Such a positive aim, in any specific sense, is outlawed on principle as a historical impossibility, which must remain wrapped in the Messianic obscurity of the future. "Since the existing generation," we read, "is itself exposed to the influence of those loathsome social conditions against which it is revolting, to this generation cannot belong the work of construction. This belongs to those pure forces that will be formed in the day of renovation." This negativism helps to explain why Peter Verkhovensky sets himself off so sharply from "Socialists" such as Shigalov, who *do* worry about the form of the future existing social order, and why, as a true revolutionary, Peter dedicates himself only to the work of uprooting the existing moral-social norms.

"But one or two generations of vice are essential now," he tells Stavrogin; "monstrous, abject vice by which a man is transformed into a loathsome, cruel, egoistic reptile. . . . I am not contradicting myself, I am only contradicting the philanthropists and Shigalovism, not myself! I am a scoundrel, not a Socialist!" (428). Marx and Engels, it should be mentioned, thoroughly confirmed Dostoevsky's distinction on this point; and the Bakunin-Nechaev propaganda was one of the weapons they used to evict Bakunin and his followers from the First International. "These all-destroying anarchists," they wrote severely, "who wish to reduce everything to amorphousness in order to replace morality by anarchy, carry bourgeois immorality to its final extreme."[11]

Peter Verkhovensky's contemptuous indifference to Socialism and Socialist theory is well brought out by his behavior at the "birthday party" at Virginsky's; and this indifference reflects a constant keynote in the Bakunin-Nechaev writings. "The modest and far too cautious formation of secret societies, without any overtly practical consequences, is, in our eyes, nothing more than a childish game, ludicrous and loathsome." Peter is a little more tactful, but he does not conceal his inexpressible boredom.

" 'You see, gentlemen'—he raised his eyes a trifle—'to my mind all these books, Fourier, Cabet, all this talk about the right to work and Shigalov's theories—are all like novels of which one can write a hundred thousand—an aesthetic entertainment' " (412).

Peter's sarcasm exactly duplicates the tone of contempt that one can find in the leaflets on the same subject. "In the Cossack groups formed by Vassili Usom in Astrakhan at the time of Stenka Razin," one leaflet declares, "the ideal goal of social equality was achieved in an immeasurably superior

---

[11] The commission appointed by the First International to investigate the Nechaev affair included Marx and Engels. Its report is printed in their works, Karl Marx and Friedrich Engels, *Werke*, 39 vols. (Berlin, 1956–), 18:396–441; my quotation from 426.

fashion to the phalansteries of Fourier, the institutions of Cabet, Louis Blanc and other learned Socialists, better even than in the associations of Chernyshevsky."

6

Even when Dostoevsky has not been accused of misrepresenting the Nechaev affair, he has invariably been charged with giving a misleading picture in *The Devils* of the Russian radical movement as a whole. Nechaev was incontestably an isolated phenomenon among the radical groups of the 1860s, and his systematic Machiavellianism was alien to the other major organizations of the radical intelligentsia (though it appeared embryonically here and there all the same). In point of fact, however, Dostoevsky never tries to give any other impression.

Peter Verkhovensky's relations with the members and sympathizers of his underground organization are a continual struggle to overcome their opposition and mistrust. Nobody at the meeting really agrees with Verkhovensky, but he browbeats them into submission by playing on their vanity and curiosity; all agree to go "full steam ahead" in order to hear his mysterious "communication" from the all-powerful organization he claims to represent. Just before Shatov's murder even the members of Verkhovensky's inner group are panic-stricken at what has occurred—the fire, the various murders, the riots and disorders—and decide that, unless Verkhovensky gives them a "categorical explanation," they will "dissolve the quintet . . . and found instead a new secret society 'for the propaganda of ideas on their own and on the basis of democracy and equality' " (554). Shigalov, at the last moment, refuses to have anything to do with the murder as a matter of principle; Virginsky never stops protesting even while it is taking place. It is quite clear that, however much Dostoevsky caricatures them as people, the members of the "quintet" do not believe in systematic amorality and universal destruction as panaceas for the ills of the Russian social order.

No character in *The Devils* has aroused more comment and more indignation than Shigalov, whom Dostoevsky originally calls by the name of V. A. Zaitsev in his notes. This radical publicist was distinguished among his confrères by his extreme theoretical élitism and his ill-starred defense of Negro slavery on the basis of Social Darwinism; he believed that the black race would be wiped out in the struggle for life unless protected by their slavelords. Shigalov too is an honest democratic radical who ends up, much to his dismay, favoring the "slavery" of the masses to an omnipotent radical élite. "I am perplexed by my own data and my conclusion is in direct contradiction of the original idea from which I start. . . . Starting from unlimited freedom, I arrive at unlimited despotism" (409). A "lame teacher" who has read his manuscript explains his idea, whose biological basis is obvious. "Shigalov suggests . . . the division of mankind into two unequal parts. One-tenth enjoys absolute liberty and unbounded power over the other nine-tenths. The others have to give up all individuality and become, so to speak, a herd, and, through boundless submission, will by a series of regenerations attain primeval innocence, something like the Garden of Eden" (410–11).

One might imagine that Dostoevsky here has simply let his satirical fantasy run wild, and that there would be no source whatever for Shigalov's plan to create "the earthly Paradise" by selective Socialist breeding. No such source can be found in Zaitsev, to be sure; but it *can* be found in the writings of Peter Tkachev, once a contributor to Dostoevsky's magazine *Vremya* (Time), and who was associated with Nechaev in agitation among the Petersburg students in 1869. Like Zaitsev much influenced by Social Darwinism, Tkachev believed that justice could not be achieved except in a world of total equality. But this, he wrote, "must by no means be confused with political or legal or even economic equality"; it meant "an *organic, physiological* equality conditioned by the same education and the same living standards" (italics added). For Tkachev, such equality was "the final and only possible aim of human life . . . the supreme criterion of historical and social progress."[12] Dostoevsky was surely parodying Tkachev when Peter Verkhovensky exclaims: "Shigalov is a man of genius [because] he's discovered 'equality.' "

> Great Intellects cannot help being despots and they've always done more harm than good. . . . Cicero will have his tongue cut out, Copernicus will have his eyes put out. Shakespeare will be stoned—that's Shigalovism! Slaves must be equal: there has never been either freedom or equality without despotism, but in the herd there's bound to be equality and that's Shigalovism! (424–25)

It would be possible to continue this demonstration with further examples, drawn not so much from the Nechaev affair as from the general social history of the period. For example, Peter's mad plan to seize power by turning Stavrogin into Ivan the tsarevich, the pretender to the throne of the tsar, is manifestly inspired by the Russian folk tradition that had impelled all the leaders of peasant uprisings in Russian history to claim to be the rightful and legitimate tsar. This tradition of peasant obedience to the tsar, whatever their hatred of the land-owning class, had been exploited without much success by the radicals of the 1860s, particularly during the Polish rebellion; and there is a mocking reference to such attempts in Dostoevsky's notes. But the evidence already given should be enough to show the procedure that Dostoevsky used, and the extent to which the usual accusations against him must be qualified.

[12] Cited in Franco Venturi, *Roots of Revolution*, trans. Frances Haskell (New York, 1960), 399.

Nothing in *The Devils* on the political level (the same is true for the cultural, though this is not the place to argue the point) is simply invented out of whole cloth. Either Dostoevsky dramatizes the "fantasy" of the Nechaev movement's own dreams and hopes, or he takes equally extreme and morally dubious events of a similar complexion and works them into his canvas. In so doing, he succeeded in creating the most brilliant and haunting work ever written about the moral quagmires, and the possibilities for self-betrayal of the highest principles, which—as we have learned most recently from Solzhenitsyn—continue to dog the destiny of "the Revolution."

CHAPTER TWELVE

Approaches to the *Diary of a Writer*

1

THE NAME Dostoevsky, for an average Western reader, is apt to evoke the figure of a tormented genius existing on the edge of madness and creating novels of hallucinatory power out of the fantasies of his semidemented psyche. The very last thing one would ordinarily associate with Dostoevsky is the practice of such a mundane activity as journalism. And yet a good part of Dostoevsky's life was devoted to writing of this kind; even more, during the years when he single-handedly wrote and published his *Diary of a Writer* (a unique, one-man monthly magazine) he was the most successful publicist ever to have appeared on the Russian scene. The *Diary of a Writer* managed to acquire a hitherto unheard-of number of subscribers, and to evoke an unprecedented public response. Indeed, according to one well-informed observer—Elena A. Stakenschneider, a good friend of Dostoevsky's who kept a sharp eye on Russian cultural life—the enormous fame he acquired in his later years was far more attributable to his *Diary* than to any other single factor. "Dostoevsky's fame," she writes in her own far more personal *Diary*, "was not caused by his prison sentence, not by *The House of the Dead*, not even by his novels—at least not primarily by them—but by the *Diary of a Writer*. It was the *Diary* that made his name known to all of Russia, made him the teacher and idol of the youth, yes, and not only the youth but all those tortured by the questions that Heine called 'accursed.' "[1]

It may seem strange, at first sight, that a great creative artist like Dostoevsky should have turned his hand to journalism at the very height of his creative career (the *Diary of a Writer* occupied Dostoevsky between the composition of *A Raw Youth* and *The Brothers Karamazov*, and he resumed its publication after the *Karamazov* volume was completed). But in point of fact, the boundaries between literature and journalism have always been more fluid in Russia than in Western European countries. Why this should be so has been well explained by Nikolay Chernyshevsky,

[1] *F. M. Dostoevsky v Vospominanyakh Sovremmenikov*, ed. A. S. Dolinin, 2 vols. (Moscow, 1964), 2:307–8.

the major spokesman for the radical democrats of the 1860s, whose ideas Dostoevsky furiously opposed but whose observation in this instance he would certainly have accepted:

> In countries where intellectual and social life has attained a high level of development there exists, if one may say so, a division of labor among the various branches of intellectual activity, of which we [Russians] know only one—literature. . . . As things stand, [Russian] literature absorbs virtually the entire intellectual life of the people, and for that reason it bears the duty of occupying itself with such interests which in other countries, so to say, have come under the special management of other kinds of intellectual activity. . . . That which Dickens says in England is also said, apart from him and the other novelists, by philosophers, jurists, publicists, economists, etc., etc. With us, apart from novelists, no one talks about subjects which comprise the subject of their stories.[2]

The reason for this situation, of course, was the severe censorship exercised by the tsarist government on all discussion of social-political issues. (The Soviet régime, until the recent proclamation of *glasnost* by Mikhail Gorbachev, had imposed even more rigid controls). It was only in literature and literary criticism that such problems could be broached at all; hence the Russian novel and even Russian poetry became organs of public opinion and public expression to a much greater extent than elsewhere. A Russian writer, in most cases, felt himself willy-nilly to be performing an important public task and not merely giving utterance to a personal reaction about the universe. As a result, he made no sharp separation between his role as man and citizen and his vocation as an artist; it would be difficult to find equivalents in Russian literature of the early and mid-nineteenth century for the attitudes of a Flaubert or a Mallarmé, who looked on the creation of Art as the supreme end of existence and considered all other human activities as subordinate or insignificant. Dostoevsky, as a Russian writer, thus felt no incongruity whatever—neither did Tolstoy, nor does Solzhenitsyn at present—in moving from the role of novelist to that of publicist and journalist, and speaking out on the great public questions of his day. Nothing could be more false than to see him in the terms mentioned earlier, that is, as a genius creating solely out of his own inner life, and as obsessed exclusively with and by his own personal fantasies. For Dostoevsky's novels are steeped in the social-cultural reality of his time, and cannot really be understood unless we grasp his relation to such reality and his ideas about it. For this purpose the *Diary of a Writer* is indispensable; and it should be far better known than it is and far more widely read.

[2] Cited in Richard Pipes, *Russia Under the Old Régime* (New York, 1974), 278–79.

2

Dostoevsky's activity as a journalist began almost from the very beginning of his literary career. Shortly after the publication of his first novel, *Poor Folk* (1845), and his sudden leap from obscurity to literary fame, he earned a little extra cash by writing four feuilletons for a local newspaper, the *St. Petersburg Gazette*. The feuilleton was simply a column of a certain length, written in a free and informal style, and dealing with some topic designed to interest the reader. Dostoevsky manages to fill the bill very satisfactorily in these early articles, which contain depictions of Petersburg life and landscape, sketches of various social types, and comments on the latest cultural events. Everything seems to be very casual and haphazard; but in fact the role assumed by Dostoevsky—that of the Petersburg *flâneur*, idly walking through the streets and chatting with his readers about everything that happens to meet his gaze—also allows him to insinuate a good deal of serious social commentary. Indeed, the manner and tone of these early articles anticipates that of the *Diary of a Writer* to a marked degree; and in launching the *Diary* Dostoevsky was only renewing contact with one phase of his own past.

As is well known, Dostoevsky was arrested as a revolutionary conspirator (with some justification) in 1848, and sent to serve a term of four years in a Siberian prison camp. The effect of this sentence on his future life and career was incalculable, and it is from this period that he dated what he later called—in one of the most important articles of his *Diary*—"the regeneration of my convictions." It is worth noting, though, that Dostoevsky also approached his prison experiences with the attitude of an inveterate journalist. Nobody in Russia had ever written a book describing life in a prison camp and portraying its inhabitants, who for the most part came from the Russian peasantry. Despite the hardships of his own lot, which brought on his first attack of epilepsy—a disease from which he suffered for the remainder of his life—Dostoevsky found time to keep a little notebook, sewn together from scraps of paper, in which he jotted down peasant linguistic idioms and key words and phrases that would remind him of stories he had heard and incidents he had witnessed. And the book he eventually wrote about these prison camp years, *The House of the Dead*, is not a novel but a series of journalistic sketches that, for the first time, threw open the barred gates of the prison stockades and gave the Russian public a penetrating glimpse into the pullulating life going on inside. With this book Dostoevsky initiated a minor tradition of Russian literature, which includes such muckraking works as Chekhov's *Sakhalin Island* and to which Solzhenitsyn has recently made the most impressive and massive contribution with his overwhelming *Gulag Archipelago*.

On returning to European Russia in 1860, Dostoevsky immediately plunged into the thick of the journalistic fray. With his older brother, Mikhail, he founded and edited two magazines, *Vremya* (Time) and *Epokha* (Epoch), which, in the format of what the Russians call "thick" journals, contained both literary contributions and articles dealing with the most pressing issues of social and political life so far as these could be discussed at all (it is astonishing how much *was* discussed in those years by comparison with the period of established Communist hegemony). Dostoevsky's name could not legally appear on the masthead because he was an ex-convict; but as unofficial editor-in-chief he read all of the contributions, and would often comment on them in unsigned editorial notes when he thought a point had to be clarified or the position of the magazine made explicit. Major works of his own (*The House of the Dead, The Insulted and Injured, Notes from Underground*) also appeared in these journals, adding considerably to their prestige and their reader appeal. In addition, Dostoevsky wrote a good many pages on literary topics as well as on questions of current interest that demonstrated his skill and vigor as a polemicist.

It was in the articles he wrote for *Vremya* that Dostoevsky first began to express some of the sociopolitical ideas that, in a more impassioned and apocalyptic style, he was later to popularize in his *Diary of a Writer*. Here, for the first time, he openly gave voice to his conviction that the Western world was doomed to destruction, and that it was the future mission of Russia to harmonize the conflicts of competing European nationalisms within a new and pan-human world order. Such Messianic hopes were not by any means original with Dostoevsky; they can be found uttered much earlier in Russian speculations about the possible world-historical significance of the grandiose Russian Empire. Alexandre Koyré has pointed out that, as far back as the 1820s, it had been suggested that Russia would produce "its *own* civilization, a civilization higher and more perfect, which [would] be, at the same time, the culmination of the entire historical evolution of the West."[3] The same Messianic idea later appears in some of the articles of Vissarion Belinsky, the most important critic and publicist of the 1840s, who hailed Dostoevsky's first novel as a masterpiece and exercised an enormous personal influence on him as well as on Russian culture as a whole. But if Dostoevsky picked up this idea of Russia's pan-human world mission from Belinsky and others, nowhere was it preached with such flaming ardor, or supported with more vivid and evocative eloquence, than in the pages of Dostoevsky's *Diary*.

Dostoevsky's journalistic bent displayed itself not only in his indefatigable zeal as editor, critic, and commentator, but also by a series of scintil-

[3] Alexandre Koyré, *La Philosophie et le problème nationale en Russie au debut du XIX siècle* (Paris, 1929), 209.

lating travel sketches (*Winter Notes on Summer Impressions*) that he wrote in 1863 and published in several issues of *Vremya*. These *Winter Notes* convey his "impressions" of Europe after his first trip there in the spring and summer of 1862; and they anticipate the *Diary of a Writer* both in style and substance. Squarely in the foreground is Dostoevsky himself, making no pretense at being objective or informative, but describing his frequently irreverent reactions to the "wonders" of European culture that every Russian was supposed abjectly to worship. Among such "wonders" was the Great Exhibition of 1851 in London, housed in the famous Crystal Palace built for the exhibition, and containing within its nineteen acres of floor space the triumphs of science and technology that were the supposed glory of European civilization. Dostoevsky describes all this in a chapter titled "Baal," which compares the scene explicitly to a vision of the Apocalypse come true. For what is being celebrated as the culmination and very last word of European civilization is, in his view, nothing but the triumph of the old flesh-god of materialism over the spiritual principle (Christianity) that had once inspired European mankind. "You feel that something definitive has been accomplished here—accomplished and completed," he writes. What has been completed is the life cycle of European civilization, which has nothing to offer mankind except what we now call "the affluent society" shorn of any moral ideal or higher goal. This is exactly how Dostoevsky would continue to see Europe and its world-historical role in the *Diary of a Writer*.

Dostoevsky's negative image of Europe, like that of all Russians, was merely the obverse of his positive sentiments about his native country; and he does not fail, in *Winter Notes*, to instruct his readers as to what these sentiments are. In his chapter on Paris, where he evokes the specter of Socialism haunting the French bourgeoisie (as Marx and Engels had done thirteen years earlier in *The Communist Manifesto*), Dostoevsky shows himself to be by no means hostile to the Socialist ideal of a society based on "fraternity." Such a society, in the eyes of the ex-humanitarian radical Dostoevsky, is at least better than that of "Baal" and is unquestionably inspired by a moral ideal. But it is impossible for Western man to create such a society, Dostoevsky explains, because "fraternity" cannot simply be installed artificially; it must exist as a natural instinct somewhere deep in the sociocultural psyche of a nation or of a civilization. Far from feeling drawn to "fraternity," Western European man has developed a civilization based rather on the principle of extreme individualism and self-aggrandizement of the ego; and this wrecks all hope of ever being able to attain the Socialist dream.

"Fraternity" can only be realized, Dostoevsky writes, in a people where "the need for fraternal communion is part of human nature, where [one] is born with this need or has acquired it as a disposition over the course of many centuries." Dostoevsky had no need to spell out for his initial readers that he was here referring to the Russian people, who embodied this instinct for "fraternity" despite "the barbarous crudeness and ignorance that had taken root in them, despite the slavery of centuries and the invasions by other peoples." Such ideas, in the 1840s, would have been considered more or less as a Slavophile aberration; but by 1863 Russians of all political persuasions had begun to come round to accepting the Slavophile idealization of the peasant and to see peasant social institutions as based on a national instinct for "fraternity." Not only Dostoevsky but the revolutionary Alexander Herzen accepted such a view; and when Dostoevsky later outlined his conception of a peaceful and voluntary "Russian Socialism" in the *Diary of a Writer*, he was employing a term that Herzen had first coined and given currency among the left-wing youth.[4]

3

The demise of both *Vremya* and *Epokha* terminated Dostoevsky's journalistic output for the moment; luckily for Russian literature and for the world, he devoted himself exclusively to his novels for the remainder of the 1860s. This was the period when he produced, in rapid succession, *Crime and Punishment*, *The Idiot*, and *The Devils* (better known in English as *The Possessed*). All during this time, however, he never abandoned the idea of eventually returning to the journalistic arena; and even while hard at work on *Crime and Punishment*, he wrote his friend Baron Wrangel: "I have in mind a periodical publication, but not a journal. Useful and profitable. Perhaps I'll be able to get it under way next year."[5] Dostoevsky's eagerness to undertake such a publication was certainly augmented by having been forced to live abroad for four years (1867–1871) in order to escape his creditors. Writing as he did at night, he spent most of his day—as we know from the diary of his second wife, as well as from his letters—poring over Russian newspapers from the first page to the last, and pondering the significance of the seemingly endless parade of items that came within his ken. "In every issue of a newspaper," he writes in a letter, "you come across reports of the most actual and surprising facts. For our writers they are fantastic; and that's why they don't concern themselves with such matters; and yet they are our actuality because they are *facts*. Who will notice them, clarify them, and write them up? They occur every minute and every day,

---

[4] Of course what Herzen and Dostoevsky meant by this term differed considerably; but both accepted the idea that the Russian national character and "Socialism" possessed some special affinity. For Herzen's use of the term, see Andrzej Walicki, *The Slavophile Controversy*, trans. Hilda Andrews-Rusiecka (London, 1975), chap. 16.

[5] F. M. Dostoevsky, *Pisma*, ed. A. S. Dolinin, 4 vols. (Moscow, 1928–1969), 1:424.

and they are by no means *exceptional*. . . . We allow all of actuality in this way to slip by under our noses" (italics in text).[6]

Dostoevsky even worked some reflections on this subject into the text of *The Devils*. The ill-fated Lizaveta Nikolaevna, enamored of the supreme egotist Stavrogin and ultimately a sacrifice to his overwhelming vanity, toys with the idea, at the beginning of the novel, of publishing a unique kind of gazette or yearly almanac, and enlists the aid of the equally ill-fated Shatov to realize her plan. Her idea was not to collect everything, which would obviously be impossible, but for the editors "to confine themselves to a selection of events more or less characteristic of the moral life of the Russian people at the present moment. . . . Everything would be put in with a certain view, a special significance and intention, with an idea that would illuminate the facts looked at in the aggregate, as a whole. . . . It would be, so to say, a presentation of the spiritual, moral, inner life in Russia for a year." There can be little doubt that Lizaveta is here proposing the project that Dostoevsky cherished himself, and which later inspired his *Diary of a Writer*—though in the form of a monthly rather than a yearly publication.

What became the *Diary* first took shape after Dostoevsky returned from Europe in 1871, and once again, after *The Devils* had been completed, resumed his old occupation as a journalist. He agreed to accept the post of editor of a weekly called *Grazhdanin* (The Citizen), which was owned by a minor novelist and rather shady court favorite, Prince Meshchersky. Dostoevsky took his editorial responsibilities very seriously, and even went to the printing plant each week in order to read the final galleys; he also did a good deal of incidental writing to fill up gaps when this became necessary. Much of the weekly commentary on foreign affairs appears to have been from his pen, and selections from such commentary are included in at least one Russian edition of the *Diary of a Writer*. Strictly speaking, however, these articles do not form part of the *Diary*, though its first entries did appear in *Grazhdanin*. What Dostoevsky called his *Diary of a Writer* was a column published at irregular intervals under his own signature, which soon became one of the chief attractions of the journal. The articles collected in the *Diary* from the year 1873 all appeared in this weekly publication, and are the original nucleus of his later independent venture. The success of Dostoevsky's column was instantaneous, and even political opponents of *Grazhdanin* such as N. K. Mikhailovsky, the leading spokesman for the radical Populists, referred to it in quite laudatory terms.

Dostoevsky, however, soon found his editorship, though financially advantageous, burdensome both for personal and ideological reasons. Meshchersky did not allow Dostoevsky a free editorial hand as he had initially

[6] Ibid., 2:169–70.

promised; and the prince's own contributions, which Dostoevsky was forced not only to print but frequently to correct for style and grammar, took a much more reactionary position on current problems than Dostoevsky was willing to accept. Moreover, creative ideas for stories and novels also began to surface once again in his thoughts, and he bewails in his letters the impossibility of working on them while overwhelmed with editorial obligations. Dostoevsky thus resigned his post after about a year and turned to his next novel, *A Raw Youth*, which began to appear in 1875. During this very same year, he started to collect material for the publication he had been dreaming of since the mid-1860s—his *Diary of a Writer*. In December, he requested permission to publish such a journal from the government agency in charge of the press. "I desire to give an account in it," he said, "of all the impressions I have really experienced as a Russian writer, an account of everything I have seen, heard and read." It was to be issued in monthly installments, to cost twenty kopeks a copy, and be available to subscribers at two rubles a year. Dostoevsky's energetic and practical second wife had by this time organized the publication of his novels as a family enterprise, and it was the Dostoevskys themselves who were the sole owners and publishers of the new periodical. The first issue appeared in January 1876, and its enormous success—approximately eight thousand copies of each number were soon being sold—established the foundation of the relative affluence that Dostoevsky was able to enjoy in these last five years of his life (he died in 1881).

4

The *Diary of a Writer* is a book of over a thousand pages, and filled with a bewildering variety of material. It is hardly possible, in the course of this brief introduction, to comment on all its multiple facets, or to do more than supply the prospective reader with a few indications of its overflowing richness. What may be useful is to suggest some of the ways in which it can be read, some of the alternative itineraries that, as in a modern "aleatory" novel, the reader may follow through its pages to enrich his knowledge of Dostoevsky and to satisfy particular tastes and interests.

The first and most obvious path is that running between the various short stories that Dostoevsky inserted into his *Diary*. One of the editorial principles he followed unswervingly was to offer his readers as much variety as possible; and he did not wish them to subsist on a steady diet of topical articles alone. Hence there is already a satirical grotesque, "Bobok," among the 1873 entries, and the more famous "A Christmas Tree and a Wedding" in the first issue of the new series (January 1876). A few months later, in March, there is the sketch of an old woman, "The Centenarian," who died peacefully and serenely while on a visit to one of her granddaughters living in the back of her husband's shop with a brood of children. In November there is the much more ambitious "The Meek One: A Fantastic Story," one of the short masterpieces of Dostoevsky's last period. This consists entirely of the interior monologue of a bereaved husband keeping a vigil at the bier of his dead wife, who had committed suicide by leaping out of a window clutching an icon. And finally, in April 1877, "The Dream of a Ridiculous Man: A Fantastic Story," which is Dostoevsky's first and only attempt (and a brilliantly haunting one it is!) at a Utopian tale of life on another planet, which turns into an anti-Utopia when the denizen of "the earth" corrupts the idyllic Paradise he finds by introducing self-consciousness into its midst.

To follow such a path, as a first approach, is all the more recommendable because there are unexpected and fascinating views to be had if one strays a little and looks around. For nowhere more easily than in the *Diary* can one follow the process by which Dostoevsky transformed the *faits divers* of his time, the ordinary common newspaper report of some momentarily sensational event, into the substance of his art. Just a month before printing "The Meek One," for example, Dostoevsky wrote about two suicides that had recently come to his attention, one being that of "a young seamstress who had jumped out of a window *holding a holy image in her hands*" (italics in text). The newspaper account attributed the death to economic causes ("she was utterly unable to find work for her livelihood"); but what evidently struck Dostoevsky was the detail of the icon, the combination of the sin of despair with such profound piety. "This holy image in the hands is a strange, as yet unheard-of trait in a suicide!" he writes. "This was a timid and humble suicide." Clearly, this detail had spurred Dostoevsky's imagination and set it to work; the result is his poignant story, which rises to its final, desolate vision of a world totally bereft of the love symbolized by the holy image. Dostoevsky offers, in this way, his entirely imaginary response to the banal newspaper item; but it is a response, he would have insisted, that remained "true" to the inner meaning of the "fantastic" event, even though totally fictitious in every detail except that of the suicide with the icon.

Another alluring path to follow through the *Diary* is that of the life history of Dostoevsky himself; and here the reader will find himself in the very good company of all of Dostoevsky's biographers. For the *Diary of a Writer* is one of the main sources on which they have drawn, and it is filled with glimpses into Dostoevsky's past and the most important shaping incidents of his life. Not the least of its attractions, for its first Russian readers, was precisely the sense Dostoevsky gave them of being admitted, on a footing of quasi-intimacy, into the company of one of their great contemporaries. And the same will still hold true for all those who wish to learn more about Dostoevsky at firsthand and from his own pen.

The place to begin is with the second number (February 1876), where we see Dostoevsky as a young boy rambling in the small wood on his father's impoverished "estate," gathering nuts and berries and enjoying nature in a fashion that one would not expect from the tonality of his novels. "And in all my life nothing have I loved as much as the forest, with its mushrooms and wild berries, its insects and birds and little hedgehogs and squirrels; its damp odor of dead leaves, which I so adored." This recollection is set in a frame narrative from a much later period of Dostoevsky's life, and we shall return to the latter in a moment. But now we can turn back a month to an account of the tenth anniversary of the foundation of the Russian Society for the Protection of Animals, which fades into an evocation of the seventeen-year-old Dostoevsky departing from Moscow, in the company of his father and his older brother, Mikhail, to take up studies as a military engineer (much against his will!) in St. Petersburg.

Both boys had long ago in secret made up their minds to become writers, and Dostoevsky was "busy planning in my mind a novel dealing with Venetian life." (At this point we can skip over to the May number, in which Dostoevsky includes a moving eulogy of George Sand on the occasion of her death, and note the remark that he had read her *L'Uscoque*—a novel of Venetian life—at the age of sixteen.) But the important thing is what he saw through the window of the way station at which his carriage stopped to change horses and take a little refreshment. A government courier arrived kicking up a cloud of dust, dashed into the station to down a few glasses of vodka, and rushed out again to a new carriage and a new, young peasant driver. As a matter of routine the courier mechanically began to beat the driver on the back of his neck, and the driver whipped up the horses in the same rhythm as they disappeared over the horizon. "This disgusting scene has remained in my memory all my life," Dostoevsky writes; and he links up his "most unrestrained and fervent dreams" in the late 1840s (the period of his revolutionary activity) with this traumatic memory of the casual and dispassionate brutality of the ruling class toward the peasant.

We can then trace Dostoevsky's career further in the January 1877 issue, and in two famous articles among the 1873 entries—"Old People" and "One of the Contemporaneous Falsehoods." The 1877 item begins with a description of a visit to the then-dying Nekrasov, the famous poet who had been a friend of Dostoevsky in the 1840s, but from whom he had drifted apart later for ideological reasons. And this visit evokes the recollection of their early days together, when Nekrasov had taken the manuscript of *Poor Folk* to Belinsky and Dostoevsky suddenly became famous overnight. These vibrant and moving pages have become classics in the annals of Russian literature, and no one can read them without experiencing some of the freshness and exaltation that Dostoevsky had felt himself in this glorious springtime of his career. Moreover, the image given of Belinsky is full of the reverence that Dostoevsky had once felt, but that, in the intervening years, had turned into bitter enmity against the passionately vehement godfather of Russian radicalism.

This change of attitude appears in the two other articles, both written three years earlier but portraying a slightly later stage of the Dostoevsky-Belinsky relationship. Here we see Belinsky indoctrinating his young protégé "into the whole *truth* of the future 'regenerated world' and into the whole *holiness* of the forthcoming Communistic society." (Actually, Dostoevsky was not really the sociopolitical innocent he portrays himself as being; but he accurately depicts Belinsky's historical role.) In "Old People," Belinsky's animadversions against Christ upset the young Dostoevsky to the point of tears—not because he was naively religious, but because his Utopian Socialist idealism glorified Christ as the supernatural harbinger of the social regeneration of earthly life. In both these articles, too, we see the supposed result of Belinsky's effect on Dostoevsky several years later—the young writer and his companions of the Petrashevsky Circle are now awaiting death by a firing squad in Semyonovsky Square. Inwardly, however, they were strengthened rather than shattered by their ordeal. "But the deed for which we were convicted; those ideas and conceptions that ruled our spirit were regarded by us not only as not requiring repentance but even as something purifying—as martyrdom, for which we would be forgiven much."

Luckily the execution never took place and had only been staged to display both the power and magnanimity of Nicholas I; Dostoevsky and the others were sent to Siberia for terms of hard labor and then army service. We catch another glimpse of Dostoevsky during his imprisonment at the assembly point of Tobolsk, just before his departure for the prison camp at Omsk where he was to spend four years. The wives and daughters of the Decembrists in Tobolsk—the Decembrists were a small band of aristocratic army officers, inspired by progressive ideas, who had tried to prevent Nicholas from taking the throne twenty-five years earlier—arranged an interview with the new wave of political prisoners, and consoled them as best they could. "They blessed us who were about to start on a new journey; they crossed us and gave us copies of the New Testament—the only book permitted in prison." (Dostoevsky does not add the detail, known from other sources, that ten rubles had been concealed in the binding of each copy.) But this is not the end of the journey in the *Diary*; we can follow Dostoevsky into the prison camp itself, and read a few crucial pages that, for some reason, he omitted from *The House of the Dead*, the volume of prison memoirs that brought him back to literary notoriety once again in 1861. These pages are the frame narrative, enclosing the boyhood recollection that we spoke of earlier; and they are published under the title "The Peasant Marei" in the February 1876 issue.

Dostoevsky here portrays very graphically his initial reaction of shock and horror at the brutality and moral squalor exhibited in the behavior of the peasant inmates of the camp. The sights and sounds to which he was exposed were so overwhelmingly repulsive that "all this in the course of a two-day holiday [Easter] had exhausted me to the point of sickness." But when, while taking a walk outside, one of the Polish political prisoners expresses Dostoevsky's very own response by saying to him, "Je hais ces brigands!" (I hate these criminals), Dostoevsky's emotional solidarity with his fellow Russians overcame his repugnance. He goes back to the barracks, lies down on his plank bed, and evokes from his subconscious the childhood memory of wandering in the forest already mentioned; along with it comes the additional image of "the peasant Marei," one of his father's serfs who had been kind to him as a little boy. "The meeting was a solitary one, in a vacant field, and only God, maybe, perceived from above what delicate, almost womanly tenderness may fill the heart of some coarse, bestially ignorant Russian peasant serf, who, in those days, had even had no forebodings about his freedom." This memory of "the peasant Marei" transforms Dostoevsky's entire relation to the peasant convicts, whom he could no longer regard simply with educated loathing—"why, he may be the very same Marei; for I have no way of peering into his heart." From this moment dates that exalted view of the peasant, and of the Russian national character, expressed so passionately (and so uncritically) throughout the *Diary*.

5

These are only two of the possible itineraries; many more could be suggested—for example, to follow Dostoevsky as a literary critic through the pages of the *Diary*—but it would unduly prolong the length of this introduction to outline any more of them in detail. Instead, let me say a few words in conclusion about two other aspects of the *Diary* that may help the reader to understand its significance for Dostoevsky and some of its larger implications.

Writing to a friend, in April 1876, who had regretted that Dostoevsky was wasting his time and talents on the comparatively trivial material treated in the *Diary*, Dostoevsky replied that such an objection was really beside the mark. There was no distinction for him between his creative work and the *Diary*; indeed, he viewed the latter as an essential step in the preparation of his next novel. "This is why," he says, "getting ready to write a lengthy novel [the future *Brothers Karamazov*] I proposed to immerse myself especially in the study—not so much of reality in particular, since I am already quite familiar with it—but of the particularities of the present moment."[7] The use of the word *Diary* in his title was thus much more than an advertising device; it referred to one of its actual uses and functions as the notebook of a working writer, a preparatory stage in the gestation of his artistic ideas. Time and again, as a matter of fact, anyone familiar with *The Brothers Karamazov* can see the themes and motifs of that great work crystallizing in various articles of the *Diary*.

A good deal of space in the *Diary*, especially in the early issues, is given over to the question of child abuse; and Dostoevsky paid particular attention to court cases involving the mistreatment of children. Many of the details in Ivan Karamazov's speech for the prosecution against God's world—a world in which innocent children are allowed to suffer cruelly and unjustifiably—are taken from facts brought to light in such cases. Moreover, Dostoevsky's careful scrutiny of court procedure, and his analysis and parody of legal language, may well have inspired him to give so much space to a courtroom scene in his novel. Many of the arguments placed in the mouth of Fetyukovich, the defender of Dmitry Karamazov, are precisely the kind that Dostoevsky castigates in these entries; and the figure of Fetyukovich is modeled on that of V. D. Spasovich, one of the most successful defense lawyers of his time, who is attacked in the *Diary* by name. Anticipations of the legend of the Grand Inquisitor also abound in Dostoevsky's obsession with Roman Catholicism as a world-political force, in the articles devoted to "spiritism"—that is, parapsychic phenomena, then being much discussed in Russia—and in his constant allusions to the temptation of Christ in the wilderness and the New Testament phrase "that these stones be made bread."

What is likely to seem, for modern readers, the most out-of-date part of the *Diary* are the numerous articles on the uprising of the Balkan Slavs against Turkey in 1875–1876, which culminated in the Russian declaration of war against Turkey a year later. Dostoevsky's *Diary of a Writer* was instrumental in publicizing the point of view of the war party in the government (Alexander II had been initially opposed to active intervention), and in encouraging the motley volunteer movement organized to aid the Slavs, which included in its ranks both regular army officers and many of the left-wing Populist youth. After war had broken out, Dostoevsky's journal glorified the triumphs of Russian arms and minimized and discounted their defeats. Passions ran high on this issue, and Tolstoy, who expressed a very dim view of the Russian volunteers in the eighth part of *Anna Karenina*, thus comes in for a sharp attack in the *Diary* (July–August 1877), even though his book is praised extravagantly at the same time (what Dostoevsky really thought of it is difficult to determine).

[7] Ibid., 3:206.

In any case, Dostoevsky's thrusts against his great rival contain a skillful parody of the Tolstoyan manner too amusing to let pass unnoticed. Discussing the scene in which Tolstoy's hero, Levin, has just attained faith through conversation with a peasant, Dostoevsky asserts that he will quickly lose it again; and he satirically imitates how Tolstoy's central characters often reason themselves out of fixed convictions (Kitty is Levin's new, young bride):

> Kitty started to walk and stumbled. Now, why did she stumble. If she stumbled, this means that she should not have stumbled; it is only too clear that she stumbled for such and such a reason. It is clear that in this case everything depended upon laws which may be strictly ascertained. And if this be so, this means that science governs everything. Where, then, is Providence? What is its role? What is man's responsibility? And if there is no Providence, how can I believe in God? And so on and so forth. Take a straight line and extend it into infinity. (792)

These entries in the *Diary* show Dostoevsky in his least attractive posture as a flaming jingoist and war propagandist;[8] and some critics prefer to draw a sharp line between this side of Dostoevsky and the creator of the Christlike Prince Myshkin and the saintly Father Zosima. But we cannot understand Dostoevsky unless we realize that he saw (and felt) no inconsistency between advocating war to advance the national interests of Russia on the one hand, and upholding the Christian values of love and forgiveness as a supreme moral standard on the other. For the reign of these values on earth could only come about through the victory of Russia over her enemies and the extension of Russian influence. It was only in Russia, and among the Russian people, that the authentic faith of Christ had been kept alive; Russia was thus destined to preside at the instauration of the true kingdom of God through the creation of a new, pan-human world order.

There is no point in wasting ink to criticize Dostoevsky's delusions,

---

[8] Another unpleasant and disconcerting aspect of Dostoevsky, regrettably evident in his *Diary*, is his anti-Semitism. This question has been well discussed in the best book on the subject, David I. Goldstein, *Dostoevsky and the Jews* (Austin, Tex., 1981). My own point of view, however, as I indicate in my preface to that work, would introduce a few nuances into Goldstein's scathing and, on the whole, perfectly justified indictment.

Dostoevsky's anti-Semitism was part of a general xenophobia and Great Russian chauvinism that made it almost impossible for him to acknowledge any merits or virtues in other groups. All the same, he was clearly embarrassed and uneasy about being considered an anti-Semite—at least in public—and took pains explicitly to deny the charge made in letters from the numerous Jewish readers of the *Diary* (March 1877). Goldstein tends to regard such disclaimers as being tactical and unconvincing; but I am willing to give Dostoevsky the benefit of the doubt, and to feel that he was perhaps more in conflict with himself on the matter than Goldstein allows. It is worth noting, after all, that Dostoevsky's article on "The Jewish Question" ends with an appeal for, and an evocation of, brotherhood between Christian and Jew—which, despite all the nasty insinuations that the article also contains, is still not the same as calling for a pogrom.

which in any case, as he knew very well himself, were just as much a matter of irrational faith as his belief in God. It is important to understand, though, that in expressing this faith Dostoevsky was by no means simply giving voice to the ideological aberrations of a man of genius. Quite the contrary, he was articulating ideas that found a ready response in his numerous readers. No better illustration of this assertion can be given than the thunderous acclaim he received for his speech on June 8, 1880, at the famous ceremonies accompanying the unveiling of the Pushkin monument in Moscow. The speech was immediately printed in the *Diary of a Writer* (August 1880); and it provides an impassioned summary of all Dostoevsky's ideas about the exalted Messianic mission of Russia, using Pushkin's works to furnish him with examples and claiming that the very quality of Pushkin's genius—his ability to absorb and transform the manifold influences he drew on from various cultures—was symbolic of Russia's future role in the destiny of mankind.

"I read loudly and with fire," Dostoevsky wrote his wife on the evening of the same day.

> Then when at the end I proclaimed the *universal union* of mankind, the hall was quite hysterical, and when I finished—I can't tell you about the roar, the yell of enthusiasm: strangers in the audience were weeping, sobbing, embracing one another and *swearing to be better, not to hate but to love one another in the future*. . . . Turgenev, to whom I had introduced a favorable reference in my speech, rushed weeping to embrace me. . . . I tried to escape into the wings, but everybody had broken in from the hall, especially the women. They kissed my hands and would not leave me alone. Students came running up. One, in tears, fell down in a fit of hysterics in front of me and lost consciousness [italics in text].[9]

Other accounts of the event confirm the accuracy of Dostoevsky's report that his words unleashed an outbreak of what can only be called hysterical pandemonium.

If Dostoevsky was able to evoke such a mass response with his ideas, the reason was that these ideas tapped the subliminal emotions even of those who, as progressives and Socialists, might have been expected to put up some resistance to his ideological extravagances. D. N. Ovsyaniko-Kulikovsky, in his still-unsurpassed *History of the Russian Intelligentsia* (1911), writes as a liberal member of the generation that came to maturity while the *Diary* was being published; and he perceptively analyzes its effect:

> Among the readers of the *Diary* the progressive intelligentsia of the 1870s unquestionably occupied a prominent place. Here they found—with reference to the people, and to the relations between the people and the upper classes—many

[9] Dostoevsky, *Pisma*, 4:171–72.

thoughts and feelings akin to their own. Dostoevsky's Slavophile point of view, the conclusions of what can be called Dostoevsky's "program," could not, of course, be accepted by them, but his fundamental "dogma" about the exalted qualities of the Russian people and about their sublime mission in the future regeneration of mankind was the very "dogma" on which they based the possibility of their efforts to propagandize Socialist ideas among the people. . . . This "dogma" was expressed by Dostoevsky with such deep faith, with a sincerity infused with so much force, that his preachment unwittingly (?) threw oil on the fire. While rejecting the teachings of European Socialism, and negating its propaganda among the people, Dostoevsky at the same time energetically . . . encouraged among the youth that system of ideas and feelings that was the psychological foundation of the revolutionary illusions of our Socialists.[10]

Dostoevsky's most extreme and farfetched Messianic ideas were thus by no means alien to the main movement of Russian thought and the sociopolitical reality of his time; nor have they ceased to continue to exert their influence up to the present, despite the triumph in Russia of everything that Dostoevsky abhorred and the gigantic transformations that have taken place in his homeland. Thirty years after Ovsyaniko-Kulikovsky, we find the very well-informed E. J. Simmons, who was by no means hostile to the Bolshevik régime, remarking of the *Diary of a Writer* that "if one substituted Communism for [Dostoevsky's] mission of the Orthodox faith, and world revolution for his notion of a Pan-Slav war against Europe, the identity of his whole position with that of modern Soviet Russia would be striking."[11] This is not as surprising as it may appear at first sight, and was even foreseen by Dostoevsky himself. (See the June 1876 article "My Paradox," in which he argues that the most ardent partisans of Western ideas in Russia invariably gravitate toward the extreme Left and end up wishing to destroy European civilization in its existing form—thereby proving that they are really good Russians at heart despite themselves!) Is this not essentially what Ovsyaniko-Kulikovsky also meant when he spoke of the "psychological foundation" of the "dogma" shared by Dostoevsky and the Russian Left of his time as being exactly the same, even though the terms of their "program" were different? And did we not hear the voice of Dostoevsky once again more recently in Solzhenitsyn's Harvard Commencement Address (1978), when he told his scandalized American audience that they were morally inferior to the Russian people because the latter had suffered more and been spiritually elevated by their suffering? Was not Solzhenitsyn repeating Dostoevsky's old charge that Western civilization had

[10] D. N. Ovsyaniko-Kulikovsky, *Istoria Russkoi Intelligentsii*, 3 vols. (St. Petersburg, 1909–1911), 2:205.
[11] Ernest J. Simmons, *Dostoevsky: The Making of a Novelist* (London, 1950), 253.

lost any moral ideal, and that it had sold its soul for a mess of money and material goods?

We have not, it would seem, heard the last of Dostoevsky's "paradoxical" ideas by any means, unpalatable though they may be and uncomfortable as they may make us feel. And if we wish to obtain a more penetrating insight into the "psychological foundation" of the culture that has shaped the great world power confronting us—if we wish to understand the puzzling fact that both those Russians who accept, and those who refuse, the present Soviet system speak of Western civilization in much the same accents and from much the same moral posture—we can do no better than to turn to Dostoevsky's *Diary of a Writer* for enlightenment. It has lost none of its relevance from this point of view as an extraordinary document, illuminating not only the past but also the present and, as Dostoevsky fervently believed, perhaps the future as well.

CHAPTER THIRTEEN

Dostoevsky: Updated and Historical

JOHN JONES's book about Dostoevsky is very personal, very idiosyncratic, and very aggressive.[1] Jones has his own special vision of Dostoevsky, and he gives short shrift to what he considers to be conventional and mistaken approaches to a writer for whom he feels a special devotion (not all Dostoevsky, to be sure, since he refuses to include *The Idiot* at all, except in passing remarks, and calls it "forced, hysterical, hyperbolic, nasty and boring"). Such language conveys some of the assertiveness of Jones's tone; and he is just as self-assured in what he affirms as in what he denies.

The usual view of Dostoevsky is that he was a writer who lived in Russia during the middle of the nineteenth century; that he wrote within the conventions of Realism like Balzac, Dickens, and others of his contemporaries, but of course with his own inimitable originality; and that he was deeply concerned with human emotions, human psychology, and the social problems of his world and time. Since he was writing about Russian life, the characters he portrayed were also plagued by problems of ultimate moral values and religious faith. But according to Jones, all those who study such aspects of Dostoevsky's work are just not "getting it right" (to use one of his favorite expressions), and producing so much "waste paper." To get it right, one must look elsewhere.

Where one must look, as Jones sees it, is to the contemporary literature of our own day, to what he calls "the proleptic twentieth-century smell" (the olfactory sense seems to be an extremely important critical faculty for Jones) that he detects in *Poor People* (his title) and that he finds "even stronger" in *The Double*. This latter work, in which Mr. Golyadkin both affirms and denies his own identity, "forebodes the daunting, exhilarating intellectualism of a *coup* in Samuel Beckett"; and as the novella goes on, "we find ourselves getting thrust deeper into the Twentieth Century." What fascinates Jones in Dostoevsky is this relation to the present, and the fact that, to his sensibility, it is much more "suggestive" to link *The Double* with Kafka's Prague than with Gogol's St. Petersburg.

Jones thus resolutely sets out to "modernize" Dostoevsky, and to read his work only from this point of view. The fact that people have read it in other ways bothers him no end, and he even speaks of a "conspiracy" between Russia and the West to distort the true meaning of Dostoevsky's

[1] John Jones, *Dostoevsky* (London, 1983).

books, or at least the true character of his originality. Both sides, each in its different way, "shun the word and salute the message" in Dostoevsky, and thus both refuse "to concentrate on the man who spent his life trying to get his words right." Uttered in the opening pages, these phrases seem to presage a treatment of Dostoevsky in terms of technique and form, or perhaps of stylistic analysis. And while Jones has done a good deal of homework in the variants made available by the new Russian (Academy of Sciences) edition of Dostoevsky, and carries on a running quarrel à la Nabokov with translators, his own interest is not really as aesthetic as his words seem to imply. For if he is concerned with form and technique at all, it is only because he believes they can be used to support his intuition that Dostoevsky was *really* portraying the same sort of uncertain, unstable, metaphysically unanchored world that he finds in his favorite modern writers. For "Dostoevsky's words drop out with the rest of the stabilizing context, and we are left with no middle ground, no mediation, between earthbound objects and a weightless mental orbiting."

When such ideas are applied concretely, they certainly lead to some highly unusual readings. *Poor People*, considered by Alexander Herzen to be the first Socialist novel in Russian literature, and filled, *pace* Jones, with the thematics of compassion common to the Natural School of young Russian writers in the 1840s, suddenly metamorphoses into a metaphysical fable about characters who have nowhere to go and nowhere to be, a work whose "real issues are forwarding-looking: dramatized chaos and inertia, the Double Act (self-cancelling repetition) the lacuna (missing letters and so forth), the resources of authorlessness which Dostoevsky will be exploring all his life." These are so many devices, according to Jones, for shaking the characters and action loose from any sort of fictional "real" world and suspending them in the "instinctive mental orbiting" that is Dostoevsky's trademark of "instinctive modernity."

The same metamorphosis occurs when Jones discusses Dostoevsky's next important work, *The Double*, which turns out to be the story "of a man busy about nothing, this story, with no future and no past, is contextless choice facing not mind but naked (*goli*) will." Readers familiar with *The Double* may have some trouble recognizing the work that Jones describes if they recall poor Mr. Golyadkin, whose subordinate status in the social hierarchy is carefully delineated, desperately trying to gate-crash a party to which he has carefully *not* been invited, and then sinking into hallucinatory madness because unable to cope with the psychic burden of his rebellious impulses in a world where perfect obedience and compliance is the social norm. For Jones, though, "when Mr. Golyadkin pays his cabby to do nothing, *The Double* leaps into focus as an absurd fable contemporary in spirit with Camus and a metaphysical one even more akin to Sartre."

Well, since we have gradually come to accept the idea that all reading is "misreading," why not?

Jones is of course uneasily aware that all this flies in the face of everything that we know about Dostoevsky and about what concerned him. So he cavalierly dismisses all *that* "as a cluster of mother's-knee Christianity and student Socialism," and believes that in doing so he is actually rescuing Dostoevsky from those who belittle his genius. For in paying attention to anything but the metaphysical paradoxes and identity jokes that he singles out (and it is easy enough to find them, if one simply disregards what they mean *in context*), "we turn a universal genius into the next rarest, the much commoner thing in literature, a great writer."

But Jones is not always consistent in such rigorous delimitation, and he finds Dostoevsky "proleptic" not only "formally" but also "in vision, prefiguring such pseudo-élites as our media men and terrorists, but equally our inert and superstitious millions, our hedonism, apathy, intellectual vandalism, and a kind of senseless public noise: so that when I first saw the slot in the jukebox into which you put money to buy silence, something in me responded to the madness and terrible humor of it by exclaiming: 'Ah, Dostoevsky!' " So while the relation of Dostoevsky's work to his own society is so much useless rubbish, its relation to ours is "prophetic"; and it never occurs to Jones to wonder whether there might not be some connection between the two. A closer look at that "mother's-knee Christianity and student Socialism" would have perhaps enabled him to understand on what Dostoevsky's gift for prophecy had been nourished.

The book follows Dostoevsky's career in roughly chronological order, weaving back and forth between the works because Jones believes that no real differences exist between them. The same Beckettian sensibility controls them all, and this is of most importance; experience does not really change Dostoevsky, but simply provides new and diversified material to allow him to fill out the established framework. This is by no means an original perspective, and there are certainly lines of continuity that run through Dostoevsky's work both in thematics and character types. But Jones carries this idea to an extreme when, in his chapter on *The Possessed*, he speaks of Dostoevsky "writing the same novel all his life." More unexpected is the devaluation of the later, major novels implicit in the remark that, after his beginnings in the 1840s, "Dostoevsky worked his way back into the nineteenth-century novel." In doing so, his characters begin to "find common ground with their international contemporaries" (Dickens, Balzac), and they thus lose the specific Dostoevskian originality of the more abstract and metaphysical earlier work. "You can," according to Jones, "date within a decade or two" the narrative tonality of Myshkin's arrival in Petersburg on the train; but "savour the implications of 'Suppose I do know the meaning; but where does that lead?'—and you can't."

All the four major works on which Jones concentrates (*Notes from Un-*

derground, Crime and Punishment, The Possessed, The Brothers Karamazov) are approached from this angle, with Jones always searching for the scene or detail that will illustrate the "nobody to be and nowhere to go of Dostoevsky's inexhaustible inventive fascination." He does not so much provide any new interpretations as rather a series of notes and observations that he works around, often with considerable ingenuity and always with bludgeoning insistence, to express his sense of Dostoevsky's world. And since there are aspects of Dostoevsky that lend themselves to such a vision, and he did directly influence all the modern writers that Jones sees him as "anticipating," the comments of the critic are by no means devoid of pertinence. The passage in which he illustrates, quite convincingly, how Beckett drew on *The Double* is particularly interesting. It is the more regrettable that Jones's dislike of *The Idiot* prevented him from responding to the one character in all of Dostoevsky who comes closest to the black comedy of Beckett, namely, the tubercular student Ippolit, who is dying all through the novel and makes a thorough fool of himself at the same time.

One wishes (or at least this reader wishes) that Jones had written a book—or better, a longish essay, since he repeats himself a good deal—frankly devoted to Dostoevsky's relations to Beckett and the French Existentialists. This would surely have allowed him to produce his Dostoevsky to the world, and to avoid becoming entangled, as he does, in questions of historical plausibility and accuracy. What goes wrong with his book is not the updating (this is a legitimate critical enterprise), but the failure to separate it from the argument that Jones is somehow giving us the *true* Dostoevsky—*tel qu'en lui-même l'éternité le change*—as against all those pedestrian scholars who spend their time worrying about what the actual Dostoevsky said, read, thought, and felt. It was not necessary for Jones to have made this claim to justify his own readings, and his book would have been much easier to accept if he had boldly presented it as the personal response of a modern writer (*Dostoevsky Our Contemporary*, as it were, after the model of Jan Kott's book on Shakespeare). For the pretense that the Dostoevsky he gives us is what Dostoevsky really meant can only be considered wildly inaccurate and totally implausible, and unfortunately makes it more difficult to recognize the genuine value of what Jones has to offer on his own terms. For he does often illuminate Dostoevsky's relation to modernity by bringing certain elements in the work to a very sharp focus, and helps us to grasp how Dostoevsky has been assimilated (though also reduced and mutilated) by his literary followers.

With the *New Essays on Dostoevsky*, no confusion arises between the historical Dostoevsky and the manner in which his work has entered into the bloodstream of modernity.[2] This is a valuable collection of eight studies, six by British and two by American Slavists, which deal soberly and prof-

---

[2] Malcolm V. Jones and Garth M. Terry, eds., *New Essays on Dostoevsky* (Cambridge, 1983).

itably with various aspects of Dostoevsky's world. Not that his relation to modernity is neglected, either from a literary or a thematic point of view. Stewart R. Sutherland shows convincingly how the central ethical issues dramatized in the major novels (freedom and determinism, or the possibility of realizing freedom purely as an assertion of individual will) are of concern to analytical Anglo-American philosophy and not only to wild-eyed Existentialists. Indeed, Dostoevsky's fictional handling of these questions is quite relevant to discussions of the same problems by, among others, Sir Peter Strawson. Similarly, Christopher Pike, in an extremely useful and balanced survey of Formalist and Structuralist approaches to Dostoevsky, mentions the various critics (Julia Kristeva, Nathalie Sarraute, Alain Robbe-Grillet, Michel Butor) who had admired Dostoevsky "as a precursor, for the modernity of his fragmented reality, the disintegration of traditional categories and authorities and the 'new' psychology of his characters."

Two of the best contributions, however, are devoted to analyzing Dostoevsky in his historical context. One would imagine that this had long been done to the point of satiation; but, in fact, many aspects of his relation to his own time still remain relatively unexplored. One reason is that Soviet scholarship, despite the excellence of the new Academy edition still in course of publication, and some very good recent works (such as the two volumes on Dostoevsky's journals by V. S. Nechaeva), can touch only lightly on his complex involvement with the Russian radicalism of his time. His criticisms are far too devastating to be openly faced, and Soviet scholars prefer to pursue other lines of research. This situation gives particular value to an essay such as that by Derek Offord, "*Crime and Punishment* and Radical Thought," which rightly locates Raskolnikov's theories as an outgrowth of ideas that can be found in Chernyshevsky and Pisarev, rather than, as Soviet scholars like to maintain, being derived from various Western bourgeois sources—thus making the novel more easily assimilable to their version of the native Russian tradition.

Another contribution of a similar kind is equally stimulating: Sergei Hackel's exploration of "Zosima's Discourse in *The Brothers Karamazov*." This article investigates the religious works on which Dostoevsky drew in his chapters on "The Russian Monk," which contain the memoirs and admonitions of Zosima, and analyzes the question of how far Dostoevsky's portrait may be said to comply with the canons of Eastern Orthodoxy. Hackel's knowledge of this rather obscure material is very extensive, and his treatment of the issue close and careful. His conclusion is that Dostoevsky follows his traditional sources only up to a certain point, and that "the most obvious cleric" used as a model "was not a product of the Syrian desert nor of the Russian *pustyn* (monastery)," but rather Hugo's Monseigneur Bienvenu, the Bishop of Digne, in *Les Misérables*. Hackel also documents Dostoevsky's refusal, even while asserting his positive religious values, to link them with specific images of Orthodox faith; they speak, in his view, "of little more than nature mysticism." This first-rate article raises fundamental issues regarding Dostoevsky's spirituality, which perhaps should be seen—as the Protestant theologian Edward Thurneysen argued many years ago—as closer to negative theology than to any positive grasp of God and Christ.[3] The other essays are all well worth reading, and the book also contains a useful bibliography of work published in Britain on Dostoevsky between 1945 and 1981.

Wayne Dowler's book *Dostoevsky, Grigor'ev and Native Soil Conservatism* is not specifically about Dostoevsky, but deals with a current of thought that has become identified with his name and was largely propagated by the two journals that he edited in the early 1860s, *Vremya* (Time) and *Epokha* (Epoch). The movement in question was called *pochvennichestvo*, which Dowler, a Canadian historian, has translated as "native soil movement."[4] *Pochva* does mean "soil" in Russian, with the accessory significance of "ground, basis, or footing"; the "native" is not contained in the word, but indicates some sense of the movement as a whole. For it was intensely patriotic, and called for Russian literature and culture to throw off the yoke of foreign ideas and values and to seek nourishment in its native soil. The search for "roots," which has become so prominent on the cultural scene everywhere in the world today (including the Soviet Union), was anticipated as a slogan and program more than a hundred years ago in Dostoevsky's journals.

The three most prominent figures of the movement were Apollon Grigoriev, Dostoevsky himself, and Dostoevsky's erstwhile "friend" and first biographer, Nikolay Strakhov, who wrote a scurrilous letter about him, after his death, to Tolstoy. Grigoriev was a tempestuous and colorful personality, a gifted poet and critic, who unfortunately shared the national vice of heavy drinking and led a wild and disorderly life. It has been suggested by two Soviet critics that he provided some of the inspiration for Dmitry Karamazov;[5] and the penchant of that character both for drunkenness and for breaking into poetry at crucial moments lends some plausibility to the hypothesis. Alexander Blok collected Grigoriev's poetry at the beginning of this century, and Soviet scholarship, though very gingerly, has begun to pay attention to his criticism again, which was more or less looked down on as a historical curiosity until fairly recently.[6] But he was

---

[3] Edward Thurneysen, *Dostoevsky*, trans. Keith R. Crim (London, 1964).

[4] Wayne Dowler, *Dostoevsky, Grigor'ev and Native Soil Conservatism* (Toronto, 1982).

[5] V. G. Seltrennikova and I. G. Yakushkin, "Apollon Grigoriev i Mitya Karamazov," *Filologicheskie Nauki* 1 (1969):13–24.

[6] A highly appreciative article was included in L. Grossman, *Tri Sovremmenika* (Moscow, 1922). An incisive and respectful analysis has been given, more recently, by B. F. Egorov,

far and away the best literary critic of the midcentury; and though he had little success in his lifetime with the public, who turned to so-called literary criticism for political propaganda in favor of revolution, his merits as a perceptive interpreter of Russian culture are gradually beginning to be recognized.

Dowler's book gives a very well-informed account of Grigoriev's career and his early association with the young editors of the journal *Moskvitianin*, a rather musty pillar of Russian patriotic nationalism. It took a new lease on life in the early 1850s, when turned over temporarily by its editor, the historian M. P. Pogodin, to a group of younger writers including Grigoriev, the playwright Ostrovsky, and the novelist A. F. Pisemsky. It was in these years that Grigoriev began to develop the ideas that became so important for Dostoevsky, though Dowler perhaps exaggerates the extent of the novelist's indebtedness to the critic. There is no question that Dostoevsky took over a number of Grigoriev's formulations and perceptions. But these did not so much shape Dostoevsky's own views as enable him to express, in terms of a philosophy of Russian culture, the intuitions and attitudes that he had arrived at independently on the basis of his own experiences in Siberia and the "regeneration" of his convictions that occurred there.

Pochvennichestvo is usually seen as a variety of Slavophilism, and so indeed it is; but the same can also be said of Herzen's "Russian Socialism," to which *pochvennichestvo* bears a great deal of resemblance. What distinguishes the "native soil movement" from orthodox Slavophilism, as Dowler excellently shows, is its acceptance of the transformations wrought in Russian culture by the Westernization of Peter the Great; where the Slavophiles looked backward to the mythical and idyllic past that Andrzej Walicki has labeled a "conservative Utopia," the *pochvenniki* looked forward to the synthesis of the educated classes and the peasantry into a new Russian nationality combining Western enlightenment with the Christian moral values still existing at the root of Russian life. They also separated themselves from the Russian Westerners by rejecting the Hegelian idea of a universal humanity evolving in a single direction—that of progress, or what we would now call modernization—and appealed rather to Schelling's idea of the "universal relativism" of the historical process, which meant that each nationality was free to work out the laws of its own internal evolution and was not part of an all-subsuming World Spirit.

The *pochvenniki* were philosophical Idealists, who fought the influence of materialism and Utilitarianism on the majority of the Russian intelligentsia, and who understood that such doctrines were an integral part of

"Apollon Grigoriev—Kritik," *Uchenie Zapiski Tartuskogo Gosudarstvennego Universiteta* 98 (1960): 194–215.

the program of sociopolitical revolution. But while the *pochvenniki* were against revolution (even to imagine that one was possible, Dostoevsky believed, was sheer self-delusion), they were by no means self-satisfied conservatives, and supported all the reform measures of the government as well as self-government through the peasant communes and local district councils. They also vigorously defended the freedom of the artist to create independent of the political pressures exercised by such radical spokesmen as Chernyshevsky, Dobrolyubov, and Pisarev. It is not true, however, as Dowler states, that "they reacted against what in Russia was called 'accusatory literature' "; at least it is·not true of Dostoevsky, who specifically took a stand in its favor. They saw Russian culture as engaged in a struggle between European (rapacious, egoistic) and Russian (meek, Christian) types of character and moral values—a struggle that had been fought through and resolved by Pushkin; and this typology unquestionably has had a lasting impact on the national imagination, even if the political influence of the *pochvenniki* in their own day was nil. It may be that only at present is *pochvennichestvo* having some political effect; for these ideas, kept alive by the powerful genius of Dostoevsky, can still be found at work in a writer such as Solzhenitsyn.

Dowler's book is certainly the best and most extensive treatment of this movement known to me, and is a fine contribution to the illumination of an essential aspect of Dostoevsky's background. Thoroughly versed in Russian cultural history, Dowler also places the "native soil movement" in the broader context of European conservatism; and he sees it as a response, just as was Russian radicalism, to the pressures exerted by modernization. His major weakness is one of omission, aside from a few errors here and there (the "literary and musical" evening in the spring of 1862, which Dostoevsky later dramatized in *The Devils*, was not so much evidence of a "mood of cooperation among the intelligentsia" as a left-wing demonstration). If Dowler had carried on a more extensive comparison with Herzen's very similar development of a left-wing, rather than a centrist, variety of Slavophilism, the value of his discussion would have been greatly enriched. For he is genuinely insightful on how little the political slogans of Right and Left meant in Russia, and how close the two were in basic attitudes when looked at from a European point of view.

One may conclude by citing part of his own conclusion, which sums up the position that has allowed him to write so unbiased a book, and to escape the usual error of regarding the *pochvenniki* simply as so many reactionary obscurantists who happened, by accident, to have a great writer in their midst. "The socially unattached intelligentsia," Dowler says,

> which was largely the product of the intensification of urban culture in the closing years of the reign of Nicholas I, addressed itself to the tensions in Russian

thought and life that were generated by the slow process of modernization. These tensions were encapsulated in the metaphor Russia and the West. The outlook of both radicals and conservatives among the *intelligenty* was shaped not only by their common intellectual roots in romanticism and utopian socialism, but also by their vehement rejection of the individualistic values and mechanical social arrangements that they believed characterized life in the bourgeois West. Both sides, consequently, ended by advocating remarkably similar collectivist or communalist social objectives. (182)

Just so; and a little more documentation of this crucial convergence would have been all to the good.

CHAPTER FOURTEEN

Dostoevsky and the European Romantics

DOSTOEVSKY, LIKE Dickens, was a stunningly effective reader of his own works, as well as a brilliant vocal interpreter of Russian poetry in general. One of his favorite pieces, which he was frequently asked to perform at public gatherings, was Pushkin's poem *The Prophet*. At the celebration organized for the unveiling of Pushkin's monument in Moscow in 1880, Dostoevsky whipped the audience into a frenzy with his speech, which included a declamation of this poem; and the audience shouted that he himself was the prophet described in Pushkin's verse. Dostoevsky, to be sure, scarcely thought of himself as a prophet in any literal religious sense. But in calling his work "fantastic Realism," or Realism "in a higher sense," he certainly included the possibility of being able to foresee the drift of coming events—which is why he was always so naively delighted when the newspapers appeared to confirm the characters and ideas he had depicted in his novels.

The appellation of "prophet," in any case, has clung to Dostoevsky ever since his death, and the word often appears in the titles of books about him—for example, Dmitry Merezhkovsky's *Prophet of the Russian Revolution*. Alex de Jonge does not use the word *prophet* in his title, but it would not have been inappropriate.[1] For the burden of his thesis is that Dostoevsky, paralleled in this respect only by Baudelaire, *was* the prophet of the "age of intensity" in which we are all living. His work, de Jonge claims, "read properly, which is to say with the understanding offered us by hindsight, provides the most penetrating and comprehensive account of the steady disintegration of European culture, and foretells the coming of an age of terror, of Rimbaud's *temps des assassins*" (5).

Dostoevsky and the Age of Intensity thus takes its place among those works that view Dostoevsky essentially as a cultural symptom, expressing the ills of his own time (and our own by anticipation), rather than as a writer engaged in creating works of literature. The two, especially in Russia, cannot ever be completely separated, nor is it my intention to imply that they should be; but some balance between them ought to be maintained all the same. Dostoevsky himself, in his controversy with the radical critic Nikolay Dobrolyubov, argued that inferior works of literature were ineffective even as sociopolitical propaganda; and while this view was excessively idealistic,

[1] Alex de Jonge, *Dostoevsky and the Age of Intensity* (London, 1975).

it at leasts indicates that Dostoevsky's passionate involvement in the moral-social issues of his time and country did not exclude a concern for art.

There is thus no warrant whatever for de Jonge's assertion that Dostoevsky was "sublimely indifferent to the technical details of execution" of his novels (has he ever looked into Dostoevsky's notebooks?), and that "he relies on instinct and intuition more than on calculation." Of course, if de Jonge had been willing to give Dostoevsky some credit for knowing what he was doing, it would have been more difficult for him to claim that his own view "provides a framework which structures the loose and baggy monsters of Dostoevsky, showing that they have a much greater degree of inner coherence, stemming from a unified creative vision, than has hitherto been suspected." No one has ever before applied Henry James's phrase for Tolstoy's novels ("loose and baggy monsters") to Dostoevsky's very different works; indeed the best Russian critics—Mikhail Bakhtin is only one example—quite rightly see the two as polar opposites in their approach to the novelist's art. The careless use of this phrase reveals how little attention de Jonge has paid to the actual quality of Dostoevsky's books, and leads one to suspect that he has perhaps himself fallen victim to the very cultural malady that he deplores—the replacement of precise discrimination of values by the "intensity" of shock effect.

Luckily, Dostoevsky's "art" is swept under the carpet very quickly, and the book gets down to its real subject. This is defined by the all too accurate observation contained in the quotation from Nadezhda Mandelstam that de Jonge uses as an epigraph. Why has "the nineteenth century with its glorification of humanism, freedom, and the rights of man," led straight to "the horrors of the twentieth," which "has surpassed all previous ages in its crimes against humanity"? It is this momentous question that de Jonge sets out to answer, with the help of Baudelaire and Dostoevsky; and his response will be familiar to all those who remember Irving Babbitt's *Rousseau and Romanticism* (still eminently worth reading) and/or the anti-Romanticism that T. S. Eliot took over both from his old teacher Babbitt and from Charles Maurras and other defenders of the French classical tradition. So far as one can tell, de Jonge is not directly influenced by this now unfashionable current of ideas; but he seems to have arrived at many of its conclusions by way of brooding over the dilemma posed by Nadezhda Mandelstam and seeking some answer in the cultural history of the past century and a half.

What is to blame, according to de Jonge, is the breakdown of values whose effects can be observed in the creations of European Romanticism—a Romanticism, to be sure, seen solely through the jaundiced eyes of Mario Praz as "the Romantic agony." Sweeping aside all attempts to discriminate between various kinds of national Romanticisms, and ignoring the simple fact (pointed out long ago by Benedetto Croce, in his cogent objections to Praz) that one type could be socially integrating and restorative while another was morally nihilistic, de Jonge treats the complex movement as a whole only as a symptom of cultural collapse. The eighteenth century, whatever its perturbations and conflicts (it was, after all, the century of *Candide* and *Le Neveu de Rameau*), still possessed some sense of a stable world order and of what de Jonge—perhaps a little uneasy over the word *religion*—euphemistically calls "whole meanings." The nineteenth century, ushered in by the historical trauma of the French Revolution, could only dream about the sense of certainty that had been lost and attempt to restore it in imagination. The Romantic experience, therefore, is one of a "degraded present," of time as impermanence and destruction, of a *mal de siècle* that turns Romantic heroes into social misfits and causes them to seek alleviation for their ontological insecurity in the pursuit of sensation for its own sake. "Intensity of experience is the most important concept developed by Romantic culture."

Its quite easy for de Jonge to apply this view to Baudelaire, a poet who did seek escape in sensations of any kind ("De vin, de poésie ou de vertu, à votre guise. Mais enivrez-vous") as a relief from the tedium of existence. But even with a writer who seems such a perfect illustration of the "intensity" syndrome, one quickly begins to feel that the term is too loose and undefined, too much a sloganized catchall, adequately to serve the purpose of critical illumination.

"Intensity" may be either the entire content of an experience that exists *only* on the level of sensation, or it may be a component of one that also contains a spiritual dimension. Baudelaire, we read, "excites himself by contemplating the likelihood of his own imminent damnation, having reached the stage when any stimulus will serve; just as the heroin addict comes to love the needle which is the cause of his own destruction. The hero gradually grows so bemused that he quite loses the ability to evaluate the experience he undergoes" (43). While perhaps true of the heroin addict, this last sentence scarcely applies to a Baudelaire contemplating "his own damnation"; self-destruction may result in both cases, but to know oneself as evil is clearly not the same as losing all distinction between evil and good. It is a fundamental defect of de Jonge's key term that it forces him to blur this crucial differentiation.

The bulk of de Jonge's book is devoted to discussing Dostoevsky's novels in the perspective provided by Western Romanticism, with Baudelaire arbitrarily selected as its archetypal representative. Dostoevsky, too, was fascinated and horrified by the *fourmillante cité*, and used it very effectively as background for the social misery and despairing isolation of his characters. Rather than dwelling on the specifically Russian symbolism that links Dostoevsky's treatment of Petersburg both with Pushkin in the past (*The Bronze Horseman* and *The Queen of Spades*), and Andrey Biely's *Petersburg* in the future, de Jonge concentrates on the city as the site of moral disintegration and loss of organic community as we also see it used in Balzac and Dickens. It may be local patriotism that impels him to single out Dostoevsky's short visit to London in 1862 as a decisive moment in his grasp of this theme, and to claim that London "first seems to have focused the image of the city for Dostoevsky." Not at all; Dostoevsky's first novel, *Poor Folk* (1845), makes effective use of Petersburg as a humanly destructive environment, and the whole Natural School of Russian literature in the 1840s, deriving from Gogol's Petersburg stores and the French *physiologies* (sketches of Parisian life), used the city in the same way. Dostoevsky's visit to London confirmed all his forebodings about the horrors of industrialism and Western "progress," which he saw as a consequence of the materialism also being advocated by the Russian radicals of the 1860s; but it did not have a crucial impact on the image of the city in his works.

The modern city was the home of the "new ideologies" of rationalism, materialism, and Utilitarianism, which Dostoevsky abhorred, and which he attacked in one work after another beginning in the early 1860s. Devoting a series of chapters to such attacks, de Jonge draws out the moral-social implications of selected Dostoevskian characters and motifs by stressing their relations to issues that are still very much with us. Social engineering, with its intolerable restraints on human freedom, leads to the exasperated revolt of the underground man. Raskolnikov and Luzhin in *Crime and Punishment* reveal the morally repugnant consequences of the consistent application of a Utilitarian pecuniary ethic. Both Prince Myshkin in *The Idiot* and Versilov in *A Raw Youth* suffer equally from a sense of cosmic alienation. The social chaos resulting from these new ideologies is dramatized most explosively in *The Devils*, and by implication haunts *The Brothers Karamazov*.

After surveying Dostoevsky's hostile diagnosis of the modern world in an interesting (if somewhat repetitious) fashion, de Jonge then goes on to argue the much more disputable case that Dostoevsky's characters turn to "intensity" as a substitute for "the whole meanings" in which their lives are lacking. This is done in a section devoted to the "modes of intensity" exhibited by their behavior—such "modes" being gratuitous spitefulness, gambling, masochism, the desire to abolish time, and finally libertinism. All these distractions are freely indulged in by one or another Dostoevskian type; but the *significance* of such conduct cannot simply be reduced to the craving for "intensity." We are back again with Baudelaire and the heroin addict, and the same issue arises even more acutely because Dostoevsky's characters are so manifestly conscience-stricken and guilt-ridden. It is simply not true to say, for example, that libertines like Svidrigailov and Stavrogin have "no sense of identity, and hence no capacity for self-recrimination and guilt." If so, why are they haunted by the memory of their atrocious crimes? Such a thesis constantly forces de Jonge to misread Dostoevsky in this way.

Even more, it impels him to accuse Dostoevsky himself of "complicity" in all the horrors that he depicts. (Would de Jonge apply the same sort of reasoning to the Shakespeare of *Titus Andronicus* or, for that matter, of *King Lear*?) The reason for this unpleasant charge seems to be that, if Dostoevsky can be thought to be secretly sympathetic to what he nominally castigates, it is easier to maintain that in his delineation of "modes of intensity" he genuinely confuses and confounds all moral distinctions. Dostoevsky, for example, is indicted for being unable to tell the difference between positive (that is, moral) suffering and sadistic pleasure derived from pain, even though he satirizes precisely this inability at the conclusion of *Notes from Underground*, where the underground man viciously tries to excuse his humiliation of the prostitute Liza with the reflection that her suffering will "do her good." And after citing a passage in which Dostoevsky himself labels the masochistic behavior of a character as an "egoism of suffering" (thus implying a clear distinction between this and a nonegoistic suffering stemming from repentance and humility), de Jonge flatly concludes that Dostoevsky reached a point where "he could no longer distinguish between good and evil, pleasure and pain."

Such a position, however, can only be maintained with the help of a severely limited and one-sided reading of Dostoevsky—or rather, not a reading of his works at all, but of fragments torn out of context and interpreted in an arbitrary and tendentious fashion.

To his credit, de Jonge is uneasily aware of this problem, and lets the cat out of the bag in one paragraph. He writes:

> Now, of course, the Dostoevskian view that suffering must be accepted without question, that it provides a path to purification and ennoblement, is a vital part of his Christian metaphysics. His view of the universal guilt is the basis of a Christian resolution of his culture's plight. He invites us all to take on, in so far as our strength permits, the tiniest share of the burden which Christ bore for us all. . . . It would be an unforgivable distortion of an aspect of Dostoevsky's thought, *which is not directly relevant to our analysis*, not to accord pride of place to this aspect of the theme of acceptance of suffering and universal guilt [italics added]. (177)

Here we have the admission that de Jonge has simply left out of consideration all those elements of Dostoevsky's world showing that he was perfectly well aware of the distinction between good and evil, and in no danger of mistaking one for the other.

What is valuable in de Jonge's book is the demonstration of Dostoevsky's undoubted links with the more morally questionable aspects of Western Romanticism, and the analysis of his insight into the moral and spiritual dangers of a cultural process that has now indeed put a premium on intensity of sensation as a supreme value. But Dostoevsky is neither the Marquis de Sade, Rimbaud, nor Lautréamont; neither a Dadaist, Futurist, nor Surrealist; de Jonge has just been carried away by his thesis. And his attempt to turn the greatest and most devastating opponent of moral Nihilism in modern literature into its surreptitious advocate must be rejected as unconvincing and regrettably misleading.

PART FOUR

The Dilemmas of Radicalism

CHAPTER FIFTEEN

Nikolay Chernyshevsky: A Russian Utopia

1

IF ONE were to ask for the title of the nineteenth-century Russian novel that has had the greatest influence on Russian society, it is likely that a non-Russian would choose among the books of the mighty triumvirate—Turgenev, Tolstoy, or Dostoevsky. *Fathers and Sons? War and Peace? Crime and Punishment?* These would certainly be among the suggested answers; but they would only testify to the endemic ignorance of Russian culture that the worldwide popularity of Russian literature has not yet overcome. No, the novel that can claim this honor with most justice is Nikolay Chernyshevsky's *What Is to Be Done?*—a book few Western readers have ever heard of and fewer still have read. Yet no work in modern literature, with the possible exception of *Uncle Tom's Cabin,* can compete with *What Is to Be Done?* in its effect on human lives and its power to make history. For Chernyshevsky's novel, far more than Marx's *Capital,* supplied the emotional dynamic that eventually went to make the Russian Revolution.

The first installment of Chernyshevsky's book appeared in April 1863 in the pages of the radical journal *Sovremenink (The Contemporary).* Translated twice into English in the second half of the nineteenth century, the book was out of print here for over fifty years. But a reprint of one of these earlier translations has recently (1986) appeared with an excellent introduction by Kathryn Feuer, and a new annotated translation in a more up-to-date English by Michael Katz has just been published.[1] The American reader thus again has available a work that no one interested in either Russian literature or politics can afford to neglect. For by its influence on succeeding generations of Russian radicals—and most notably on Lenin himself—the effects of Chernyshevsky's novel can still be traced in the attitudes and behavior of men who are leading the Communist world at this very moment.

Chernyshevsky's novel did not have to wait for the future to guarantee its status and prestige. Testimonies to its authority abound in Russian lit-

---

[1] Nikolay Chernyshevsky, *What Is to Be Done?*, trans. N. Dole and S. S. Skidelsky, intro. by Kathryn Feuer (Ann Arbor, Mich., 1986). This text, however, still contains some slight cuts made by the translators. An exact rendition of the original can be found in the version by Michael R. Katz (Ithaca, N.Y., 1989), with annotations by William G. Wagner. My page references, however, are to the first American edition of Dole and Skidelsky (New York, 1886).

erature; one of the earliest may be culled from the pages of Dostoevsky, who had an unrivaled flair for spotting the significant developments in the Russian culture of his time. Dostoevsky sensed the importance of *What Is to Be Done?* immediately on its publication, and tried to counter its effect in *Notes from Underground*. Ten years later, a passage in his novel *The Devils* confirms its extraordinary proselytizing powers.

Stepan Trofimovitch Verkhovensky, the old liberal Idealist of the 1840s, tries to fathom the baffling mentality of his Nihilist offspring Peter Verkhovensky and can only turn to the source—Chernyshevsky—for enlightenment. The narrator of the novel goes to visit the old gentleman, and reports: "An open book was on the table. It was Chernyshevsky's *What Is to Be Done?* . . . I realized he had got hold of the novel and was *studying* it with the sole purpose of knowing their arguments and methods beforehand from their 'catechism' so that when the inevitable conflict with the 'shriekers' came he would be ready to refute them triumphantly." Dostoevsky further adds the historically accurate detail that, without renouncing Chernyshevsky, who had by this time become a "catechism," Peter Verkhovensky sardonically offers to bring his benighted father even "better" books.

From another side of the Russian political spectrum, and twenty years later, we may invoke some remarks on *What It to Be Done?* in the first version of G. V. Plekhanov's important book on Chernyshevsky (1890). "Who has not read and reread this famous work?" asks the father of Russian Marxism, and for a good while the adored idol of his young disciple, V. I. Lenin. "Who has not felt its attraction, who has not become, under its beneficent influence, purer, better, stronger, and bolder? Who has not been struck by the moral purity of the main figures? Who, after reading this novel, has not reflected on his own life, has not subjected his own strivings and inclinations to rigorous examination? All of us have drawn from it both moral strength and faith in a better future."[2] The emotional vibrancy of this passage displays the impact of Chernyshevsky on the radical sensibility, even when, as in Plekhanov's case, it was still possible to admit the glaring artistic deficiencies of the novel. Today, when *What Is to Be Done?* is printed in the Soviet Union in editions of millions of copies, no Soviet critic would dare intimate that it is anything but a literary gem of the purest ray serene.

But whatever disagreements may exist between East and West over the literary merits of Chernyshevsky's opus, all will readily concur that the conditions of its publication are a remarkable comedy of errors. Chernyshevsky, who had been arrested on charges of subversion in July 1862, began the novel in prison while his case was being investigated and tried. Cut off

---

[2] G. V. Plekhanov, *Izbrannye Filosofskie Proizvedenia*, 5 vols. (Moscow, 1958), 4:159–60.

from the possibility of carrying on his propaganda through cleverly "Aesopian" articles—which nominally discussed events outside Russia, but which were always angled to convey his opinions on Russian affairs—he decided to follow the example of such French Encyclopedists as Voltaire, Diderot, Montesquieu, and Rousseau, and take to fiction to spread his ideas. He therefore asked permission of the commandant of the Peter-Paul prison, Prince Golitsyn, to work on a novel for which he had already received an advance from the magazine *Sovremmenik*.

The obliging prince granted his prisoner's request, and Chernyshevsky ardently began to write. The first part of the novel was then submitted to the prison censor, who, leafing through it rapidly and finding only what appeared a harmless love story, stamped it as publishable and dispatched it to the censor of the magazine. This latter gentleman might well have been capable of a little more literary perspicacity; but confronted with the imprimatur of Prince Golitsyn, he did not feel obliged to wrestle either with the manuscript or with his conscience and passed it on to the editor of *Sovremmenik*, the famous poet N. A. Nekrasov. Nekrasov, whose private life was rather hectic, promptly lost the precious manuscript in a cab and successfully advertised to obtain its return through the official newspaper of the St. Petersburg police. It was thus the Russian police themselves who conscientiously rescued the most subversive novel in Russian literature from oblivion.

2

A first approach to the book is likely to inspire the reader with a good deal of sympathy for the unhappy prison censor, who no doubt had to pay dearly for his oversight in passing the manuscript. In truth, the first chapters of the novel hardly seem very explosive. Chernyshevsky captures the reader's interest immediately by presenting him with the account of a mysterious suicide, whose circumstances retain enough strange features to create an atmosphere of suspense. Then he goes back to give the history of the vanished Mr. Lopukhov, who turns out to have employed an unusual (though rather cumbersome) method of protesting against the general obscurantism of the Russian attitude toward divorce. What Lopukhov has done is to stage a fake suicide in order legally to disappear from the scene and allow his wife to marry another man. This only becomes clear, however, much later on. Once the initial description of the suicide has whetted the reader's curiosity, the book narrates the history of Lopukhov and his wife, Vera Pavlovna Rosalsky, in more or less chronological order.

In the first part of the book, this history revolves around Vera's struggle against the strangling constraints of Russian family tyranny. Vera's widowed mother is trying to force her into a wealthy marriage against her will.

Lopukhov, a young medical student who tutors Vera's brother, falls in love with her and rescues her from parental enslavement by an elopement. The book thus appears to be only another of the numerous Russian novels of the early 1860s devoted to the intricacies of the "woman question"; and such works were not considered a major threat to the stability of the Russian Empire. But while Chernyshevsky, like all Russian radicals, was genuinely concerned with the emancipation of the female, he used this issue in his novel to play for much higher stakes. The "woman question" only serves as a convenient device for portraying the ideas and attitudes of the "new people," the younger generation of the 1860s, whose lives were presumably lived according to the precepts of Chernyshevsky's own ethical philosophy.

This doctrine, expounded by Chernyshevsky in 1860 in an article called "The Anthropological Principle in Philosophy," had stirred up a furious and bitter controversy in the Russian press. Curiously enough, although the title of the article is taken from Feuerbach, the ethical precepts that Chernyshevsky advocates reject Feuerbach's emphasis on altruism and I-Thou solidarity in favor of a "rational egoism" derived from the Utilitarianism of Bentham and Mill. But as in the case of Mill himself, Chernyshevsky's "egoism" is more a matter of terminology than of actual behavior. For Chernyshevsky convinced himself and his readers that, while everybody always wished to act in a manner dictated by the most arrant selfishness, reason proves conclusively that self-interest is best served by the most selfless and altruistic conduct (though it is strictly forbidden to use these latter terms as *reasons* for one's action). Utilitarians had appeared in literature before, most notably in Dickens's novels, under the guise of hypocritical villains wrapping their opportunism in a cloud of Benthamite terminology. But it remained for a Russian—and, even more oddly, for a Russian Utopian Socialist!—to make English Utilitarianism the credo of his heroes, and to attempt to portray its beneficial effect on their lives.

The first test of Lopukhov's principles comes when he decides to elope with Vera. Originally, he had intended only to help her obtain a job as governess and marry after he had obtained his medical degree; but when this proves impossible, and the pressure on Vera becomes intolerable, he throws overboard a brilliant academic and medical career to spare her any further suffering. Chernyshevsky realizes that, to the corrupt and cynical average reader, this may well seem very strange behavior for an "egoist." So he hastens to explain that Lopukhov had "made up his mind, conscientiously and resolutely, to renounce all material advantages and honors, so as to work for the benefit of others, finding that the pleasure of such work was the best utility for him."

As a result, Lopukhov finds it quite easy, even child's play, to give up everything he had striven all his life to attain. What worries him is only whether he is being perfectly consistent with the rules of rational egoism. Might he really be giving way to the enemy and making a "sacrifice"? Lopukhov reassures himself, as he is mulling over his decision, by the consoling reflection that "the notion of sacrifice is a false term; a sacrifice is equivalent to such nonsense as 'top-boots with soft-boiled eggs!' One acts in the way that's most agreeable." Indeed, the fact that his own action might be interpreted as a "sacrifice" merely proves the omnipresence of egoism. "What a hypocrite!" he says of himself. "Why should I take a degree? Can't I live without diplomas? Perhaps, with lessons and translations, I'll make even more than a doctor." On the basis of such reasoning the troubled Lopukhov quiets his fears that he might be infringing the wonder-working prescriptions of rational egoism.

After marriage, Vera and Lopukhov arrange their lives according to the latest theories of equal rights between the sexes. Neither is allowed to enter the other's room without permission; nor will either appear before the other in dishabille. The bewildered shopkeeper who is their first landlord can only conclude that they belong to some new religious sect. Chernyshevsky obviously intends this as an ironic thrust against the general benightedness of Russian society; but the shopkeeper struck far closer to home than even Chernyshevsky was aware. Vera and Lopukhov, in any case, do not spend too much time enjoying the delights of "rational" cohabitation. For Vera, who has received a thorough Socialist education in the meantime, decides to set up a cooperative dresssmaking establishment.

This, of course, turns out to be delightfully simple. It is only necessary to choose girls of "good character," who are able to understand, after a little indoctrination from Vera, that it is in everybody's interest to divide profits equally regardless of skill or degree of responsibility. With the help of the French mistress of an important Russian bureaucrat—who, even in her degraded condition, still symbolizes all the innate virtues of the revolutionary French working class—the shop succeeds in attracting a fashionable clientele. As time goes on, by the inevitable force of Socialist economic logic, the girls all realize that it is more profitable not only to work, but also to live, in common; and the shop turns into a full-fledged Fourierist phalanstery for the unmarried girls and their families. Finally, with everything running without a hitch, the shop is transformed into a university even during working hours; and the lower-class working girls surprise visitors with their breeding, refinement, and culture.

Only one cloud ruffles the horizon during this triumph of reason and common sense over antiquated prejudice. Vera discovers that she is no longer in love with Lopukhov, although they have lived together in perfect serenity; but her own development has brought to light new aspects of her nature that Lopukhov is no longer able to satisfy. Poor Lopukhov likes privacy and solitude after a hard day's work, while gay Vera likes opera and the stimulus of society; on this fatal reef their marriage comes to ship-wreck. Instead of Lopukhov, it is his best friend, Kirsanov—one of the bright lights of international medicine—who now best satisfies Vera's re-quirements; and the result, as might be expected between two such egoists, is a strange duel of renunciation and withdrawal.

Lopukhov can think of nothing better to do than hand Vera over on a silver platter: strict egoism impels this move because he knows it is impos-sible to countermand the dictates of nature. Kirsanov too, who acts with all the scrupulous delicacy of a Henry James heroine, also behaves only on the basis of the most "material" calculations: he reasons that having Vera on his hands would simply take up too much of his time. Nothing can be more involuntarily comic than the solemnity with which Chernyshevsky's virtuosos of virtue argue themselves into the conviction that strict egoism alone determines all their conduct. And the upshot, as we have seen, is that Lopukhov simulates suicide to allow Vera to marry Kirsanov (marriage is a regrettable but necessary concession to the reigning prejudices). At the end of the book, Lopukhov turns up again in disguise as a citizen of the United States and a staunch Abolitionist. He becomes engaged to a friend and disciple of his ex-wife; and the two couples settle down side-by-side as the best of friends to await the imminent advent of a brave new world.

3

What Is to Be Done? created a sensation among its first readers by its attack on the inviolability of marriage, its portrayal of the "rational" relations be-tween Vera Pavlovna and her two husbands, and by the interweaving of this sentimental plot with propaganda for female education and Socialist cooperatives. Another important source of the novel's effect, however, cer-tainly derives from its relation to Turgenev's *Fathers and Sons*. At the time of Chernyshevsky's arrest, the Russian intelligentsia were immersed in the throes of a violent controversy over *Fathers and Sons*; and Chernyshevsky's inspiration obviously takes its point of departure from the issues raised by this vitriolic quarrel.

Turgenev's novel has usually been misinterpreted in the West as an at-tempt to glorify the new Russian radical of the 1860s—powerful, self-as-sured, arrogantly secure in the certitude that science and materialism would triumph over all obstacles in the way of progress. The new genera-tion, though, was far from unanimous in giving its approval to Turgenev's portrayal of its position and the human qualities it supposedly engendered. The result was a split in the ranks of the radical intelligentsia that was to have important later effects on Russian literature and life. One group, led by the rising young critic Dmitry Pisarev, took Turgenev's Bazarov as their ideal whatever his defects, and became the advocates of a "Nihilism" that came dangerously close to justifying negation and destruction for its own sake. But the other group—the followers of Chernyshevsky, who clustered around the *Sovremmenik*—attacked *Fathers and Sons* as a vicious attempt to malign the new generation in the eyes of Russian society.

Turgenev himself had the unfortunate habit of making conflicting statements about his own work at various times, depending on his mood of the moment and the character of his interlocutor or audience. Consequently, there is no way of establishing definitely just what he really intended in his novel. The most likely hypothesis is that, as the *Sovremmenik* group suspected, he had originally proposed to take revenge for the implacable campaign of this magazine against the older generation of the 1840s—a campaign in which his own works had been a prominent target. As the course of composition progressed, however, he was carried away by sympathy for his creation; and he ended up by making Bazarov a much more imposing and impressive figure than any of Bazarov's ideological rivals.

In any case, it is a matter of historical record that the entire Russian reading public—including Dostoevsky, who, Turgenev said in a letter, was one of the two people to have really understood the book—took the work as an indictment of radical youth. Even before *Fathers and Sons* appeared in print, the rumor had gone around in radical circles that Turgenev had based his main character, Bazarov, on a vicious caricature of the young critic N. A. Dobrolyubov, who had died just a year before. Despite Turgenev's numerous denials of this charge in later years, he could never shake off the onus of this suspicion, which became deeply implanted in Russian left-wing circles.

On the other hand, the more conservative party of society applauded the book heartily as a well-deserved riposte to radical extremism. The Russian secret police, who kept a solicitous eye on literary developments, even wrote in one of their reports that *Fathers and Sons* had "had a beneficial effect on opinion.' Turgenev, in their judgment, "had branded our adolescent revolutionaries with the biting name of 'Nihilist,' and had shaken the doctrines of materialism and its representatives" to their very roots.[3] In view of this state of affairs, it is little wonder that Chernyshevsky undertook the task in *What Is to Be Done?* of giving what he considered a more authentic picture of those whom Turgenev had labeled "Nihilists."

E. H. Carr, who is usually better informed, has remarked that Chernyshevsky's book "is not so much a retort to *Fathers and Sons* as a proud acceptance of it."[4] On the contrary, Chernyshevsky's "new people," as Dobrolyubov had called the younger generation (the subtitle of *What Is to*

---

[3] Cited in the indispensable book of Henri Granjard, *Ivan Tourguénev et les courants politiques et sociaux de son temps* (Paris, 1954), 314.

[4] The statement is contained in a preface that Carr wrote for the Vintage edition of *What Is to Be Done?* (New York, 1961), xii.

Be Done? is *Stories about the New People*), are not at all Nihilists in Bazarov's sense; their aim is by no means only a despairing negation and destruction of the stagnant and moribund. The lives of these "new people" have a well-defined positive content—the content of Chernyshevsky's own curious and ill-digested amalgam of crude Feuerbachian materialism and determinism, Benthamite Utilitarianism, and Utopian Socialist perfectionism. And Chernyshevsky wrote his novel precisely to demonstrate the miraculous capacity of this doctrine to solve all the major problems of society and human life.

Indeed, the tranquil dénouement of Chernyshevsky's complicated love knot is clearly intended to form the sharpest contrast with Turgenev's treatment of a similar theme. Turgenev, with unerring artistic aim, had revealed the human limitations of Bazarov's ideology by causing him to fall in love. There is no place in Bazarov's materialism for the complicated torments—the bafflement, rage, and inner impotence—that Bazarov's infatuation makes him feel for the first time. Only his failure with Mme. Odintsova is capable of undermining his colossal vanity and self-confidence. Chernyshevsky boldly accepts this challenge of love for his heroes and demonstrates how a "rational egoism" can triumph, with hardly even an occasional twinge, over the petty perturbations of old-fashioned romantic passion. Such trifles no longer present any problems for the "new people," who, as medical men of lower-class origin, correspond with Bazarov externally in every respect. Turgenev's attempt to prove otherwise had merely shown his bad faith, and the characteristic incomprehension of the senile Romantics of the 1840s for the temper of the "new people."

4

Besides this general demonstration of the moral dilemmas that could be solved by rational egoism, there are two other aspects of Chernyshevsky's book of great historical importance. One is the character of Rakhmetov, the professional revolutionary. Rakhmetov plays no important role in the main line of the romantic action, but Chernyshevsky cannot help dwelling at some length on this revolutionary Superman—the highest exemplar of his human ideal in the present "irrational" organization of society. And it is amusing to see that Chernyshevsky himself, despite his continual sniping at Romantic literary conventions, uses all the tricks of the trade to endow Rakhmetov with as much glamor as Robin Hood, Childe Harold, and Young Lochinvar.

Rakhmetov, for one thing, is not a lowly commoner—far from it! He is the descendant of one of the oldest families of the Russian nobility, and immensely wealthy to boot. Chernyshevsky has taken very little trouble up to this point to make his fiction jibe with his materialistic determinism.

Vera Pavlovna, for example, can only exclaim surprisedly at the "wonder" of her own moral purity of spirit amid the corrupt surroundings of her girlhood. But for Rakhmetov, in very unscientific fashion, Chernyshevsky himself makes a self-conscious exception to the laws of nature. No matter "how bad the soil may be," he writes, referring to Rakhmetov's aristocratic forebears, "it may have some tiny portions that will produce healthy grain." Indeed, the more he dwells on the majestic figure of Rakhmetov, the more *all* the principles of Chernyshevsky's philosophy go flying out the window. For Rakhmetov is nothing if not a prodigy of self-discipline, whose "firmness of will" is a living refutation of Chernyshevsky's denial in theory that anything such as "will" existed in human nature.

Rakhmetov came to study in St. Petersburg at the ripe age of sixteen, just another innocent and good-natured lad from the country; and his awe-inspiring development begins from the moment he sets foot in the capital. When he meets Kirsanov, the latter's Socialist ideas strike him like a clap of thunder. "He wept, he interrupted him with exclamations of curses against all that was to vanish, and blessings on all that must live." It is not only Dostoevsky's characters, we see, who are capable of becoming obsessed by ideas in the Russian novel. For after this encounter Rakhmetov reads steadily for eighty-two hours (Chernyshevsky is very precise with figures) and gives up only when he collapses on the floor from exhaustion. This marks the moment of his conversion—and very soon he has outstripped his teachers.

Leaving the university, and secretly using his fortune to provide scholarships for poor students, he travels the length and breadth of Russia working at itinerant trades. As a bargeman on the Volga he achieves the legendary status of a Russian Mike Finn, whose feats of strength ring up and down the river; and on returning to St. Petersburg he virtually becomes a monkish ascetic of the revolution. He renounces wine, women, and personal happiness, refuses to eat anything that is not available in the humblest peasant household, and finally tests his endurance by sleeping on a board studded with nails. All this is to prove that, while the radicals are asking for the political and sexual emancipation of women, and for "the full enjoyment of life," they are not doing so "for the gratification of our personal passions, not for ourselves personally, but for humanity in general."

Rakhmetov has all of Bazarov's gruffness, boorishness, and rudeness, but nobody resents his lack of ceremony because it is not taken personally. Rakhmetov is obviously engaged in underground revolutionary work (referred to euphemistically as "the affairs of someone else or . . . matters not relating especially to his own person"); he simply has no time for the trivial amenities of social intercourse. He arranges his day with mathematical precision and exactitude, feels at perfect liberty to interfere with and arrange other people's lives, and is a perfect monster of complacent self-sufficiency. Rakhmetov, in other words, is a Bazarov wholeheartedly dedicated to revolution, unshakable and unconquerable in his strength, and deprived even of the few remaining traits of self-doubt and human awareness that still manage to make Bazarov sympathetic. But Chernyshevsky can hardly contain himself when he comes to eulogize Rakhmetov, who surpasses Vera and her admirers to the same extent as they surpass the run-of-the-mill citizen. People like Rakhmetov, he assures his readers, are "few," but through them flourishes the life of all; without them life would become dead and putrid."

5

Chernyshevsky not only depicts his human ideal in the present, but he also allows the imagination of his reader to take wings into the future and revel in the delights of the Socialist Golden Age. This Utopia is pictured in Vera Pavlovna's resplendent fourth dream. Here Chernyshevsky brushes in a sweeping tableau of the evolution of humanity in the pseudo-apocalyptic style of Lammenais, Ballanche, and the French Social Romantics of the 1830s. Neither the pagan sensuality of Babylonian Astarte, nor the captivating physical beauty of Greek Aphrodite, nor the image of Chastity adored by the medieval knight can equal the beauty of the modern goddess of love who takes on the features of Vera Pavlovna. "If you want to express in one word what I am," says the new goddess, "this word is 'Equal Rights.' Without it enjoyment of the body, delight in beauty, are tedious, gloomy, wretched; without it there is no purity of heart; there is fallacious purity of body" (377).

The advent of this new goddess, however, whose reign was first announced in Rousseau's *La Nouvelle Héloise*, is only the prelude to the world of the future—a world in which virtue will have created the Earthly Paradise. Chernyshevsky describes this Fourierist Paradise at great length and in loving detail; but there is no need to enlarge on the particulars. Suffice it to say that the earth has been transformed into a radiant garden; that the life of the humblest worker equals the opulent ease and enjoyment of ancient kings; that no passion is trampled on or disdained; and that man has been transformed, morally and physically, into a creature whose beauty, virtue, and wisdom surpass that of all the greatest ages of civilization rolled into one.

One detail of this evocation is worth dwelling on at greater length because it has—through Dostoevsky—become so familiar a symbol. This detail is Chernyshevsky's description of the marvelous cast-iron-and-glass dwelling, shimmering with subdued electric light and glowing with aluminum furniture, that houses the lucky denizens of Utopia:

An edifice; an enormous edifice, such as can be seen only in the largest capitals—
or, no, at the present time there is none such in the world. It stands amid fields
of grain, meadows, gardens, and groves. . . . What is it? What style of architec-
ture? There is nothing like it now; no, but there is one that points toward it—
the palace which stands on Sydenham Hill, built of cast-iron and glass, cast-iron
and glass and that is all. . . . This integument of cast-iron and glass only covers it
as by a sheath; it forms around it wide galleries on all floors. . . . But how rich
everything is! Everywhere is aluminum and aluminum, and all the spaces between the windows are adorned by large mirrors. And what carpets on the floors!
. . . And everywhere are tropical trees and flowers; the whole house is a large
winter palace. (378–79)

Chernyshevsky's allusion to the "palace" on Sydenham Hill links this
structure to the famous Crystal Palace of the World's Fair in London in
1851; and this, of course, is the "Crystal Palace" attacked in Dostoevsky's
Notes from Underground. Dostoevsky, as it happened, had used the Crystal
Palace as a symbol himself even before Chernyshevsky's novel appeared.
During his trip to Europe in the summer of 1862, he had been struck with
horror at the Crystal Palace, which he took as a triumphant image of the
soulless materialism that he felt was undermining European life. In his
Winter Notes on Summer Impressions, written during the winter of 1863, he
had depicted the vast influx of visitors from all over the world come to
admire the Crystal Palace as a symbolic expression of modern man's surrender to the fleshly and material power of Baal. Whether Chernyshevsky
could have read these *Winter Notes* during the writing of his novel is difficult to say; but we can well understand that Dostoevsky should have felt
the glorification of the Crystal Palace in *What Is to Be Done?* as a direct
challenge to his own position.

Indeed, it is only in the light of an exact understanding of Chernyshevsky's Utopia that we can really do justice to Dostoevsky's point of view.
This Utopia, it should be kept in mind, was not merely the application of
"reason" to the solution of social problems; it also involved exactly that
deification of the material that Dostoevsky had already rejected, and that
he now returned to attack once again with brilliant vehemence. In Chernyshevsky's Utopia all material want had vanished, and since all passions
are considered equally legitimate, man could satisfy any and every inclination without let or hindrance and without inner conflict. For Chernyshevsky, this made every man totally free to do exactly as he pleased; but for
Dostoevsky it meant that man had simply become the plaything of his
drives and impulses. He would no longer have to choose between good
and evil, and would thus surrender the moral autonomy of the personality
that consisted precisely in the necessity of having to make such a choice
and the capacity for doing so.

Such a Utopia of total freedom was, for Dostoevsky, total slavery to the material—and a slavery, moreover, that he was deeply convinced human nature would never accept. If "reason" meant a world in which man no longer had an opportunity to feel the *inner* freedom involved in choice, then he would go mad and destroy such a world simply to prove his freedom to do so. Dostoevsky's attack on Chernyshevsky, however, was hardly noticed at the time it appeared (except for a parodistic résumé of its contents by the satirist Saltykov-Schedrin), and continued to be ignored almost up to the turn of the century. It had no effect in shaking the authority Chernyshevsky had obtained over the radical mind.

6

Chernyshevsky's novel, as should be amply clear by this time, is a strange hodgepodge of the most diverse mixture, by turns infuriating in the innocence of its fatuity and self-complacency and touching in the fervid candor of its glowing faith. Nothing reveals more clearly the deep-rooted spirit of romantic and sentimental idealism that still inspired these Russian "realists" and "egoists" of the 1860s. And the great success of Chernyshevsky's absurd novel unquestionably springs from its ability to tap these latent emotional yearnings under the guise of "science" and "practicality." All the evidence concurs to prove that *Fathers and Sons* was decisively vanquished, and that not Bazarov but Vera Pavlovna, her two husbands, and Rakhmetov became the ideal of radical youth.

The younger generation, writes Prince Kropotkin in his *Memoirs of a Revolutionist*, found Bazarov "too harsh, especially in his relations with his old parents, and, above all, we reproached him with his seeming neglect of his duties as a citizen. Russian youth could not be satisfied with the merely negative attitude of Turgenev's hero. Nihilism, with its affirmation of the rights of the individual and its negation of all hypocrisy, was but a first step toward a higher type of man and woman, who are equally free, but live for a great cause. In the Nihilists of Chernyshevsky, as they are depicted in his far less artistic novel *What Is to Be Done?*, they saw better portraits of themselves."[5]

All through the nineteenth century, accordingly, enlightened Russians tried with more or less success to arrange their emotional lives on the pattern provided by Chernyshevsky. Innumerable cooperatives were also established, in imitation of Vera Pavlovna's dressmaking establishment, among student groups in universities and colonies of Russian exiles. Alas, not always with the same happy results. Most important of all, however,

---

[5] Peter Kropotkin, *Memoirs of a Revolutionist* (Garden City, N.Y., 1962), 197–98.

was the inspiration provided by the example of Rakhmetov to the budding revolutionary underground.[6]

The ideal of the disciplined, dedicated revolutionary, coldly Utilitarian and even cruel to himself and others, but warmed by a love for mankind that he sternly represses for fear of weakening his resolution; the iron-willed leader who sacrifices his private life to the revolution, and who, since he looks on himself only as an instrument, feels free to use others in the same way—in short, the Bolshevik mentality, for which it is impossible to find any source in European Socialism, steps right out of the pages of *What Is to Be Done?* It is Chernyshevsky, the son of a Russian priest and the graduate of a Russian theological seminary, who first made the fateful fusion between the hagiographic pattern of Russian religious kenoticism and the coldly dispassionate calculations of English Utilitarianism that forms the essence of the Bolshevik character.[7]

We have already noted the admiration of Plekhanov for Chernyshevsky's novel; and this admiration was fully shared by Lenin. Nikolay Valentinov, who knew Lenin well in the early years of this century, reports him as saying that after the execution of his brother Alexander in 1887 he began to read *What Is to Be Done?* knowing it had been one of his brother's favorite books. "I spent not days on it but weeks. Only then did I truly understand its profundity. It's a work that inspires you for life."[8] Lenin's wife, Krupskaya, also tells us in her memoirs: "I was astonished to see with what attention he read this novel [Chernyshevsky's], and how he noted its subtlest aspects."[9] It is thus no accident that Lenin should have taken over the title of Chernyshevsky's novel for one of his most famous pamphlets.

No doubt Lenin adopted the title *What Is to Be Done?* partly for the inspiring associations it would evoke in the minds of all his readers. But there is also an inner appropriateness in the title that must certainly have been consciously intended by so astute a mind as Lenin's. For this pam-

[6] The influence of *What Is to Be Done* was by no means limited only to Russia. Soviet Russian scholarship is fond of citing its inflammatory effect in Eastern Europe, but my colleague Edward J. Brown has called attention to its impact on our own shores as well. "Emma Goldman, the American anarchist leader famous in song and story, set up in her New York apartment a sewing cooperative for young, possibly wayward, and in any case poor and helpless girls that was modelled directly on Vera Pavlovna's enterprise. . . . And Goldman's associate, Alexander Berkman, when he took off to assassinate the steel magnate Henry Clay Frick in the course of the brutal Homestead strike in 1892, used as a pseudonym the name of . . . Rakhmetov." Edward J. Brown, "So Much Depends . . . Russian Critics in Search of 'Reality,' " to be published in the *Russian Review* (1989).

[7] A highly original analysis of Chernyshevsky's novel, which skillfully examines its use of such secularized religious motifs, can be found in Irina Paperno, *Chernyshevsky and the Age of Realism* (Stanford, Calif., 1988), esp. chap. 3.

[8] Nikolay Valentinov, *Encounters with Lenin*, trans. Paul Rosta and Brian Pearce (London, 1968), 64.

[9] See *Reminiscences of Lenin by His Relatives* (Moscow, 1956), 202.

phlet is the work in which he broke with the Western idea of a democratic, working-class party as suitable for the purposes of revolution, and stressed the need, instead, for a group of full-time, professional revolutionary conspirators to take absolute control and guide the revolutionary struggle. Rakhmetov here is triumphing over Karl Marx—and there is thus a clear line of historical affiliation between Chernyshevsky's novel and the Leninist ideal of the Bolshevik. One can only speculate on whether Rakhmetov still exercises the same fascination in present-day Russia as he did one hundred years ago; there is very good reason to believe that his grip (at least on adolescent readers), as recent Soviet émigrés have informed me, has by no means weakened. And God knows where else in the world his image still continues to loom very large, and where in Africa or Asia, at this very moment, he is being idolized and emulated!

CHAPTER SIXTEEN

Sons against Fathers

THE TITLE of Eugene Lampert's book *Sons against Fathers* is adopted from Turgenev's famous novel called in Russian *Fathers and Children*, and translated into most other languages as *Fathers and Sons*.[1] This masterpiece, as fresh and apposite today as when first written, depicts the conflicts that broke out in Russian culture around 1858 between two generations. One was the generation of the 1840s, which had been formed on Romantic literature and German Idealist philosophy, and was politically liberal or Utopian Socialist in its sympathies. The new generation of the 1860s—the generation of Turgenev's hero, Bazarov—favored Realism rather than Romanticism in literature, and admired the later Gogol rather than Pushkin; its philosophical mentors were, at best, Feuerbach, and at worst such third-rate epigones of materialism as Vogt, Moleschott, and Büchner; and it was bitterly hostile to liberal reformism of any stripe. This opposition marked a fateful moment in the history of Russian culture, and was really the beginning of the revolutionary surge that ultimately led to the triumph of Communism.

An objective and dispassionate study of this period by a Western cultural historian familiar with the Russian sources would be of the greatest interest and value. No single up-to-date work of this kind exists in Russian (Nestor Kotliarevski's excellent *Kanun Osvobozhdenia*, besides stopping at 1861, was published in 1916); and since the issues of this controversy are still intimately related to present Soviet ideology, it is unlikely that the Russians themselves will be allowed to produce anything that can be considered adequate. Lampert's book has no pretensions to being a full-scale study of the period, but it contains, nonetheless, three vigorous and very well-informed essays on the leading figures among the Russian radicals of the 1860s—Nikolay Chernyshevsky, Nikolay Dobrolyubov, and Dmitry Pisarev. These essays, moreover, are preceded by a lengthy introductory section sketching the historical and cultural setting of their work and influence. Lampert thus touches on all the major problems of the early and middle 1860s, and adds a welcome contribution to the scanty number of reliable works in Western languages on the subject. The reasons it cannot be considered entirely satisfactory, however, will become clear in the course of the following remarks.

[1] Eugene Lampert, *Sons against Fathers* (London, 1965).

The most important historical event of the period was the liberation of the serfs by Alexander II, which finally occurred in February 1861. It is generally agreed that this liberation placed too heavy a tax burden on the peasantry, and that they were seriously disappointed by the failure to receive all the land they believed rightfully theirs. Disillusionment with the conditions of the liberation turned the generation of the 1860s against all reforms initiated and controlled by the tsarist government. And it was from this moment that the Russian radicals acquired their pitiless hostility to any type of liberal compromise with existing authority. Lampert rightfully stresses the indignation of the radical leaders at what they considered the betrayal of the liberation; and he staunchly opposes the views of scholars such as Victor Leontovitch, whose *Geschichte des Liberalismus in Russland* (1957) regards the radicals as having impeded the possible peaceful development of Russia toward a constitutional régime.

It is, of course, impossible to know whether such a development would have taken place. But in order to show that such hopes had no foundation, Lampert inclines far too much to exaggerate the peasant opposition to tsarism in the 1860s. In his first chapter, he objects strenuously to the "generally accepted view" that, despite the peasant unrest accompanying the liberation, the Russian peasant still retained all his religious reverence for the quasi-supernatural figure of the tsar. As evidence, he cites the uprising in Bezdna in the spring of 1863, where the peasants refused to accept the terms of the liberation edict and ceased working for the landowners. This state of affairs finally had to be put down by force with considerable loss of life; and it called forth some of the first public manifestations of opposition to Alexander II by the radical intelligentsia.

Lampert's account of this event fails to mention that the leader of the movement, a literate peasant named Anton Petrov, had promised his followers that "in due time a young man will come here sent by the Tsar. He will be seventeen years old, and on his right shoulder he will have a gold medal and on his left a silver one."[2] This messenger, the tsar's "true" emissary, would, it was believed, carry the authentic liberation decree; and the entire uprising was made presumably in conformity with the real wishes of the tsar, who was being betrayed, in the opinion of the peasants, by the local officials and landowners. The Russian radicals preferred to overlook such evidence of peasant loyalism, or, occasionally, tried to capitalize on it by issuing forged "true" edicts that would stir the peasants to revolt in the name of the tsar.

By trimming the facts in this way, Lampert creates the impression that the radical hope for a revolution against tsarism in the 1860s has the support of the historical record. Many by no means conservative Russians such

---

[2] Franco Venturi, *Roots of Revolution*, trans. Frances Haskell (New York, 1960), 215.

as Herzen and Turgenev, on the other hand, believed that these radical hopes were a delusion, and that the only possibility for immediate progress lay in implementing the tsarist reforms, imperfect and inadequate though they admittedly were. Lampert is at perfect liberty to find this idea morally unpalatable, and to prefer the uncompromising intransigence of the radicals; but this is a different matter from pretending that a less optimistic evaluation of the facts had no justification, and that its advocates were closing their eyes to "reality." Since all the efforts of the diehard radicals to provoke a revolution of the peasantry against the tsar failed miserably throughout the mid-nineteenth century, the reverse would seem to have been true.

Fundamentally, it was on this evaluation of the immediate political situation that the two generations differed; and the bitterness of the cultural conflicts of the 1860s can only be understood in the light of this underlying political disagreement. Curiously enough, after spending so much space explaining the economic and social situation arising from the liberation, Lampert fails to use it at all significantly in his essays on the three major figures. Instead of reading their works as an attempt to argue about politics, under circumstances where censorship required such arguments to be concealed as philosophy, literary criticism, or history, Lampert attempts to take the writings of the Russian radicals on their merits as "ideas." This results in giving them both too much credit and too little at the same time. By endeavoring to extract some sort of general conceptual framework from the (for the most part) topical journalism of his authors, Lampert places their work in a context in which its weaknesses become all too painfully apparent. On the other hand, by failing to view them primarily as political journalists, writing in the heat of the ceaseless struggle to express a forbidden point of view, he does less than justice to their consummate skill as propagandists and to the importance of their work as a reflection of the hopes and dreams of the Russian intelligentsia whose moods they crystallized.

In each of Lampert's three essays, the first section is invariably the best. Here he sketches the main events of the personal life of each of his protagonists; and his unvarnished presentation of the facts is a welcome relief. Soviet scholars, concerned to construct a golden legend of spotless revolutionary saints, always paint a very edifying picture of the private lives of the radicals and gloss over anything that might tarnish the sacred icon. Without in any way being cheaply debunking, Lampert fills in the picture of Chernyshevsky's surprisingly complaisant cuckoldry, Dobrolyubov's sad and despairing debauchery, and Pisarev's egomania and schizophrenia. Far from lowering the three in one's estimation, the revelation of their human weaknesses and unsolved personal problems only increases our admiration for their heroic intellectual-political battle against impossible odds.

Chernyshevsky is uncontestably the weightiest and most important figure of the three, and Lampert appropriately gives him the most extended treatment. It was only Chernyshevsky who, before being completely absorbed by his journalistic tasks, had the time and the talent to write such relatively pondered works as his master's thesis *The Aesthetic Relations of Art to Reality*, and his *Anthropological Principle in Philosophy* (though this is merely an extended book review). These books furnished the radicals of the 1860s with their meager arsenal of ideas; but it can hardly be said that in themselves they offer anything startlingly insightful or original. Chernyshevsky's "philosophy" was the naïvest sort of pseudo-scientific materialism and determinism, stitched together with Benthamite Utilitarianism and topped off by a totally inconsistent appeal to the revolutionary will. Lampert does his best to blow up this mishmash into something respectable, and does it far too much honor by invoking the names of Spinoza, Helvétius, and Marx by way of comparison. Ultimately, though, he cannot conceal from himself that Chernyshevsky's thought is impossibly crude and limited. "He drew large cheques on non-existent scientific assets in favor of his materialistic interpretations," he writes in one place, "and dismissed awkward facts by the use of such vague terms of abuse as 'metaphysical,' 'fantastic,' or 'illusionist,' much as indignant school girls use the epithets 'frightful' and 'beastly.' " This conveys very accurately the impression that one derives from a good deal of Chernyshevsky's so-called "philosophical" pages.

Despite this steady drumfire of criticism, Lampert nonetheless struggles heroically to give Chernyshevsky an important status as a thinker. And here it is clear that his admiration for Chernyshevsky's courageous rectitude as a man, and his sympathy with his political stand in the 1860s, has led to a regrettable confusion of moral intention with intellectual accomplishment. According to Lampert, while "much of the 'outside' in his [Chernyshevsky's] outlook is rough and springs from misconceptions," the " 'inside' contains a profound moral and intellectual experience, into which it is necessary to enter." This "inside," as Lampert sees it, is Chernyshevsky's impassioned humanism, his desire to see man as a whole; and his materialism, his naive epistemological Realism, and his rough-hewn Utilitarianism are all part of his attempt to get back from the bloodless heights of metaphysical abstraction to the flesh-and-blood individual. As proof of this point, Lampert produces a number of phrases in which "man" is extolled and glorified, such as, for example, "in the whole sensible world man is the supreme being."

Such phrases, however, are nothing but Feuerbachian and Left Hegelian clichés, the common coin of the period on which Marx finally stamped the most original and independent impress. Chernyshevsky, as Lampert well

knows, was a fervent admirer of Feuerbach, and he even quotes Chernyshevsky's admission, made in the closing years of his life, that he had always
been Feuerbach's "faithful follower." Lampert will have it, though, that
"Chernyshevsky rightly suspected that in raising man to the status of a
deity Feuerbach had lost sight of real man, known in the here and now;
that he had substituted an abstract idea of man, or the genus man, or humanity in general for the concrete human person." This is the criticism that
both Max Stirner and Marx made of Feuerbach, each in his own way; but
one would like to know where Lampert found it in Chernyshevsky. No
citation is given, and there is good reason to believe that even Lampert's
fine scrutiny could not unearth a supporting text. Even if such a text existed, it would still not prove that Chernyshevsky's "humanism" found expression in any truly important conceptual form. An awareness of this "humanism" can help us to understand the underlying impulses of
Chernyshevsky's thought, but it does not convert his philosophical weaknesses into strengths.

For the most part, despite a good deal of this kind of irritating special
pleading, and an occasional recourse to the Marxist tactic of morally vili-
fying the opposition, Lampert's pages on Chernyshevsky as a philosopher,
historian, and political economist give a reasonably balanced picture of his
position. The same cannot be said for his treatment of Chernyshevsky as
an aesthetician. Chernyshevsky's *The Aesthetic Relations of Art to Reality* is the
fountainhead of the doctrine of "Socialist Realism," and for more than a
century has played a baneful role in Russian culture by its establishment of
the dogma that the artist must be subordinated to "life," that is, the needs
of the social struggle. "Science and art [poetry]," Chernyshevsky wrote, in
a much-quoted passage, "are a *Handbuch* for those who are beginning to
study life; their purpose is to prepare the student for reading the original
sources and later to serve as reference books from time to time." In the face
of this unequivocal assertion, it is astonishing to read Lampert's declaration that Chernyshevsky's book "gives no support to the view that [he]
turned art into a vehicle of propaganda, [and] made didacticism an artistic—or unartistic—dogma." On the contrary, it would be difficult to find
anywhere a more outright assertion of art's primarily didactic function
than the sentence from Chernyshevsky just quoted.

Lampert again defends Chernyshevsky on the grounds of his "humanism," and places his aesthetics in the context of a struggle against a vapid
and dilettantish doctrine of "art for art's sake" that would remove art from
any polluting and vitalizing contact with man and human life. This is of
course what Chernyshevsky and his followers contended; but one wishes
that Mr. Lampert had looked at their arguments a bit more critically. He
might have recalled that the names of some of the people who combatted

Chernyshevsky's view of art were Turgenev, Tolstoy, Dostoevsky, Leskov, Goncharov, and Pisemsky. Did any of these believe that art was too "pure" to have any connection with real life, or that "artistic insight came from supernatural illumination rather than from an experience of the world of sense"? By no means! The real issue was not whether art should be concerned with "life," but whether the *value* of art depended on its commitment to a specific political doctrine. It is possible to find an occasional passage (not many) in Chernyshevsky's literary essays approving a wider standpoint; but Chernyshevsky's magazine *The Contemporary* adopted the inflexible policy of judging writers exclusively in a political perspective, and carried on a pitiless campaign against all those whose works did not fit their narrowly Utilitarian notions of art's function. It is this heritage, which Lampert praises so unreservedly, that the younger generation in Russia today is struggling to cast off.

The essay on Dobrolyubov suffers from Lampert's strictly "ideological" approach much more than the one on Chernyshevsky. Chernyshevsky, at least, had made some effort to deal directly with major intellectual matters; but Dobrolyubov merely took over his already simplistic general ideas—though using them, it is true, with a literary verve and a brilliantly satirical wit that Chernyshevsky could scarcely muster. Dobrolyubov was a political pamphleteer whose stinging and inspired pages can stand comparison with the great masters of polemical controversy; but what emerges from Lampert's account, penetrating and conscientious as it is, will hardly enlighten the reader on the reason for Dobrolyubov's importance and influence. "Not much can be said of Dobrolyubov's precise social ideals," Lampert admits. "At any rate, they cannot be defined in terms of any known economic and political theory." This is scarcely very helpful about a writer whose works helped to shape the sociopolitical ideals of a whole generation. And when Lampert does say something about Dobrolyubov's specific ideas, these turn out to be the most distressing platitudes. "Value, in the last resort, could be known only in concrete instances, in the individual case, historically; and all morality was seen by him as historically and individually conditioned."

The trouble is that the true force of Dobrolyubov's writings can only be understood in the light of his effort to project a new human image—the hard-boiled, realistic, unsentimental, and quietly determined revolutionary who, Dobrolyubov was convinced, would reshape Russian society. And his destructive attacks on the moral foibles of the generation of the 1840s, the old gentry-liberal intelligentsia, succeeded completely in ruining their credit and influence. By confining his analysis to only the bare conceptual bones of Dobrolyubov's essays, which turn out scarcely even to exist, Lampert misses the secret of their power. Moreover, while he is right in praising Dobrolyubov's occasional insight as a literary critic, he neglects to mention that, in some of his most famous essays (such as the one on Ostrovsky's *Storm*), Dobrolyubov distorts the clear significance of the text to suit his propagandistic purposes.[3]

Much the same can be said of Lampert's treatment of Pisarev, whose essays dominated the mid-1860s after Dobrolyubov had died and Chernyshevsky was silenced by being sent to Siberia. Pisarev also began as a follower of Chernyshevsky; but from the very first he struck a note of egoistic individualism that distinguished him from his master. Chernyshevsky had posed as the advocate of "egoism," but had immediately qualified this by proving (or trying to prove) that a "rational egoism" meant identity with the needs of one's fellow man. Pisarev took egoism much more literally, and objected to *any* kind of authority over the human person deriving from any source. Lampert points out the well-known proto-Nietzschean aspects of Pisarev, and remarks rightly that "he was an intellectual and a dissenter rather than a class-fighter, a moral prophet or even a revolutionary." Most important, Pisarev did not share the faith of Chernyshevsky and Dobrolyubov in the virtues and revolutionary potentialities of "the people," and placed his hopes, rather, in the leadership of the declassed intelligentsia whom he vividly dubbed "the thinking proletariat."

Lampert once again gives an excellent cross-section of Pisarev's views, interspersed with admissions of how little value they have in themselves. "Most of Pisarev's scientific knowledge was second- or third-hand," he notes; the same can be said for most of his other knowledge—except, of course, of Russian literature. Nor does Lampert inform the reader that what he calls Pisarev's "remarkable allegorical essay on *Bees*" is an outright plagiarism from Karl Vogt.[4] All this does not go very far in explaining the reason for Pisarev's influence, which replaced that of the followers of Chernyshevsky and Dobrolyubov clustered around *The Contemporary*. The battle was fought and won in the abusive polemic known as "The Schism among the Nihilists" (so baptized by Dostoevsky), which took place between 1863 and 1865 and whose course Lampert briefly describes. To account for Pisarev's victory, he can only remark lamely that "the young took sides eagerly and vehemently, and, being in a mood to enjoy great things and great ideas [?] deflated, they mostly took Pisarev's side as the more deflationary."

Pisarev swept the field, however, because the younger generation, by this time, had become disillusioned with the earlier hopes that their mentors had placed in "the people." The radicals had looked forward confi-

[3] See Rufus W. Mathewson, Jr., *The Positive Hero in Russian Literature* (Stanford, Calif., 1975), 79. Lampert does not appear to be familiar with this excellent work, which is discussed in chapter 6, above.

[4] Armand Coquart, *Dmitri Pisarev et l'idéologie du nihilisme russe* (Paris, 1946), 168. This first-rate study is far too little known.

dently to an uncontrollable uprising in the spring of 1863, when the interim period of the liberation came to an end; but nothing of the sort occurred. Also, the peasants had proved completely unreceptive to the appeals directed at them by the radicals to sabotage the suppression of the Polish rebellion in the same year. Just as the real significance of Dobrolyubov's essays had been contained in the issue of reform or revolution, so the influence of Pisarev can be attributed to his insistence that the intelligentsia must count only on itself to act in the future. Pisarev's traces, as Franco Venturi has remarked in his *Roots of Revolution*, can be found in all the various Jacobin and conspiratorial currents of Russian radicalism that began to emerge after the mid-1860s.

These comments on Lampert's approach to Dobrolyubov and Pisarev are not so much a criticism as an expression of regret that, with all its merits, Lampert's book does not come closer to the work that is needed on the 1860s. Where Lampert can legitimately be criticized, however, is in his tendency to allow his sympathy to run away with his intellectual discrimination; and perhaps the greatest weakness of his book is the failure to give the opponents of the radicals a fair hearing. It may be that the radicals were right on political issues (they were certainly right in their diagnosis of the economic consequences of the liberation); but this does not mean that they also were invariably right on philosophy, ethics, and aesthetics.

Indeed, Lampert sometimes seems to imply—as in his contemptuous treatment of a philosophical opponent of Chernyshevsky's (Yurkevich)— that the utilization of a philosophical argument by the forces inimical to the radicals impugns its philosophical value or validity. But such a point of view, as Lampert is well aware, means the end of all objective and impartial thinking. Lampert is clearly too honest and independent a writer to agree with any such proposition in the abstract, yet he seems to have adopted it inadvertently as a working principle much too often for comfort. Perhaps this is the influence of the vast amount of Soviet scholarship that he has so conscientiously ingested; but whatever the reason, it seriously biases his treatment of his subject. One of the worst banes of Russian culture has been what Nicholas Berdyaev has called its "theological" aspect, that is, the conviction that truth must be one, and that only the partisans of this one "truth" are worth a hearing on any question. It is unfortunate that, as a Western scholar, Lampert should have allowed himself to be infected even ever so slightly with this congenital Russian malady.

CHAPTER SEVENTEEN

Deadly Idealist: Mikhail Bakunin

MIKHAIL BAKUNIN, best known as the father of revolutionary anarchism, ranged like a stormy petrel across the skies of nineteenth-century European history, becoming a legend in his own lifetime. Since then he has served as a constant inspiration to various dissident groups intoxicated by his inflammatory tirades and raging pronunciamentos, and his apocalyptic vision of a new world of total freedom and perfect social justice and harmony emerging after the old one—the existing one—has been thoroughly destroyed in an all-consuming revolutionary holocaust. The present writer saw with his own eyes, during the insurrectionary spring days of 1968 in Paris, the walls of the Sorbonne adorned with Bakunin's most famous slogan (in the original German); "Die Lust der Verstörung ist eine schaffende Lust" (The passion for destruction is a creative passion). Moreover, Bakunin was the great opponent of what he called, percipiently, Marx's "authoritarian Socialism" in the latter part of his life, and his ideas have continued to attract followers for this reason as well ever since.

Indeed, Arthur Mendel tells us that he set out to write his own study of Bakunin[1] because he found that the only other biography in English—E. H. Carr's skeptical and brilliantly written portrait—"did not take seriously enough Bakunin's contribution to freedom." From such words one infers that Mendel himself was something of an admirer, if not a disciple; and he felt that Carr's rather mocking and ironic depiction did not do Bakunin sufficient justice. One wonders how anyone who had read Carr could really imagine that Bakunin had any interest in "freedom," as that word is understood in the Western democratic tradition. In any event, while setting out initially to correct Carr, Mendel's own researches have caused him to swing round full circle. He now feels that Carr's book, as well as the other literature on Bakunin (of which there is a good deal, including a magisterial four-volume biography in Russian by the Old Bolshevik Yuri Steklov, who ended as a victim of Stalin), does not "take seriously enough his [Bakunin's] threat to freedom."

What has caused such a radical shift of heart and mind? It would appear that Mendel, in digging for himself into the sources of Bakunin's life, has been appalled by the contrast he has found between Bakunin's words and deeds, the glaring discrepancy between his exalted vision of freedom and

[1] Arthur P. Mendel, *Michael Bakunin: Roots of Apocalypse* (New York, 1981).

the taste for secret conspiracy that he also exhibits—his relish for envisaging the formation of small dictatorial groups who, remaining in the shadows, would exercise absolute control over whatever revolutionary outbreaks they managed to provoke, or over which they could gain control. At the same time as he was excoriating Marx for his "authoritarian" control of the International, Bakunin was drawing up endless plans for such secret organizations, which existed, however, largely on paper and in his own grandiose fantasies. To make matters worse, he was always ready to go to any lengths with others (such as the notorious Sergey Nechaev, whose murder of an innocent student inspired Dostoevsky's *The Devils*), and agree to any and all means, no matter how terrible and Machiavellian, to attain his supposed revolutionary ends.[2] This discovery of the underside of Bakunin is what set Mendel against the man he had previously looked on, we may infer, with some sympathy.

Mendel has thus set himself the task of explaining the fascinating, tumultuous, personally appealing, and self-contradictory character and career of Bakunin. He turns to psychoanalysis for aid in grappling with the anomalies of his personality. Psychobiography is no longer the fashion that it once was, and he is somewhat defensive about his use of psychoanalytic categories; but he makes a very good case for approaching Bakunin in such terms. For one thing, Bakunin was well known to have been sexually impotent; for another, it is quite clear that he harbored a pathological aversion to sexuality along with an incestuous attraction to one of his sisters—an attraction from which he recoiled in horror while acknowledging its existence. As an exile in Siberia, he married a seventeen-year-old girl when he was forty-three, and lived peacefully with her to the end of his life while she had three children by an Italian lover who was also Bakunin's close friend and financial benefactor. Much of his early "subversive" activity as a young man, before he had acquired any genuine political interests, consisted in fighting the efforts of his family, and those of other acquaintances, to marry off their daughters, as well as keeping one of his sisters separated from her husband.

Mendel rightly believes that such aspects of Bakunin's life should be given more prominence than they usually receive, and he analyzes them in the light of a complicated theory involving recent views about narcissism combined with standard Freudian Oedipal doctrine. There is no need to follow him into the details of what, as he acknowledges himself, are highly speculative conjectures; but he summarizes his conclusions neatly in a final chapter. Bakunin, he says, "first completely rejected anything sexual, 'animal,' " and "then transferred this total rejection to society, because it so

[2] See the discussion of this work, as well as samples of the sort of propaganda Bakunin was issuing along with Nechaev, in Chapter 11, above.

inextricably involved—directly (sex, marriage) and indirectly (power, responsibility)— that oedipally repulsive 'animal' world. Finally, he disguised (and compensated for) the fear, weakness, and impotence by transmuting them into their opposites" (419)—that is, into what Mendel considers his ultimately futile revolutionary extremism, which always led to disaster, and the fantasy world of immensely powerful but largely nonexistent secret societies.

There can be no question, it seems to me, that such a view of Bakunin helps to illuminate certain aspects of his life more sharply than previous accounts, and is a valuable contribution to understanding this enigmatic and flamboyant personality. No future study of Bakunin will be able to overlook the interpretation that Mendel has presented, and his ample demonstration that the "roots" of Bakunin's obsessive vision of chaos and paradisial rebirth can be suggestively linked to a study of his psychic dilemmas. At the same time, though, it also seems to me that he rides his thesis too hard in wishing to make *every* aspect of Bakunin's life and activity merely a repetition-compulsion of his own private "psychodrama." If this were so, it would be difficult to explain his enormous influence; and Mendel realizes that this influence poses something of a problem. "Although [Bakunin] stages his dreams and nightmares mainly for his own therapy and even sanity (and no doubt experienced, as in all good theatre, the desired catharsis) countless others in search of similar self deception for whatever reason, eagerly mistook those dreams and nightmares for objective portraits of reality or serious designs for social change and acted accordingly" (423).

Such a passage simply evades the crucial issue of psychobiography—the relation between the individual and his time—rather than attempting to grapple with it in some adequate fashion. The trouble lies in Mendel's initial assumption that Bakunin, in his psychopathic recoil from a sexually charged "reality," had lost all contact with its true problems. But is this really so? And does he realize the full social implications of his implicit psychoanalytic postulate that an "acceptance" of "reality" is always desirable? Bakunin's refusal to follow a normal military career and to step into his father's shoes, for example, is seen strictly as evidence of psychic abnormality. But does this mean that there could be no good reasons for not wishing to serve Nicholas I, or for becoming a contented Russian landowner living off slave labor? And while Bakunin's untiring efforts to prevent marriages certainly were tied to his own sexual dilemmas, could he have exercised so much power over others if some of the women in question had not felt they were being forced into legal prostitution? Mendel does not raise such questions, and thus seems to identify his psychoanalytic categories of "maturity" and "normality"—certainly without intending to do so—with an unthinking acceptance of whatever social and political arrangements existed at the time.

The same tendency to reductionism can be seen in his discussion of Bakunin's intellectual and philosophical evolution. Bakunin's adoption of various metaphysical and philosophical views is seen exclusively as a response to his own personal problems, though Mendel does remark at one point, after quoting some Romantic effusions, that "we are encountering [in them] the mood of the age as much as we are aspects of Bakunin's personality." But he forgets this aspect of the matter very quickly, and fails to notice, in working out his psychoanalytic correlations of Bakunin's move from Fichte to Schelling, and then to Hegel and Left Hegelianism, that Bakunin was following exactly the same path as many of the other members of the generation of 1840 in Russian culture; he was by no means doing anything eccentric or original. This is why his famous article, "Reaction in Germany," was greeted with such enthusiasm, and hailed as a classical fusion of German metaphysics with French revolutionary ardor. Once more he coincides with "the mood of the age," and to analyze him *only* in psychoanalytic terms (however justified they may be) does not get us very far in explaining his impact.

Similarly, one wonders to what extent many traits of Bakunin's character that seem "abnormal" to a psychology based on late nineteenth-century European assumptions about human behavior—for example, his refusal to soil his hands by earning money while living off the largesse of his friends—simply derive from the fact that he was a Russian nobleman for whom the idea of gaining his daily bread by the sweat of his brow was literally unthinkable. And Bakunin can also be seen as a typically Russian phenomenon in a wider sense as well: underground conspiracy and secret societies were a Russian tradition necessitated by the social conditions of the country, and it seems irrelevant to measure Bakunin, as Mendel does, against a "norm" provided by Marx and the International. Nothing like the European working-class movement existed in Russia in Bakunin's lifetime, and to see his preoccupation with secret societies only as his way of "withdrawing" from the "real" political struggle is to overlook that he was a product of the Russian situation. His anarchism comes from a country where even loyalist Slavophiles could declare that the existence of the state, even though regrettably necessary, was an inevitable source of moral evil.

The main weakness of Mendel's book is his refusal to entertain the possibility that Bakunin's inner drives could intersect in any way with the sociocultural and political "reality" of his time, and his rejection of any categories of explanation except the psychoanalytic. Although he does not manage to overcome this congenital defect of the genre of psychobiography, he nonetheless offers a penetrating study of Bakunin within his own terms.

CHAPTER EIGHTEEN

Alexander Herzen: *Who Is to Blame?*

ALEXANDER HERZEN is best known outside Russia as the author of *My Past and Thoughts*, those sparkling memoirs that are, as Sir Isaiah Berlin has rightly said, one of the finest depictions of progressive and radical European politics in the mid-nineteenth century. They are, as well, of a literary quality equal to the greatest Russian novels. Herzen was an incomparable observer and a wittily skeptical and ironical writer (he was often called the Russian Voltaire); he was also at the center of Russian cultural life as a young man. Later, in European exile, he became a figure of international renown after setting up the first free Russian press in London, founding the weekly journal *Kolokol* (The Bell), which served as the voice of liberal opinion in his stifled homeland, and also turning out a series of works (mainly in the form of imaginary dialogues with, or letters to, friends and adversaries) that have lost none of their freshness and force as commentaries on the key issues that still plague modern civilization. Herzen's writings combine aristocratic asperity toward bourgeois values (he was, even if illegitimate, the son of an extremely wealthy Russian nobleman and had been educated as such) with democratic aspirations toward liberty, equality, and social justice. The two elements form an extremely attractive and highly individual compound, and give Herzen a unique perspective on the modern world.

As a young man, Herzen tried his hand at belles lettres and wrote a novel, *Who Is to Blame?*, which has occupied an important place in Russian literature ever since.[1] It was written in the mid-1840s, in the days of what was called the Natural School of young Russian writers, a group whose members were all supposed to have come out of Gogol's *The Overcoat*. This meant that they were carrying on the humanitarian appeal contained in that short story as well as in Gogol's satirical masterpiece *Dead Souls*. *Who Is to Blame?*—with its withering account of the corruption, cruelty, and the stupefying spiritual stagnation of life in the Russian provinces—is more indebted to the novel than to the story, which is set in St. Petersburg. And while Herzen lacks the madcap grotesquerie that allowed Gogol to create his gallery of monumental monsters, his version of Russian mores is perhaps even more depressing because his people are closer to being ordinary

---

[1] *Who Is to Blame?*, trans. and ed. Michael Katz (Ithaca, N.Y., 1984).

human beings. They are even, on occasion, capable of making generous gestures.

At the center of *Who Is to Blame?* is a romantic dilemma involving the sacredness of the marriage bond. The first part of the book deals with the meeting and marriage of two unhappy souls, Lyubonka Negrov, the illegitimate daughter of a landowner by one of his serfs, and Dmitry Krutsifersky, the son of a provincial doctor living in desperate poverty. As a young boy, Krutsifersky attracts the favorable attention of a passing notable and is thus enabled to study at Moscow University. One of Herzen's alter egos, Dr. Krupov, then obtains a post for Krutsifersky as a tutor at the Negrovs. Dr. Krupov, who appears in other works by Herzen, is the spokesman for a disillusioned, materialistic view of life, a view closed to any sort of romanticism or idealism and filled with a resigned pessimism; but Dr. Krupov always strives to behave decently, honorably, and justly within the limited range of the possible. Lyubonka and Krutsifersky fall in love and decide to marry, with the blessing of Negrov, who is only too glad to get Lyubonka off his hands without a dowry. But Dr. Krupov is filled with trepidation and warns Krutsifersky that Lyubonka is really a powerful personality ("she is a young tigress, as yet unaware of her strength") while he is "as sentimental as a German maiden." The marriage takes place all the same, with this premonition of disaster hanging over its head from the very start.

Herzen is not really a novelist, and makes no attempt to tell a story in any conventional sense. His chapters are a series of essayistic sketches, obviously related in style to his later autobiography, which expositorily paint in the social background and the character traits of his people; there are very few dramatic scenes in which the action comes to life. Herzen writes what he calls the "biographies" of his characters, and remarks rather proudly, in his role as narrator, that "I never avoid biographical digressions." So after recounting the story of Lyubonka and Krutsifersky, his attention shifts from them entirely for a number of chapters and focuses on the history of Vladimir Beltov, the first of the famous "superfluous men" who fill the pages of the Russian novel in the 1840s and whose type reaches its apogee in the threadbare splendor of Stepan Trofimovich Verkhovensky of Dostoevsky's *The Devils*.

Beltov himself is the scion of a wealthy landowning family of the region whose mother had been born a serf; his father had unexpectedly married her as a gesture of repentance for previous mistreatment. Herzen is highly critical of the education given Beltov by his adoring mother, who hires one of those irreproachable and impossible Swiss tutors one finds in Russian novels—full of Protestant uprightness and Plutarchian civic virtue—to instill in Beltov noble precepts and inspire him with ideals totally unsuited to Russian life. As a result, though Beltov enters the Russian civil service full of zeal to help his countrymen, he soon retreats before the quagmire of injustice, cupidity, and sheer animal cunning that he encounters; he then occupies himself with various substitutes—medicine, painting—which he quickly abandons because they do not satisfy his real need. As Herzen makes clear, this real need is the possibility of some form of fruitful and beneficent political activity. "Nothing in the world is so enticing to an ardent nature as a role in current affairs, history-in-the-making. Anyone who has once harbored such dreams within his breast has spoiled himself for all other activities." Here Herzen is undoubtedly speaking for himself and predicting his own career.

It was the Swiss tutor, Monsieur Joseph, who had implanted such dreams in the bosom of his pupil, and thus unfitted him for life in Russia—or anywhere else. Beltov, after the usual fruitless wanderings through Europe of the Russian "superfluous man" seeking ways to escape his "spleen," accidentally encounters his tutor again and decides to make a final, absurd attempt to realize his ambition: he will return home and run for the purely ceremonial office of marshal of the nobility. But his fellow nobles cordially despise this Europeanized wastrel and wanderer, and he never stands a chance. Dr. Krupov incautiously introduces him to the Krutsiferskys, he and Lyubonka recognize each other as kindred souls unable to adapt to the ignoble mediocrity of their surroundings, and the inevitable occurs: malicious gossip starts up and reaches the ears of the tenderhearted and hapless husband. Lyubonka wastes away after a single passionate kiss from Beltov, torn between her new love and her pity for the suffering Krutsifersky. The book ends with Beltov escaping once again to a life of boredom and futility in Europe, with Lyubonka "declining rapidly" and Krutsifersky "overcome with grief," drinking and praying to God. It is a new version of the ending of *Eugene Onegin*, but renunciation is no longer a triumphant vindication of duty over inclination and passion; it is a sacrifice that dooms all concerned to despair and death.

Ever since the publication of *Who Is to Blame?* the question posed by the title has elicited a flood of commentary, and the excellent translator Michael Katz, a professor of Russian at the University of Texas in Austin, outlines the various alternatives in his introduction to this edition. Russian criticism, particularly since the 1860s, has stressed the social morass depicted by Herzen as being ultimately responsible; and there is certainly ample evidence to make such an emphasis plausible. The numberless, almost inevitable, cruelties arising from the master-serf relationship; the complete lack of the most elementary liberties; the hopelessness of affecting any important change for the better—all these are driven home by Herzen relentlessly and can hardly be ignored. But Herzen was not a determinist, and he also believed that human beings had a hand in creating their own fate.

For all his sympathy for Beltov, Herzen nonetheless treats him with much the same irony with which he indicts the Negrovs and the other unenlightened denizens of the province. When Beltov reaches for a copy of Byron's *Don Juan* instead of occupying himself, as he had originally intended, with "an English pamphlet on Adam Smith," Herzen makes clear that his hero is more concerned with distraction than instruction. And Dr. Krupov sharply tells Beltov that, if he is bored by the idleness of his life, it is because he has never had to earn his bread. This is exactly the home truth that would cause the radical critics of the 1860s to regard the "superfluous men" (among whom they now included Herzen himself) as unworthy of even a moment's sympathy or concern. Herzen does not see Beltov and the others *only* as helpless victims of their environment; and this has caused some American scholars, reacting against the Russian emphasis, to answer the question of the book's title by stressing the characters' own responsibility.

Michael Katz believes that neither extreme is faithful to the novel, and this is my own opinion as well. What makes the book more than a tract for its time is precisely the many-sidedness of Herzen's understanding of the Russian dilemma, and his refusal to offer any easy answers. But there is no question about where his sympathies lie—with all those, like Beltov, Lyubonka, Krutsifersky, and Dr. Krupov, who are unable to reconcile themselves emotionally with the injustices existing around them and who remain faithful to some vision of a better and happier world in which much of what Herzen castigates would cease to exist. For all his skepticism about Beltov, Herzen's attitude is clearly indicated in a key passage:

> In spite of the maturity of his thought, he [Beltov] was not really an adult. In a word, now, more than thirty years since his birth, he was *just getting ready* to begin his life, like a sixteen-year-old boy, without noticing that the door that had been gradually opening was not the one through which gladiators enter but the one through which their bodies are carried out. "Of course, Beltov himself is to blame for much of this." I am in complete agreement with you, while others think that there are people whose faults are better than any virtues. (187–88)

Herzen is of course one of these "others," and he could both judge Beltov lucidly and find his "faults," which stem from his unfulfilled political idealism, to be superior to the virtues of others. One encounters a good deal of this same feeling in Chekhov's portrayal of his idealists, the good men who, as Nabokov said, could never make good.

Although the romantic intrigue of *Who Is to Blame?* may seem secondary, at first sight, to the sociopolitical theme, it actually adds an element of complexity to Herzen's vision. At this time Herzen was under the influence of the French Saint-Simonians, who preached "the rehabilitation of the flesh" and who had found a powerful literary spokesman in George Sand.

Her works were immensely popular in Russia and had produced a spate of imitations, among which Herzen's novel is usually included. But while *Who Is to Blame?* has often been taken as a protest against the legal and religious shackles that bind unhappy people together in an unsuitable marriage, and while one can find statements in Herzen's diary recommending "free relations between the sexes," his novel does not avoid the moral difficulties that can arise when such ideas are put into practice.

Nobody, after all, is really to blame that Lyubonka is a more powerful personality than Krutsifersky, whom she married freely and out of love, or that she finds qualities of "genius" in Beltov, qualities her adoring and devoted husband lacks. For Beltov and Lyubonka to fulfill their ideal love, Krutsifersky would have to be ruthlessly sacrificed; but he has done nothing to deserve such a fate and Lyubonka is too fine a human being to throw him over without a qualm. Herzen knew that the human conscience had imperatives that had little to do with the "rationality" of one or another social arrangement. When Herzen himself later discovered that his own wife was having an affair with a close friend, the radical poet Georg Herwegh, he was wounded to the depths of his being by the treachery involved, despite all his liberated ideas. It was because he could prophetically intuit such a response that his own book can still be taken seriously, and escapes the puerilities later enshrined in Chernyshevsky's *What Is to Be Done?*, where marriages are made and unmade with untroubled serenity and reduced simply to matters of mutual convenience.

The "superfluous man" as a literary type, at least in his gentry-liberal incarnation, began to go out of fashion in Russia during the 1860s. He made his last great literary stand in Dostoevsky's *The Devils* (1871–1872) with the character of Stepan Trofimovich Verkhovensky; Nezhdanov in Turgenev's *Virgin Soil* (1877) cannot compete with him in stature and bite. But while the social class from which the superfluous man came ceased to occupy the foreground of Russian literature, the sociocultural theme that he exemplified has continued to resurface. How was one to adapt to the ugly and seemingly immutable realities of Russian life without losing one's soul? The radicals replied by engaging in a heroic and self-sacrificing battle against the political régime. They saw this régime as the source of all evil; its elimination, they were firmly convinced, would solve the problem once and for all—especially since the soul was in any case a bourgeois illusion. But it is astonishing to observe, despite the enormous changes that have occurred in Russia since Herzen wrote, that a descendant of Beltov, with all his weakness, capriciousness, irresolution, and idealism, turns up as the hero of what is arguably the greatest Russian novel of our time—*Dr. Zhivago*. Yury Zhivago combines elements of Beltov's character with the profession of Dr. Krupov, and he is a poet as well, who continues to uphold the values of the spirit (including religion) in a world fashioned by the descendants of all those who fought so tenaciously to rid Russian culture of every trace of reverence for the "superfluous man." The same tyranny and suffocating oppression that produced the superfluous man once has done so again, and he has lost none of his aura or his symbolic value as a clue to Russian realities.

CHAPTER NINETEEN

The Birth of "Russian Socialism"

ALEXANDER HERZEN is certainly the most sympathetic and interesting figure among the leaders of Russian radicalism in the early nineteenth century, and the only one whose writings have more than a local or historical interest in connection with the revolutionary movement. Belinsky's literary criticism makes no important contribution to its field, though his work had undeniable importance in stimulating concern with intellectual and cultural problems in Russia; nor do Bakunin's tirades and dialectical sleights of hand give us new insights into anything except the vagaries of his temperament. The same is true of the succeeding generation of the Russian radicals of the 1860s. Their leaders, Chernyshevsky and Dobrolyubov, were incredibly hardworking publicists who turned out an immense amount of copy (including poetry and novels); but nothing that they wrote on a vast variety of subjects transcends in value the propaganda limits of their time and place. Herzen is the only true radical whose work is entitled to a place alongside that of the great nineteenth-century Russian novelists; and his most important book, the autobiography *My Past and Thoughts*, is perhaps the greatest work of its kind published anywhere in the nineteenth century, ranking with Rousseau's *Confessions* and Goethe's *Dichtung und Wahrheit* as the picture of both a life and a time.

In view of Herzen's importance, and the worldwide interest in Russian culture in general, the available literature about him for a reader restricted to the major European languages is very scanty. There is, of course, a vast amount of writing on Herzen in Russian, but only one very good, if by now somewhat outdated, book in French (by Raoul Labry); surprisingly, there is no single German work that comes to mind; and E. H. Carr's *Romantic Exiles* was for a long time the only full-length study available in English.[1] Carr's book, for the most part, is an amused depiction of the imbroglios of Herzen's complicated private life in exile, and he touches only lightly on the intellectual and political background (though these can be found broadly sketched in Sir Isaiah Berlin's effervescent, enthusiastic, and deeply penetrating essays now collected in his *Russian Thinkers*).[2] The appearance of Martin Malia's extremely erudite, wide-ranging, and masterly *Alexander Herzen and the Birth of Russian Socialism* in 1961, however,

[1] E. H. Carr, *The Romantic Exiles* (Boston, 1961).
[2] Sir Isaiah Berlin, *Russian Thinkers* (New York, 1978).

remedied this situation with impressive authority. It is thus all the more to be regretted that Malia did not give us a full-length study of Herzen but chose to cut off his account with 1855 (actually he ends in 1848, and fills in the rest of the period in one concluding chapter). Malia, as the title of his book indicates, is interested in the birth of "Russian Socialism," of which Herzen was the progenitor; and he terminates his book at the point where Herzen's basic ideas on this issue were essentially hammered out.[3]

Nonetheless, nothing can give us more insight into the tragic antinomies of Russian culture than Herzen's conflict with the radicals of the next generation, as reflected in parts of *My Past and Thoughts* and in later writings such as *Letters to an Old Comrade* (Bakunin). This conflict forms the background for such a work as Dostoevsky's *The Devils*, which was inspired by exactly the same events—the Nechaev conspiracy—as *Letters to an Old Comrade*; and Malia would have performed a great service had he undertaken as dense an account of Herzen's intellectual evolution in his later years as he does of the earlier. However that may be, one certainly cannot complain of the quality of the fare offered in the period that Malia has chosen to cover. He is admirably versed not only in the Russian material, but also in the early history of Socialism, the rise of nationalism, and, what is rarer, in the speculative intricacies of German Idealism. He writes vigorously and well, and sometimes with genuine eloquence. His book is certainly one of the fullest and most reliable pictures available in English of Russian cultural history during the crucial first half of the nineteenth century.

The intellectual evolution of Herzen, with some slight variations, is essentially that of the whole generation of the 1840s in Russia. Born the illegitimate son of a wealthy Russian aristocrat, Herzen was nourished on the dramas of Schiller, with their pathos of freedom, and on the cry for liberty that rings out in some of the poetry of Pushkin as well as in that of the Decembrists, who unsuccessfully tried to prevent Nicholas I from ascending the throne in 1825. Herzen and his friend Nicholas Ogarev swore their famous oath on the Sparrow Hills outside Moscow in 1827 or 1828, when they were still in their early teens; they pledged to dedicate their lives to fighting tyranny and to sacrifice their existence for the good of mankind. All this was very juvenile, romantic, *exalté*, but they remained true to their word, and this adolescent oath turned out to be a crucial moment in Russian history.

At Moscow University, then a little oasis of light and learning in the midst of the general desolation, Herzen imbibed the prevalent Schellingian Idealism smuggled in by professors in the faculty of science. Even at this

---

[3] Martin Malia, *Alexander Herzen and the Birth of Russian Socialism, 1812–1855* (Cambridge, Mass., 1961).

early period, however, Herzen was the center of a circle interested in the new French Socialism of Saint-Simon and his school. Herzen's sociopolitical interests were temporarily submerged by a period of exile and an ensuing preoccupation with religious mysticism; but he returned to such problems under the influence of George Sand and Pierre Leroux, whose own Socialism was strongly tinged with mystical and religious ideas. The early 1840s brought him into contact with Hegel, and he thrashed out his final position by prolonged debates with two groups—on the one hand the nationalistic Moscow Slavophiles, on the other the more liberal Westernizers. Herzen personally had a foot in both camps, though his best friends were among the second group; and he eventually broke off relations with the Slavophiles because, in the last analysis, they still supported autocracy and orthodoxy despite their moderately liberal desire for such Western inventions as freedom of speech, press, and thought.

Herzen, however, took from the Slavophiles the idea that the Russian peasant commune, with its completely democratic administration by a village council or *mir*, and its periodic redistribution of land, realized the ideals toward which European society was aspiring in such imaginary Utopias as the Fourierist phalanstery. His debates with the Westernizers, who refused to go along either with his atheism or his idealization of the people, made him aware of the internal hindrances in European culture itself—as reflected by its defenders and admirers in Russia—barring the way to the realization of the brave new world of integral freedom that he desired. One of the most original aspects of Malia's book, from the purely historical point of view, is his demonstration of the effect that Herzen's conflict with the Westernizers had on shaping his predisposition to believe that European culture was incapable of sloughing off its centuries-old involvement with bourgeois individualism, private property, and a centralized state. By the time he came to Europe in 1847 this conviction had already begun to harden; and the failure of the revolutions of 1848 simply confirmed what he already felt. Out of this concatenation emerged Herzen's Messianic and nationalistic "Russian Socialism," which counted on Russia and the peasant commune, led by the enlightened radical members of the gentry, to show the world the way to the Socialist Utopia of the future. It was this Russian Socialism that became the ideology of Russian Populism up through the rise of Marxism in 1880.

Malia is not content merely with impressively unrolling the panorama of these events as cultural history; he also attempts to "explain" them in terms of an elaborate employment of what he calls "social psychology." He links his method to that of Karl Mannheim and Max Scheler, and the neo-Hegelian, heretical Georg Lukács of the early 1920s; but despite this formidable array of authorities, the basic idea is very simple and more psychological than social. "It has been the major thesis of this book,"

Malia writes, "that the democratic ideal arose in Russia, not by direct reflection on the plight of the masses, but through the introspection of relatively privileged individuals who, out of frustration, generalized from a sense of their own dignity to the ideal of the dignity of all men" (421). Nor is this type of explanation used only to cover the Russian situation. For Malia treats *all* the major intellectual movements with which he deals—German Idealism, French Utopian Socialism, and the appropriation and assimilation of both in Russia—as essentially such "ideologies of compensation," which can best be understood in the light of the frustrations they express and whose objective value is approximately nil. It is the psychological dynamism of this frustration, he argues, that accounts for the maximalism, intransigence, and totally Utopian impracticality of Russian radicalism.

Certainly there is a good deal of truth in this point of view, which seems primarily to derive from Karl Mannheim; but Malia applies it with a rigor, a logic, and a relentless consistency that narrows his perspective to a point where it becomes distorting. In the first place, it leads him to what, in my opinion, is a perfectly false picture of the kind of human being Herzen really was. Since everything has to spring from the frustrations of his "ego," poor Herzen is turned into a monster whose every action is dictated by vanity, self-seeking, and a need for power or "recognition" (whatever that really means). Malia never seems to have asked himself why anyone should "generalize" his own need for dignity into a universal ideal, and then devote his life to struggling to attain this kind of "generalization." Is there not some essential difference in human quality between those who "generalize" and those who do not, and is it permissible to portray the former as if no such difference exists? Herzen is hardly ever allowed a moment's sincerity, generosity, sympathy, or even a movement of real spontaneity; and if we compare the actual facts of his life and behavior to the standards of his time and country, this continual denigration after a while becomes simply grotesque.

Indeed, there is a certain complacent cruelty in Malia's whole approach that becomes quite irritating, and that derives from his superior certainty that he has "seen through" all the elaborate ideological structures of rationalization by which Herzen masked his practical impotence and futility. Time and again Malia explains to us how hopeless and impossible the situation in Russia really was, and attributes to this fact the preoccupation of the Russian intelligentsia with art, idealistic philosophy, religion, and such extraneous issues as the emancipation of women, when the "real" problem was to obtain some elementary civil rights for the vast majority of the people. But after showing us that such evasions were "inevitable," Malia cannot resist characterizing them scornfully and ironically and continually belaboring Herzen for his incapacity to face up and "recognize reality." A good example occurs in the chapter on Herzen's exile, when he took refuge in religion, Masonic mysticism, and a highly exalted correspondence with his future wife as a means of avoiding total despair. "His love went to the metaphysical lengths it did," Malia comments, "because of what was grafted onto it by the frustrations of exile. Hence the association of Natalie with the idea of Providence, God, the angels, heaven, and all other conceivable occult powers necessary to save him from despair in the face of adversity. Perhaps the most preposterous aspect of the whole affair is the solicitude attributed to Providence for the welfare of the inestimable Alexander" (173). Such a sarcastic tone, by no means uncommon in the book, is entirely out of place in this context; and Malia might remember that it is unseemly even for a social psychologist to kick a man when he is down.

Perhaps the most unfortunate consequence of Malia's theoretical approach, however, stems from the view of "reality" that it implicitly assumes. Art, speculative philosophy, religion, the problems of personal life—all these are "sublimated politics" from his angle of vision, blind alleys into which the Russian intelligentsia wandered out of practical helplessness. "Reality" thus becomes equated with pragmatic politics on the Anglo-American model; and whether intentionally or not, Malia leaves the impression that every other intellectual and cultural activity or preoccupation is an "escape." But all the while he is pitilessly harrying Herzen for such "escapes from reality," one cannot help thinking that it was precisely these escapes that make Herzen so unique and attractive a figure in the gloomy gallery of Russian revolutionary fanatics.

The radicals of the 1860s would also look on "reality" exclusively in political terms, exactly like Malia, though of course with a different kind of politics in mind; and, with a more self-conscious logic, they excluded as "useless" every nonpolitical inclination and requirement of the human spirit. Herzen was the only great radical who refused to accept this politicization of man, which has had such unhappy consequences for Russian culture as a whole. Just as in the case of Marx, whose education in the era of Romantic Idealism left him with a residue of respect for great art that he never lost (though he could never manage either to make it consistent with his historical materialism), so Herzen's similar respect for the sanctities of private feeling and the necessity of beauty derives from the depth of his involvement with all those romantic "escapes" that Malia continually jibes at and decries. One of the great symbolic encounters of the modern spirit is that between Herzen and Giuseppe Mazzini described in *My Past and Thoughts*, where Herzen unsuccessfully attempts to persuade the great agitator of the importance for humanity of Leopardi's lyric cry of pain. Herzen could feel and express both the tragic human *cost* of extreme radical politics as well as its ineluctable necessity in Russia; and this is what gives him a warmth, a breadth, and a humanity that we find also in the great novelists of his generation, but that is so noticeably lacking in what Herzen called the "bilious" generation of radicals that followed.

Malia's totally negative evaluation of these romantic elements of Herzen's formation constitutes, in my opinion, the single most important deformation imposed by his approach. But whatever the limitations of Malia's emphasis and interpretation, they do not impair the substantial value of his first-rate study.

CHAPTER TWENTY

A Word on Leskov

NIKOLAY LESKOV is a Russian novelist comparatively little known in the English-speaking world; but he is perhaps the best of that galaxy of minor nineteenth-century Russian prose writers who have been completely over-shadowed by the triumvirate of Turgenev, Tolstoy, and Dostoevsky (with Goncharov not far behind as a fourth). It is good to be reminded from time to time that the Russian novel is not composed exclusively of their creations, overpowering as they may be. And Leskov has also recently be-come better known, at least to people interested in contemporary criticism, because of the growing reputation of Walter Benjamin, whose article on Leskov as a writer of tales is now often cited and referred to in discussions of the theory of prose fiction. With the publication of Hugh McLean's monumental book on Leskov, the result of many years of devoted labor, there is no longer any reason for those interested in Russian literature to remain ignorant of the career and works of this talented writer, whose books give one the "feel" of wide areas of Russian life left largely un-touched by his greater contemporaries.[1]

Leskov obtained his vast knowledge of the Russian lower classes by first-hand experience. As a young man he worked as a clerk in the criminal court of the district where he lived. Later he traveled extensively throughout the country as a commercial agent, working for his British uncle, Alexander Scott, who administered the extensive estates of wealthy Russian landown-ers. Leskov spoke of these years as providing him with a store of impres-sions and observations that he embodied in his stories and novels; and it is interesting to note that he began his literary career by writing muckraking articles devoted to matters of topical concern. He did not start off with attempts at fiction or poetry, like so many other writers; nor is there even any evidence of early literary ambition.

Leskov's work always remained close to the harsh and hard realities of Russian life and its day-to-day texture. If his writings lack the imaginative depth and ideological scope of his great countrymen, they make up for it in the vividness and understanding with which they depict a Russian world quite different from that of the ideologues and aristocrats who people the best-known Russian nineteenth-century fiction. Leskov's tender and mov-ing depiction of the provincial clergy in his excellent *Cathedral Folk*, and of

[1] Hugh McLean, *Nicolai Leskov: The Man and His Art* (Cambridge, Mass., 1977).

the fanatical religiosity of the Old Believers in *The Sealed Angel* (which also contains one of the first admiring discussions of icon painting written for the general public), broke new ground in Russian literature, as did his picaresque account in *The Enchanted Pilgrim* of how an adventurous serf finally entered a monastery.

Leskov was a proud, passionate, and frequently irascible character who, in the course of his life, managed to quarrel with almost everyone he knew, as well as with all the current tendencies and movements in Russian literature. This also tells us something about his fierce independence, his refusal to kowtow to the ideological shibboleths of the moment. His most widely known quarrel, which led to his virtual ostracism by the radicals for most of his life, involved the famous St. Petersburg fires of 1862, which coincided roughly with the circulation of the bloodthirsty *Young Russia* proclamations calling for the extermination of the royal family and all its adherents. It was generally believed that the radicals had started the blaze, and the student population in general was suspected by the populace of being in sympathy with the presumed arsonists. Leskov printed an article intended to protect the students, which asked the police, if there was any evidence of arson, to name the culprits so that suspicion could be removed from those who were blameless.

Nothing, at first sight, would seem to be more harmless than such a request; but the fact that Leskov lent some credence to the charge of arson, and seemingly appealed to the police against the radicals, was enough to make him a marked man. McLean pooh-poohs Leskov's bitter and frequent complaints about the effect of this literary quarantine on his career. It did not, to be sure, stop him from writing, but he was forced to publish in obscure and second-rate periodicals and felt unjustly deprived of his proper audience and larger recognition. Even a better-balanced personality might well have become exasperated; and there seems something uncharitable in denying Leskov the right to his resentments. Indeed, the vendetta of the radicals has continued to pursue him right up to the present: Leskov's argument with those of his time, McLean writes, "has made him an object of suspicion forever," and even today in the Soviet Union his work is published only in expurgated editions.

McLean's book is unquestionably a major scholarly achievement, certainly one of the most impressive works on a Russian writer to be published recently in the English language; and it is probably the most complete study of Leskov available anywhere. A useful summary in the preface gives the essence of McLean's views on his controversial subject:

> Although he [Leskov] toyed briefly with radicalism in the early 1860s, he remained basically a liberal and gradualist, who believed in working for reforms within the existing system rather than pulling it to pieces and starting afresh.

Philosophically, his quest for a viable Weltanschauung took him not to Western secularism and Socialism, as it did so many of his contemporaries, but back to a Christianity originally more or less in harmony with official Eastern Orthodoxy, but later developing into a thoroughgoing "Protestant" moralism that eventually merged with Tolstoy's. Leskov ardently believed in the didactic powers of literature, and he was also convinced that lasting improvements in the human condition could only be achieved by raising the moral standards of individuals, not by tinkering with social forms. (viii)

On this latter point, one might add, he was in agreement with Dostoevsky as well as Tolstoy, and profoundly in the Russian tradition still represented by Solzhenitsyn.

This quotation says little about Leskov as a writer, but McLean pays close and careful attention to style as well as theme, and grapples manfully with the difficult problem of conveying Leskov's intricate linguistic effects to the uninitiated. Much of Leskov's work is in the *skaz* form, and depends on narrative tone and attitude indicated largely through subtle shifts in language. This is one reason why he is so difficult to translate, and why his work loses so much even when the translation is conscientious. Nor was Leskov really a novelist: he did his best work in the shorter forms, and his longer works are usually ill constructed—simply a collection of stories and anecdotes strung together, sometimes in a very artificial, awkward manner.

Nothing but praise can be given to McLean's knowledge and industry, but his critical interpretations, at least to my taste, are somewhat less satisfactory. It is curious that, while lavishing so much energy on winning our interest for Leskov, he often seems to undermine his own efforts by his general depreciation of Leskov's view of life and his dominating values. The problem is that McLean has been convinced by Freud that Leskov's frequent depictions of Christian love and charity exhibit merely an ignorance of the true motives of the human libido; and as a critic he constantly feels called upon to show up Leskov's naïveté in this regard. As an example, here is a passage about *Cathedral Folk*:

> Victorian eyes were always ready to mist at . . . spectacles of sinless love and saintly virtue in humble circumstances. Twentieth-century readers, however, their innocence lost to Freud, may be aware of the self-indulgences disguised in the fantasy. Pizonsky's sexual confusion makes his motherhood hard to accept as pure Christian charity [he has adopted an orphan], and Tuberozov's admiration of such "lesser brethren" [he is a priest] may seem too patronizing to be genuine. (184)

Perhaps so; but it may be suggested that this is hardly the way to appreciate what is unique in Leskov, who writes so often of his *pravedniki*, the saintly and self-sacrificing, and who manages, despite McLean's strictures, to convince us of their human reality and possibility in a way that Dickens, for example, was quite unable to do. To take Freud as an exclusively authoritative guide to the range of human motivation and human feeling is to approach literature with blinkers. Hamlet is more than the Oedipus complex, and Pizonsky and Tuberozov are more than sexual confusion and patronizing superiority—or so, it seems to me, Leskov is a good enough writer to make us believe.

Index

DATE DUE